THE LAND THAT THYME FORGOT

www.**booksattransworld**.co.uk

Also by William Black

AL DENTE

Books by William Black and Sophie Grigson

TRAVELS À LA CARTE

FISH

ORGANICS

THE LAND THAT THYME FORGOT

WILLIAM BLACK

BANTAM PRESS

LONDON · TORONTO · SYDNEY · AUCKLAND · JOHANNESBURG

TRANSWORLD PUBLISHERS
61–63 Uxbridge Road, London W5 5SA
a division of The Random House Group Ltd

RANDOM HOUSE AUSTRALIA (PTY) LTD
20 Alfred Street, Milsons Point, Sydney,
New South Wales 2061, Australia

RANDOM HOUSE NEW ZEALAND LTD
18 Poland Road, Glenfield, Auckland 10, New Zealand

RANDOM HOUSE SOUTH AFRICA (PTY) LTD
Endulini, 5a Jubilee Road, Parktown 2193, South Africa

Published 2005 by Bantam Press
a division of Transworld Publishers

A catalogue record for this book is available from the British Library.
ISBN 0593 053621

Typeset in 13.5/14.5pt Perpetua by
Falcon Oast Graphic Art Ltd.

Printed in Great Britain by
Clays Ltd, Bungay, Suffolk

1 3 5 7 9 10 8 6 4 2

Papers used by Transworld Publishers are natural, recyclable products made from wood grown
in sustainable forests. The manufacturing processes conform to the environmental regulations
of the country of origin.

For Lola

CONTENTS

SOUTH

RECIPES

ACKNOWLEDGEMENTS

Thank you to all who have helped to get this off the ground, and assisted me along the way. In particular to Alan Bichan, and Christine and Tommy Muir in Orkney; Paul Merry in Dorzit; Jeremy Torz, Martie and Vanilla in London; the Bhatt family and Sima Patel in Leicester; Horace and Richard Cook, Stephen Doherty, Colin Burgess and Arthur Strand; Doug Young and Linda Evans at Transworld, and Daniel Balado for his editing skills.

And to Claire, for all her love and support, and Florrie, Sid and Lola, for being so interested in what Dad was up to.

A true gastronome is as insensible to suffering as a conqueror.
— Abraham Hayward, *The Art of Dining* (1852)

INTRODUCTION

IT ALL BEGAN IN THE SOUTH OF FRANCE. EIGHT OF US SITTING around a table in a little Provençal village at the foot of a blistered Mont Ventoux. The sun was setting. The *cigales* were chattering outside. There were piles of whelks, mayonnaise, succulent prawns, and a bubbling *daube* to be had. All eased on their way by endless bottles of wine. We moved on to the pristine goat's cheese, and sliced into the crusty *pain au levain*. The conversation turned, as it so often did, to food.

'Well, William, you've done Italy, what next? How about France? At least there'd be something to write about.'

'I was thinking of looking at British food, actually. It's far more interesting.'

Mirthful explosions from around the table.

'*Tu rigoles?* What on earth could you write about? Name me one single dish you have that can get anywhere near this *daube*.'

The temperature was already rising.

'Well, there's the sandwich, for one.'

1

'*Le sandwich, le sandwich? Bah!*'

'OK, then, there's roast beef, pie and mash, potted shrimps, haggis . . .'

Gallic shoulders shrugged.

'And what about these: Hindle Wakes, sooan, clapshot, singing hinnies, pan haggerty, sewin, salamagundie, stap, krappin, boxty, cabbieclaw, stotties, lobscouse, kickshaws—'

'*Quoi? Ils sont fous, les rosbifs!* Let's eat the *daube* and taste some real food.'

It seemed to be the profoundest of tragedies that every single one of those dishes was almost entirely unknown not only to anyone in the hallowed hexagon, but in the whole of Britain too, right from the heel of the Lizard to the very tip of Unst.

What has happened? Are the British really so lost in the culinary miasma? What a marvellous thing it is to have this long list of enigmatic, mysterious dishes that give absolutely nothing away in their names, and that cause you to stop, listen, and just wonder. What on earth is Hindle Wakes? Why can't we eat it any more?

Well, I, like you, had absolutely no idea. But I soon began to feel pulled by a Scott of the Antarctic moment. I felt in need of a stiff challenge, to discover what has happened to our culinary heritage – indeed, what on earth it is. So it was off to the Bodleian Library to soak in ancient texts, and try to build up a picture of what appeared to me to be a permanently recidivistic food culture, one that flirts and toys with innovation but always seems to return to the dull and the monochromatic.

And one that shows a marked tendency to play with its food, to joke and to demean excellence. One that thinks that to make food appealing to children all that needs to be done is to cut it up into teddy bear shapes. One that has a government that continually promotes fear and worry about the imminent danger from dreaded bacteria, yet so often shields us from the truth, and promotes an industrial ethic in food production at all levels. One that has been comprehensively traumatized by premature industrialization, and by the excessive dominance of a few powerful mega corporations that have us well and truly by the short and curlies and one that increasingly seems to prefer the microwave to the stove.

But I was absolutely convinced that somewhere there was a vibrant regionalism just waiting to blossom. And that, in a sense, is the *raison d'être* of this book. It's quite easy to argue the case. Just visit a farmers' market and you can hop and skip your way back to the car park laden with earthy carrots and glory in this apparent revival. But . . . as always, the but. It's what we do with the ingredients when we get back home that really matters.

Why do we seem to be so utterly uninterested in the intricacies of taste? In food's sublime subtleties? In the sensation of the bite of a freshly picked apple, whatever its shape, on the tongue? In the fabulous twang of a farmhouse Cheddar? In the warming, delicate softness of a slice of well-hung beef? I had long been troubled by the thought that the British seem to have a problem with taste. We love to use a culinary bludgeon: ketchup on our bacon sarnie, Marmite on toast, the chilli blast of a strong curry, horseradish with beef. That sort of thing. Somewhere along the line we seem to have been desensitized to the elaborate subtleties of food. Are we overwhelmed by a lingering puritanical resonance? And if this is true, will it ever change?

So I planned a journey, a guided dabble, to try to tease this all out. I hope that by the end of the book you will, like me, be a little clearer on the subject of the foodstuffs we enjoy as a nation, those we ignore, and the history that has shaped and informed the status quo. And I say 'hope' for the British have an undeniably complicated relationship with food. Our cooking is as widely denigrated as our raw materials are praised.

We are said to prefer simple cooking, unfussily presented, where the raw and natural flavours sing out, yet we are more than partial to that sharp blast from the sauce bottle. Our beef was once thought to be the finest in the world, yet we have given the world BSE. Our fish is the sweetest, but fast disappearing through overfishing. Our milk the richest, but most of our organic milk is now imported. It's all deeply paradoxical.

Yes, it seemed an excellent idea to set off into the mists to ponder and muse on the strange world of what the British eat and drink, to grapple a little with the intricate tangle of a nation's gastronomy. My journey took me to the wild island of North Ronaldsay, to the industrial deserts of northern England, and right across southern parts from Lowestoft to west Wales. I met vicious cows, ogled Tudor cauldrons, and watched naked people chase cheese down a precipice. I supped with Chinese ladies, and Gujarati gentlemen. I wrestled with the quince, and ate boiled pig's head. I waded through rivers and seas, and finally, for the first time in my life, I really began to fall in love with this bizarre and ancient country whose national dish, chicken tikka massala, is never cooked at home and doesn't really exist.

I never did get to taste most of the dishes I wanted to. They simply don't exist any more. No-one seems to cook lobscouse, salamagundie or singing hinnies, but I sincerely hope, indeed confidently predict, that they will. We have discovered French, Italian, Greek, Indian and Chinese food, so why not a British revival? Our heritage is ripe, and ready for the picking. The recipes still exist and the raw materials are to hand, so as our national culinary consciousness re-emerges, we will begin to revisit these distant waters. It hasn't all gone to dodoland. It is a rich and wacky heritage out there, so go and test the waters. I hope this book will awaken those dormant appetites and get your imagination a-wandering.

NORTH

PRESTON

Tripe and Cowheel

'OOO, NOO, I WOULDN'T PUT ANYTHING LIKE THAT IN *MY* MOUTH! I'm funny like that!'

The lady in Preston's Tourist Information Office was bursting with Lancastrian charm but not exactly overworked. She fixed me with a stern look, and laughed.

'But my dogs love it!'

Tripe was on my mind, the stomach of a ruminant that has been scraped, washed and endlessly boiled – or 'dressed', in tripe parlance – in the offal heartlands of northern England, just as it has been for hundreds of years. Tripe was once eaten enthusiastically by one and all. Millions of tons of flubby cow stomachs were lovingly fried, stewed with onions, or eaten with an invigorating splash of finest malt vinegar. They became part of the working-class heritage. But somewhere along the line tripe seems to have lost its culinary charms to such delights as the hamburger and the hot dog. The Lancastrians' famed love of offal seems to have vanished into the breeze, and now hangs on by the merest pig's trotter in odd pockets of the north-west. The only thing was, I wasn't at all sure why.

Tripe. For reasons that we have yet to reason about, tripe is funny. Mocking rather than embracing the industrial past is what we like to do best in post-industrial Britain. Perhaps this is part of its problem. Maybe tripe is just too redolent of brass bands, Grimethorpe and flat 'ats. The one thing much of northern England has had to grapple with over the past thirty years is how to manage its post-industrial soul. Inevitably, life is different now. Maybe it's a psychological thing. But the golden days of tripe are over.

In the cash-rich lottery days of the new millennium, huge amounts of money have been pumped into the north of England. It all seemed slightly ironic to me. It took terminal decline to help build art galleries, magnificent iconic bridges, and the inevitable chain of heritage museums. There are end-less shopping malls that reach their apogee in the enormous Metro Centre in Gateshead. Docks have received the customary makeover (actually, that's a brilliant idea: why don't we see more urban makeover shows on TV, with Richard Rodgers and Norman Foster teaming up with Diarmuid Gavin for a change?), and they now have natty little walkways, granny flats, and endless things to do with leisure. Where once stevedores sweated, now waiters perspire. Cafés, boats and lakes cohabit. It is quite relaxing really, but since I completely fail to understand the mysterious art of economics I cannot quite see how all this compensates for the demise of the one unifying link – manufacturing and mining. OK, two.

The manufacturers are long dead and buried, and the phantom of heavy industry struggles on elsewhere, off to haunt countries where labour is that much cheaper. Much of the architectural legacy of this industry has been absorbed into the loft culture. People are attracted by the idea of being able to walk back home drunk instead of driving inebriated. What we are left with seems to me to be depressingly homogeneous. Once self-possessed, proud and beautiful parts of the country all begin to look remarkably similar. Bar culture is pupating the country.

For a Londoner by birth, it always amazes me just how quickly the countryside can begin and urban sprawl end in and around some of the towns and cities of the industrial heartland of northern England. True to form, the train I took from Oxford zipped in and out of Stoke and Bolton, emerging suddenly each time into lush countryside before pulling in at Preston, where I had managed to track down one of Lancashire's last tripe dealers, still plying his trade in the market. Proud Preston, they call it – proud, that is, of its status as Britain's newest city, and as proud of its industrial past as it is of its magnificent football team, Preston North End. This gallant Victorian team were known as the Invincibles, and they battled with mighty rivals such as Accrington Stanley and Sheffield Wednesday. They once went through a whole season unbeaten, a record that stood until Arsène Wenger's Arsenal repeated the feat in 2003/04. Arsenal have called themselves the Untouchables, to avoid upsetting the deep memories of the Preston supporters. But Preston's achievements didn't stop there. Oh no. They are the only team ever to have had a goalkeeper who wore glasses. That was in an FA Cup final (in 1922). Predictably, perhaps, they lost to Huddersfield Town. In 1886 they even fielded the first black player to play in the British football league, another goalkeeper, Arthur Wharton. But the game they are perhaps proudest of is their massive 26–0 FA Cup-tie win over Hyde United in 1887. Hyde never really got over the humiliation.

While football evolved from a gentleman's game into the beating heart of working-class leisure, tripe also managed to capture this lucrative mass market, though it was a little hampered by its slippery texture. It proved impossible to create a portable version, so eventually tripe's bitter rival, the pie, won out. But by some commercial fluke, tripe took to the moral high ground and became almost genteel in the hands of a company called UCP (United Cattle Products), the tripe grandmasters if you like, the only company to take tripe firmly between their entrepreneurial teeth and run with it.

And so to Preston. When you have finished ogling at the architectural wonders of Winkley Square, head towards Preston Market. Feel the adrenalin begin to rush as you notice a towering iron structure, busy and full of browsing Prestonians looking for bargains. But don't get too excited, for as is so often the case the food market has been moved inside, to a dull, anodyne structure, leaving the glorious old Victorian market outside to be filled with second-hand booksellers called Derek reaping tiny profits from Mills and Boon seconds. 'All four for a pound. Come and buy your lovely Mills and Boon now. Four for a pound . . .'

When you do finally get inside, look for the one and only stall that sells tripe and you'll find Arthur Strand at work. Actually, Strand's now sells more than just tripe: it's 'Quality Cooked Meats, Pies, Black Puddings and Tripe' to be exact. Arthur has been dealing in the stuff for over thirty years. So let's take a tour of the waning world of the tripe dealer.

But first, a brief lament on the dying art of tripe dressing. There are very few tripe dressers left these days. All Strand's tripe comes from over the border in Dewsbury, Yorkshire. His supplier, Chris Heys, runs the tripe stall in Leeds. They are part of the tripe elite of northern England.

'You know, it's sad really,' Arthur confided, 'but not long ago every town and city had its own tripe dresser. There were four here in Preston; now there's Heys in Dewsbury, and one in Brighton, and that's it as far as I know. They were mostly one-man bands like. It were a good trade really.'

As he talked, I peered into his refrigerated cabinet, and noticed the pure white rubbery slabs of tripe almost apologetically lying in the corner. Honeycomb, seam, and the enigmatically named ladies tripe. There is something weirdly fascinating about honeycomb tripe. Its intricate geometric patterns call to my mind the biomes of the Eden Project, neatly interlocking in their geometric oneness.

'The thing people don't realize,' Arthur told me, 'is that all this tripe has already been cooked. You can eat it right away if you want. I think everyone's forgotten that; they think you've got to cook it for hours and hours. I get all mine in ready to use.

'Now, this is the honeycomb, which I think is the best tripe to eat. It comes from the second stomach, the reticulum. And this one' – he pulled another slab of slime from the fridge – 'is what we call seam, or belly, which is from the first stomach, the rumen. And then this one 'ere' – he dragged out something a little darker than the others – 'is what we call ladies tripe. I'm not too sure why, to be honest, but it's the best one to fry like, with chips. And that's from the omasum, the third stomach.'

Now, the story could in a sense stop here. A food goes out of fashion, expertise and know-how dissipates, but there is more to it than that. There were the UCPs. In their heyday in the 1950s, United Cattle Products had over 150 outlets throughout the area. Every major Lancastrian town and city had its very own UCP.

'There was one here in Preston,' Arthur explained, 'and I remember there was a lovely one at Blackpool, right by the station. It was all very clean and proper. And it was silver service. Imagine that nowadays, a whole chain of restaurants that were silver service.' And serving tripe.

A lady queuing at the stall heard what we were talking about.

'I remember the UCP,' she said. 'It was lovely. I used to go and have tripe and onions at lunchtime. It was all so clean and, well, nice really!' She laughed.

Another old lady joined in. 'I liked my tripe with chips.

But it wasn't *just* tripe, you know. We went there for a cup of tea sometimes. Ah, the UCP! They 'ad vans an' all. Their own vans delivering tripe. Fancy that!'

This sense of niceness that UCP strove so hard to achieve lives on. Considering that they were working with that most intractably unpleasant part of an animal's body, it is undeniably a fine achievement.

Later in the day I managed to track down one of their recipe books in the local library and felt the prim and proper soul of the company oozing from the pages. Did I know, for example, that tripe has played an important part in the diet of democracy? The pamphlet continued in the same glorifying vein: 'Any Pecksniffian prejudice arose through the misuse of the word itself, or because tripe was sold in a careless, un-hygienic fashion.' So, even if UCP couldn't get over the bald fact that tripe in colloquial English meant rubbish (a word that has generally been replaced by the equally colloquial 'bollocks'), they valiantly continued to work on the image of tripe to their dying day. The recipe booklet told me that UCP embodied one of the 'most interesting movements in the history of food'. And, yes, it was true: they had over eighty vans delivering the stuff every day, and created a snappy, easily recognizable logo that gave the chain commercial gravitas. UCP were proud to boast that they printed – and got rid of, presumably – over 295,000 copies of their first recipe book. Not a bad figure at all, I assure you, for anything in print.

UCP evolved from the tripe stalls that plied a brisk trade by the factory gates at the end of the working day, the men stopping off on their way home to stave off their hunger. It was particularly popular to eat tripe on Fridays, apparently; to line the stomach with stomach lining for the evening's drinking. Tripe bars were often to be found in town too, but none on the grandiose scale of the UCPs. Factories were built to be as 'lilywhite as a model dairy, exploiting every invention of science to maintain purity; each factory prepared and cooked tripe which has resuscitated its ancient fame'. UCP tried to persuade the consumer that they were part of a long and glorious culinary heritage. And it's true, tripe eating does have a long and relatively glorious past. Falstaff loved it. Sam Pepys too.

Nothing unusual there perhaps. But what astonished me was just how far tripe has fallen. Then, it was clearly far from its present-day image as yucky, greasy and fatty, as something almost inedible. UCP reflected the widely held view that tripe was a food 'rich in nutriment [*sic*] and body building qualities, the most digestible possible food that is peculiarly suitable as a base for the most delicately appetizing dishes'. Tripe, we were told, 'has been saved for the national diet. Tripe is a cheap food (9d per pound); but it is also a splendid food for the sedentary brain worker, for the invalid, the child and the nursing mother.'

But don't imagine that it was only tripe that was eaten with such gusto. There was more lurking in Arthur Strand's cold cabinet. As we were talking, an elderly man asked for a bit of cow'eel, and I watched as Arthur took up a cooked cow's foot in his hand and scraped some of the gelatinous outer layers onto the scale. 'That's fifty pence, please,' he told him, and I thought I'd ask the old man what he was going to do with it.

'Excuse me,' I said in my best English, 'but   '

He turned his head, his eyes mixed with a curious combination of terror and loathing, snapped, 'Can't you see I'm busy?' and stumped off.

Cowheel is nothing more than the boiled foot of a cow, and it exudes a preposterous amount of gorgeous gelatinousness. Perhaps it's worth reminding ourselves that gelatine itself, the very substance that once united fruit under the guise of wobbly jellies, was once derived from rendering down the bones of animals, but cow and particularly calves' feet were always prized. In cooking, cowheel adds substance to a stew, a steak and kidney pie, a Lancashire hotpot even, and is of course cheap. But then there's the other side of the coin that places cowheel, and more particularly calves' feet, as a restorative, well suited for that good old cook's addendum, the invalid. Calves' feet jelly is a classic Victorian remedy that has also lost its attraction these days. And nutritionally speaking, it is more than mere superstition. A light, meaty broth, like the Jewish mother's chicken soup, does restore. Indeed, the very word 'restaurant' comes from the French *restaurer*, 'to restore', and it began life in the 1760s when one Monsieur Boulanger sold a bouillon of sheep's trotters to eager Parisians with the specific purpose of being a restorative – not everyone's choice, perhaps, but it worked well in Paris in those days. He called his establishment a restaurant – a place, in other words, that would restore good health.

Tripe and cowheel stew

Serves 6

1.5kg dressed honeycomb tripe
200g cowheel jelly
2 large carrots, thinly cut
3 white onions, peeled and thinly cut
1 bunch fresh thyme
3 cloves
salt and pepper
100ml beef stock

Place the cut vegetables, thyme and cloves in a casserole. Cut the tripe into even strips about an inch wide and place on top of the vegetables. Add the cowheel jelly and the stock, and mix. Season, and cook in a moderate oven for thirty minutes.

Adapted from the *UCP Cookbook*

I turned my attention back to the tripe and wondered out loud if it was the fattiness that had put people off. Arthur Strand told me that his father would have had nothing to do with the tripe he was selling these days. He would have expected a great thick layer of the stuff around the cow's stomach, but in our crazed, misguided world the consumption of fat was, pre-Atkins and during the cholesterol concern decades, considered to be virtually suicidal. Tripe may well have had great gobbets of fat on it, and people were none the worse for it, but then work was often hard and physical, and life expectancy that much shorter. Our animals are now bred to be lean. Too lean for good tripe.

Perhaps it might just be the texture that people dislike, plus that gelatinous, slightly intestinal taste you get from tripe, trotters and the like, no longer appreciated by the British household, allied to their deep suspicion of anything different. Whatever the truth, people are rarely ambivalent towards tripe. You either love it or loathe it. And these days loathing wins out. And what of the wacky world of the UCP? Even they couldn't survive the changing tastes of a changing Lancashire. They were bought out by a company called the Golden Egg, which served what I would call excruciatingly horrible food and had it all inscribed on an egg-shaped menu.

Despite all this, Arthur Strand is deeply committed to Lancashire and its culinary traditions. 'Come back any time and I'll show you all my books on tripe,' he said as a parting shot. 'You're welcome to have a look. Anything that helps us Lancastrians keep our food from disappearing completely!'

Elsewhere on the stall he had piles of good, solid, round, crusty butter pies, which I had never heard of. I bought a couple to take home, ate one on the train and the other later on. They were exquisite. Arthur Strand had been encouraging his local piemaker to start production again, for these were also on the way out until the locals discovered vegetarianism (butter pies are made with cheese and potatoes). There were even trays of Lancashire hotpot, a dish that unlike tripe has somehow managed that huge conceptual leap from working-class favourite to the restaurant menu. But, Arthur warned me, 'It's not really genuine 'otpot, you know, cos it's made from beef. But it's good, mind.' 'Real 'otpot' was made with mutton and served in a particular curved earthenware pot so that the chops could fit neatly into the edges.

When I had finished my tripe session, I staggered out into the pouring rain laden with bags of cow'eel, tripe and the finest Lancashire cheese I had ever tasted. 'Crumbly or creamy?' they had asked me. Lancashire is a young cheese, ideal for cooking, almost spreadable when fresh. Then, outside the solid Victorian art library, I came across a stall selling parched peas. Parched peas? Yup, parched peas. A delicious gastronomic irony here: they are always served swimming in juice. 'Gutter slush' they used to call it. Parched peas are made from black or pigeon peas, soaked overnight then boiled, sometimes with a little beef dripping, and served with lashings of salt and vinegar. They sound unappetizing, but they aren't. In fact, they were so good I bought another little cupful, casting to the breeze any thoughts of the train passengers I was about to gift with lashings of good old intestinal gas.

Parched peas used also to be made from Carling peas, which are almost impossible to find these days. Carling peas were grown mainly in the north and were said to have saved the Lancashire cotton workers from starvation once when a shipment of them arrived one Carling Sunday, and were quickly cooked. I'm not too sure whether this is why they are called parched peas or not. But they remained a firm local favourite.

What really struck me here on the streets of Preston was that there was a lingering food subculture. It was quite encouraging, coming as it did at the start of my odyssey. Yes, there were the usual culprits – burgers, pizzas and the like – but Preston market was studded with tasty food that was genuinely and ineluctably regional.

2

BOLTON

Black Pudding

MORNING. FOR MANY OF US THE NIGHTS ARE WASHED AWAY WITH a quick shower and a cup of tea. Fluorescent cereals tumble from unfeasibly large packets to be splashed with a milky stream of semi-skimmed, and onto the floor, where the Labrador waits with drool issuing from its stinking jaws. Ah, the joys of an everyday domestic family scene somewhere in the depths of Middle Britain.

But to Jack Morris, the mornings once meant something even more picturesque. Blood. Gallons of it. Buckets of warm, fresh pig's blood to be precise. Fortified with tea, Jack would set off from his butcher's shop in Farnsworth, just outside Bolton, pick up his trusty old forty-gallon milk churn, scrubbed clean and smelling lightly of bleach, and go and meet his old friends at the abattoir. An everyday scene in 1960s Lancashire.

Jack Morris made black pudding, you see, and did so for over forty years until he handed over the business to his son

17

Richard at the dawn of the new millennium. Happily for the enthusiast, the company he created still churns them out by the ton. In fact it is widely considered that they make the best black puddings in the land, and Jack has overseen a curious revival of this most ancient of foods — remarkable considering just how squeamish the British can be. I had been reminded of Morris's black pudding by Arthur Strand, who told me that he had been dealing with Morris's for well over thirty years now and knew of none finer. So I arranged, almost literally, to backtrack (my train to Preston had already torn in and out of Bolton a few days earlier), thus to move seamlessly from tripe to blood, and to meet the great man himself.

Jack was a butcher by trade, and he realized that he was selling so much Bury black pudding up in Farnsworth that it might be well worth his while making his own. Bolton and Bury are the cultural core of black puddings and their stubby, hand-linked sausages are easily identifiable to the practised eye. So he looked up a few old recipes and began to do just that. Hence the blood, of course, for black pudding is principally a mixture of blood and cereal, possibly some fat, and little more.

In the 1970s, Jack was elected president of the Bolton Butchers' Association and began to worry about the business of butchery, and the perceptible decline in local specialities. Then he read of a world-famous black pudding competition over in Normandy, in a rather sleepy town called Mortagne in an even sleepier region called Le Perche, famous for its thick-set carthorses, as well as its *boudin noir* competition. One fateful day, Jack took the plunge and entered the cut and thrust of international competition. Eventually he triumphed, and his Bury black pudding achieved the ultimate — the Gold Medal. It was a proud and lachrymose man who returned to the streets of Farnsworth, glorying in this great honour. Things were never to be the same again. Jack had at last found fame, and he developed quite a taste for this highly prestigious event of international butchery. 'One year I was judging the German section,' he told me. 'You taste the black pudding, you drink the wine. And you then can't remember a thing about it! I loved that French competition.'

Jack reckoned that maybe he could try and recreate a little of this black pudding magic back home in Lancashire, so he started the Best Black Pudding of Great Britain competition whose duty was not just to boost the public profile of this estimable sausage but also to raise money for charity.

Now, it has to be said that after several decades Jack Morris has the patter down to a fine art. He has been fêted by chefs and stars since he appeared with Gary Rhodes on British television and amused us all with his tales of blood and guts. He became a blood pudding megastar. 'It was a grand time, really,' he recalled. 'I met them all. Larry Grayson, Les Dawson . . .' And this at a time when the idea that perhaps chefs could make use of local produce rather than getting poor souls like me to pluck the finest mini cauliflowers in France and truck them over was almost eccentric.

But by 2001 the small-scale local butcher was in severe decline. It proved almost impossible for them to survive while punters succumbed to the powerful temptations of the super-market, where meat – indeed everything – was cheaper and could be bought at once. Corporate Britain won through, the country's food supply became controlled by a handful of mega corporations (where it remains to this day), and the com-petition was stopped. Still, it is an inescapable fact that wherever there are pigs there will be blood. And wherever there is pig's blood there will be black pudding. In Scandinavia it is called *blodpudding*, like the *boudin noir* made as a variation on the theme of blood as a by-product of butchery, stuffed into an animal casing and boiled. In Italy you will find *sanguinaccio*, a curious mix of blood and chocolate, and in Spain it's *morcilla*. It is, indeed, a pretty universal offering.

But why 'pudding', you may wonder? Why not black

sausage? A pudding was not always a sweet and sticky thing, but once implied something stuffed into a container of some sort. So, black pudding was blood mixed with cereal stuffed into a piece of the gut of a pig – the 'bung end' as it was called. It could easily be boiled along with flitches of bacon and whatever else would fit into a canny household's cauldron. There are also historical echoes of pudding crossover in what we now call Christmas pudding. It was once more usually called plum, or even plump, pudding, made with sweet ingredients as well as suet, or the fat that is found around animals' kidneys.

Without giving me the precise recipe – it's secret, you see – Jack gave me a rough idea as to what you add to the pig's blood, and reminded me, 'You had to be careful not to let the blood set, coagulate like, so somebody would keep stirring it with a stick. When you got the blood back to the shop, you'd add some barley flour, or maybe some oatmeal – all that helps bulk it out, you see. Then some diced fresh onions. And then some herbs and seasoning.' It's important to use something that will absorb the blood. In the Lancastrian version barley flour and oats are used, in France it's mainly chopped onion, so the two puddings have very different tastes and textures.

'I don't suppose you're going to tell me what herbs you use, are you?' I asked.

'Well, no, I can't do that. We do use a bit of celery salt, and nutmeg. I'll tell you that much!'

Ancient texts suggest that pennyroyal – called, locally, pudding grass – was also used. This member of the mint family once had a reputation for driving away irksome fleas, but became part of the northern English cook's store cupboard.

So this glorious thick purple mass was then piped into its casing to become recognizably a sausage rather than a bloody mush. The Morrises use a natural casing, but it's bovine. Porcine is better, but tender and more difficult to use. These days, some of the cheaper black puddings even use a plastic casing.

Tradition has it that each Bury black pudding be studded with a cube of white pig fat. Although I like the idea of this deliberate poetic contrast between the dark, vinous purple of blood and the pure marble-white fat, its origin was probably due to the need for cheap calories for breakfast in the days when copious amounts of fat provided the fuel for working men and women, and even children, in the industrial heartland of Britain.

Cutting the fat used to be one of Jack Morris's other early-morning duties. 'It was actually about the first thing I used to do in the mornings,' he said, 'before I went down to get the blood. But the pigs were fatter in those days. We used what was called the flair fat, and I had to cut it up into squares. It was so tender you didn't even have to cook it.' These days, since pigs have been put on a collective diet, back fat is used. But being that much tougher, it needs to be cooked. The issue of fat neatly divides the market into two. Traditionalists expect it, novices and younger enthusiasts may baulk at it, so Morris's now produces a contemporary lean black pudding for those who worry about their fat levels.

Transylvanians among you may be saddened to learn that it is not as easy to find prodigious quantities of fresh blood as it used to be. Small local abattoirs are closing down all over the country, so Morris's now uses dried, reconstituted blood. Not as good in Jack's opinion, but there is little choice in the matter. To reproduce that essential bloody blackness some producers even add a vegetable dye. Morris's doesn't, instead travelling the high road to black pudding purity by adding a handful of soda.

When all is stuffed and ready, cooking the black puddings is simple. 'We put them in water that's just below boiling point,' Jack explained, 'and keep them on a very slow boil for about forty-five minutes. Traditionally, up here in Lancashire, we used to boil the puddings for ten minutes, then serve them. Then some people liked to slice and grill 'em. You might have them served with mash and veg for dinner, and some people would add them to a stew.

'But,' Jack added, lowering his voice a notch, 'I like to cook them like this: you slice 'em in half, cut into quarters and dip them in batter, then serve 'em on a bed of stewed apples. That's absolutely fantastic!'

I returned home laden with black puddings, and bags of tripe. The family crowded round, had a look, and backed away. Odd, that. It was tripe for dinner that night, some splashed with vinegar, the rest served with a thick onion sauce. Soft, and gelatinous, I could imagine myself toothless, watching Preston North End or Bolton Wanderers in my carpet slippers, enjoying the experience. And the black pudding? Class, indeed. Breakfast the next day was a freshly laid egg, a rasher of the very best bacon, and a Morris's black pudding.

But it was time to put offal to bed for a while and set off on the trail of a Lancastrian dish the sound of whose name I loved – Hindle Wakes.

3

BLACKPOOL

Hindle Wakes and Rock

WHAT'S PINK AND HARD IN THE MORNINGS? WHY, THE *FINANCIAL Times* crossword, of course! Is that just a little bit vulgar for you? If it is, don't come to Blackpool, the Mecca of vulgarity, a town with one of the highest teenage pregnancy rates in the country and the home of one of the stickiest and hardest pink things you will ever put in your mouth – Blackpool rock. As Muhammad Ali was once supposed to have said, 'Boy, it's harder than Joe Frazier!'

My wanderings around Lancashire looking for Hindle Wakes ended in Blackpool, but on the way, having had my taste buds tickled by Arthur Strand and Jack Morris, I became passionately curious about the county and its food, a blessed mix of the homely and the thrifty – dishes such as Lancashire hotpot, but perhaps most of all about the long list of the region's culinary creations that have the most marvellously bizarre names. Meet pan haggerty, a mixture of soft Lancashire cheese and potatoes. Then there is lobscouse, scouse or simply lobby, once a Liverpudlian speciality, a slowly cooked stew of silverside, dried peas and spuds. Lobscouse was supposed to have come over from Germany, settled down and given the city's inhabitants their name – scousers. Neither is difficult to make. Neither is easy to find. And where have all the wet nellies gone? This variation on the theme of bread pudding still exists in Walsall but is said to have originated in Liverpool. It was one way in which a great port could show its appreciation to that great lipsmacking naval hero Horatio, Lord Nelson. Then there was Lancashire foots. Not, I emphasize, Lancashire feet. They were pasties, also called Colliers foots, made to fit the miners' tin lunch boxes that hung from their belts, and were cooked at home in the morning, baked with cheese, bacon and onions.

Mind you, not all Lancastrian food seems to have foundered so profoundly. Chorley cakes and Eccles cakes, for example, have both managed to survive the cruel Darwinian treadmill. Being sweet, cheap and portable has probably helped – not the case, sadly, I discovered, for Hindle Wakes. I needed a steaming plate of Hindle Wakes whatever it took, whatever it was. Its name gives you not the mildest hint, the vaguest scintilla of a clue as to what it might be. Maybe Hindle the mad axe murderer awoke and had this dish cooked for him before he was hanged at the gallows. Or, the town of Hindle awoke one morning to see that the plague had spared them and cooked this dish to celebrate. Nah! None of this.

What I found out was this. A wake was a time for communal fun and japery that originally started when churchgoers stayed awake all night to celebrate the local saint's day. It was very much a celebration, a time for bizarre rituals, played out in the valleys and hills of much of pre-industrial northern Britain. It often involved much drinking, to the distinct disapproval of the Church. But it was particular to a local community. The word is also used in 'funeral wake', when people would literally stay awake to celebrate the life of the dearly departed, then depart themselves to the valley of despondent drunkenness.

But what of this word Hindle? Well, it seems it is a dialect mumbling of 'hen de la', which should immediately suggest chicken, and a foreign tongue. The most likely explanation is that it is a dish that was brought to Lancashire by Flemish weavers tempted by the profitable woollen trade in the sixteenth century, and it became particularly associated with Bolton.

When you get down to the nitty gritty you begin to sense how totally unsuited the dish is to modern life. You take a capon, or more commonly a boiling fowl, stuff it with prunes, lemon and breadcrumbs, and then steam it for four hours. And that's not all. When your pinger finally pings, you need to get the whole thing out and roast it for another half an hour. So it's not exactly the ideal dish for a harassed, poverty-stricken, working family of the Lancashire mills. Which quite possibly explains its demise.

Hindle Wakes

1.4kg boiling fowl
450g prunes
6 pieces of rindless streaky bacon
2 lemons
50g breadcrumbs
1 small onion, chopped
1 pinch thyme
1 pinch basil salt
pepper
gravy

Wash the lemons and pare the rind thinly; simmer in water for 15 minutes. Add the strained juice of the lemons. Wash and stone the prunes, then pour the lemon juice over them. Blend them with the onion, thyme, basil and breadcrumbs, then stuff the chicken with the mixture. Steam for 4 hours, then wrap the chicken in bacon and roast for 35 minutes. Serve with rich gravy and prunes.

This might suggest to you, as it does to me, that Hindle Wakes would be a magnificent candidate, as would so many of our redundant national dishes, for the attentions of the Slow Food movement. But this phenomenally successful movement, created in the 1980s as the antithesis to the growing global fast food culture, and with its roots firmly planted in Italian soil, exists to promote, preserve and protect products rather than dishes that are finding it hard to survive, be it through changing tastes, crazy bureaucratic directives from Brussels, or just plain geographic isolation. There is nothing in the recipe for Hindle Wakes that cannot be readily found on a supermarket shelf. Still, it's true to say that Slow Food has yet to sink its teeth into the complexities of British regional cooking.

However, while the dish itself might have died, the wakes lived on. Wakes took many forms. In some of the valleys and towns of Lancashire and Yorkshire there evolved a strange custom called rush bearing. Church floors were strewn with rushes and everyone had a fantastically good time going to the hills to find them. In 1780, the vicar of Rochdale took exception to all this enjoyment and forbade any rush-bearing jollity to sully his church. However, the population still took to the hills on the Saturday, collected their flowers and rushes, and carried them back through the town, enjoying themselves hugely in the process. On the following Monday no-one worked, and they watched the carts bedecked and piled with rushes move through the streets. The idea caught on and eventually the processions became almost unmanageable, as rival towns tried to outdo one another, got drunk and fought. Thus was born the idea of a mass holiday, towns choosing their own particular weeks. The practice was eventually accepted by the mill and factory owners who knew that productivity plummeted when the workforce was completely cowed and exploited. So the Wakes Week holiday pleased everyone.

This was the origin of the annual migration to the sea, which fed the infamous Blackpool landladies with endless streams of holidaymakers from early July right through to September. First the Pottery towns arrived. Then it was the Scots Trade Weeks. Then Preston, Blackburn – all in a repetitive and highly predictable pattern. Burnley had its Peterstide Fair, and all the towns and cities entered into the municipal spirit of things by setting up Wakes Committees to ease the planning as the town left en masse. Coaches were commandeered, trains booked. Everyone was encouraged to 'put something by' for the holiday, and as the Wakes Week approached the excitement was palpable.

There are still many who remember those days. And there are still many who go to Blackpool every year, as they always have done, and stay in the same guesthouse, as they always have done. One landlady told me, 'You know, they used to sit on the wall outside, and they'd know just about everyone! Hello Mrs this and that. Where are you staying this year? What's your landlady like? It was all very gossipy in them days.'

But it needed the train to make Blackpool into the rocking success it became in the late nineteenth century, golden days that lasted right up to the 1970s, when people began to discover the package tour. At last they could eat chips in the sun! Which is, in a way, Blackpool's great paradox. The idea of a seaside holiday is to lie in the sun, soak up the rays, and then sip something a little stronger. Blackpool's skies are almost permanently leaden.

'You know what I think the problem is? I think somewhere along the line we all forgot how to have fun.'

These wise words came from the mouth of a true

Blackpudlian, a 'sand grown 'un' as they say, and a real pillar of the community. Elaine Smith is retired now but was once a hotel owner, a woman born and bred in the salty air who knows a thing or two about what makes the town tick.

Blackpool landladies once had a reputation for being formidable, for running their little fiefdoms with an iron hand and woe betide anyone who didn't play the game. Back by eleven and out by ten in the morning, so that by ten thirty, come rain or the rare moments of sunshine, Blackpool's streets were full of people looking to have some fun (they still are). The much-maligned landlady was left to get on with the business of running the guesthouse while the guests went out and enjoyed themselves.

But when you look at what she had to do, her reputation may not surprise you. For it became the tradition that the guests brought their own food with them to be cooked by the landlady for lunch, dinner and even tea. Imagine it. This poor woman had to imitate and stand in eternal comparison to Mum's cooking, and keep the place clean and tidy to boot.

Breakfast was perhaps the easiest meal of all, for everyone liked, and still expects, a Full English Breakfast. It's almost a criminal offence to start the day without lashings of good old pork fat streaming through your aorta, and slices of toast, all washed down by a strong cuppa. But lunch and dinner must have been far more challenging. Elaine told me how they did it. 'They had a frying pan divided into sections, so one family would have this, and the next something else, and that's how it worked.'

Frying has a special place in the hearts and minds of Britons. And it's not just that it keeps coronary surgeons in work. It is a relatively economical way of cooking food, important at a time when fuel was expensive and hard to get, and, as we have seen, a cooked breakfast was a good way of fuelling the collective corpus of manual workers throughout this prematurely industrialized part of the country. Fried food began to be hawked through urban streets by itinerant food sellers in the nineteenth century, which provided working-class homes with cheap snacks and helped develop the national love affair with the chip.

Elaine Smith can still remember the bizarre ritual of the pigeonholes. 'Everyone had a pigeonhole on the wall,' she explained, 'and would put what they wanted to eat that day in them, and that was that. All the landlady charged for was the "use of cruet"! You just hoped there was enough. I used to help my aunt get the food ready when I was little, and would run off down to the shops if something was missing.' Where else would you find such a deeply anal attitude to food? Experimentation? Bah! None of it! Let's just stick to what we know, to those familiar dishes, and then moan behind the landlady's back for not cooking like Mother does. That seemed to me to be the logic behind this crazy idea.

And then came dinner. Elaine's son Mark owned one of the best family-run guesthouses in Blackpool, the Old Coach House, right at the southern end, within good screaming distance of the Pleasure Beach. Although he and his wife Claire have now sold up and are busy building the town's first 'boutique hotel', as they called it, with plasma screens, gorgeous towels, nice jam and home-made bread, when they started the Old Coach House they learned the hard way.

'When we changed the time of dinner at the beginning from five o'clock to seven o'clock,' Mark recalled, 'we couldn't work out why our takings dropped so much.'

It was all down to one of Blackpool's least trumpeted but much-loved institutions, the WMCs, or the Working Men's Clubs. Born in the spirit of Victorian philanthropy, the WMCs were formed in the second half of the nineteenth century by well-meaning men with bushy beards and women with names like Mrs Cooper and Mrs Wilson (who may also have had bushy beards). The idea was to give the working classes somewhere to talk and socialize away from the pub. Many were initially supposed to be alcohol free. These were the days of Temperance, and hey, teetotals had their rights too. In seaside resorts such as Blackpool WMCs were widely approved of and hugely popular.

The founder of the Club and Institute Union, Henry Solly, wrote in 1867, 'The Halls are opened from six to ten o'clock every week evening, and from two to nine on Sundays. Refreshments are supplied at a low fixed rate. Smoking is allowed, but the use of intoxicating drinks on the premises is prohibited. A large number of publications . . . are placed on the tables; and provision is made for fourteen games in the Halls and skittle-grounds.' All very uplifting. The intention all along, of course, was to help the working classes become the way the upper classes thought they should be. Solly again: 'Working men . . . often need the very culture which alone would make their Club profitable to them . . . A proportionately greater vital force is required to lift working men, and to help them lift themselves, out of the various evils, temptations and hindrances, social, physical and moral, which now oppress them.'

Thus the movement started. It flourished, and continues still. In Blackpool there is the Brunswick Club in Bethesda Road, which has moved on a little, as they all did, to become part cabaret, part theatre, with a snooker hall and vicious games of bingo at lunchtime. Many of these clubs have decided that elevating the masses is no longer quite the thing to be seen to do, and they nurse talent instead. Some of the acts are well past their prime, easy stuff, but through the ranks of the WMCs have risen some of the greatest comic talents of all time.

'Well, there's Jack Duckworth, Rita Sullivan,' Elaine began, rattling off a list. 'Oh, and Les Dawson!'

And Peter Kay, I might add. He actually exists. Watch *Phoenix Nights*, if you haven't.

So why the collapse in business at the Old Coach House?

Well, because the clubs opened their doors at six and everyone wanted to get the best seats – the tradition of first come first served still holds true. Dinner had to be at five and that was that, so the poor old landlady had even less time to put her feet up and have a rest.

For those guests on a really tight budget, there was always a Holland's meat pie to be had in the interval. Holland's still have a passionately devoted Lancastrian following. They have supplied the fish and chip trade with their pies since the middle of the nineteenth century, and a true Lancastrian will go misty-eyed at the thought of a meat pie barm with salt and vinegar. To us non-Lancastrians, that's a pie sandwich.

Sea, sun, and yes, sex. Blackpool thrived on its phallic tower, its smutty jokes, on the clubs that nurtured comic talent and made fun of fat mothers-in-law and demonic landladies. Full of testosterone, in the days long gone by when everyone was supposed to be in bed by eleven on pain of a jolly good thrashing (oooh, sir, that sounds nice!), the streets vibrated to the nocturnal rhythms of the 'knee-trembler' – a quick shag, in other words, against a wall. It was, and is still I suspect, a Blackpool speciality, although you have to wander around a bit before you notice that there is something odd going on with the guesthouses these days.

It reminded me of Amsterdam, the way you can walk past and observe the whores in the windows of the red-light-district buildings. The fronts of guesthouses are just as full of explicit messages. OVERNIGHT GUESTS WELCOME means that you can bring anyone back. And vice versa. Many are adorned with porcelain cats and begonias, and curiously vivid lights; there are 'nice' tablecloths on the tables. The bars are clean, mini pubs run entirely by the owner.

Groups come up for the weekend, get drunk, get laid, and sleep for the minimum number of hours. It's the British doing what they do abroad back home again. A domestic Faliraki.

Apparently, the guesthouse owners who profit from all this are much keener on groups of boys, who tend to end up somewhere other than the rooms they have booked.

But at the other end of the scale there's old Blackpool and the stiff-upper-lipped charms of the Grand Ballroom, with its glorious rococo ceiling, and the mighty Wurlitzer that still rises up from the bowels of the theatre at the stroke of the hour, the organist smiling, enticing us all to get onto the floor for a rumba, a waltz or a tango. These days few do. Few know how to. It's a little sad to see photos of the black and white glory days when the floor was packed out. There's just the odd couple now, dancing with consummate skill, entirely straight-faced, to these rhythms of, as the French call it, *le troisième age*.

But what was the town to do in the winter? How on earth can a seaside resort survive on such a short season? Well, many haven't. Take a day trip to Hastings on the south coast and you'll see just what I mean. The town is a miserable place, run down and full of Hogarthian horror scenes, of junkies and alcoholics, and all this despite a heritage of such magnitude – there was a battle there once in 1066, you know – and a unique fishing fleet that launches the boats from the beach. But the place is just too grim to enjoy this. Sorry, Hastings, but do something before it's too late. Maybe it is already.

Blackpool did do something. They built the town in the full realization that it will more than likely rain for at least seven days out of ten. So, if anyone did decide to come back they would be far better off offering them something to do. Hence the tower, the piers – all three of them – the Winter Gardens, the magnificent Pleasure Beach, the Illuminations, the Trams, the Circus . . . You can bathe in the freezing cold sea, and be thrown about on the Pleasure Beach. You can spend a whole day up Blackpool Tower, eating bucketloads of greasy food, or even experience the joy of a Holland's meat pie. The town thrives on stags and hens drinking themselves into oblivion, and throwing up on the beach as a grand Blackpudlian finale. Then there are the smutty postcards, the depressed donkeys on the beach, the kiss-me-quick hats. And the thousands upon thousands of hotels, guesthouses and bed and breakfasts. Life can be rough and hectic in Blackpool. But forget about anyone offering you Hindle Wakes. They won't.

It would, however, almost be immoral to leave without that evocative hard pink thing somewhere in your luggage. A stick of Blackpool rock. Wherever you go in this civilized world of ours you can be fairly sure that the rock you hold in your sticky hands will have been made right here in this the most kitsch of towns, the queen of Britain's seaside resorts. Sugar and glucose syrup – the fundamental ingredients that maketh rock, along with a homoeopathically tiny dose of dye and a tad of artificial flavouring – may sound a simple creation, but it requires a team of dedicated rockers whose skill, it appears, is in their teamwork.

Happily, rock-making seems to be very much alive in Blackpool. The Coronation Rock Company was saved from ignominy by Ian Atkinson, a Lancastrian who had sought his fortune in metropolitan London as an accountant. Incomprehensibly, the joys of accountancy soon palled, and he took off back home where he bought a rock-making business whose finances were deeply precarious (we might almost say rocky). Ailing no longer, they now send rock quite literally around the world. One of their most faithful customers is in Australia where there is a thriving subculture of expats who simply swoon at the prospect of a stick of Blackpool rock. The sales team spends hours dreaming up innovative, sickly-sweet things to eat, such as artificial sausages, and fried eggs and chips. When I passed by they were experimenting on something even more mesmerizing.

'Here, try this,' Ian told me, slipping me a little sweet something. 'Tell me what you think it is.'

A strange memory of the 1970s came flooding to my brain, a hazy vision of Rizlas and joss sticks. It was a sneak preview of their latest invention, Ganja rock, the letters running through from beginning to end to remind you where you are in case you become too insensible. Ganja rock has the pointed leaf of a *Cannabis sativa* in the middle, and is chopped up into manageable munchy-size bites, with flavours that range from Super Skunk to Northern Lights. It has apparently gone down a storm in the cafés of Amsterdam, and is set to conquer the world. If it can get its act together, that is.

The basic mix of a stick of rock is fairly simple: two-thirds best cane sugar and one-third glucose syrup boiled to about 320 degrees in a fine copper cauldron, then poured seething and steaming into a long cooling tray. Add the dye, and the flavouring, and there you sort of have it. This huge mass of warm, sugary protean rock, sweet-smelling and malleable, cools briskly and is then set upon by a team of burly men – the rock-making team. And then the masterstroke, the touch of genius: the letters are added.

At first, these are written on a Brobdingnagian scale. A 'C' will be a loop of coloured dye wrapped around a mass of the aerated inner part of the stick of rock to be. And so on. And I say this with the profoundest respect, for it must be a frustratingly fiddly job. The whole sweet mass is then carried across like an elephantine foetus to the batch roller, where it is rolled and stretched and pulled, the stretching making the whole thing smaller and smaller while keeping the logo and letters intact, and in proportion. Sounds simple? It isn't. For, as they say up here, the longer it takes the harder it gets (tee hee), so they have to work quickly. The white central core is sent along to be properly seen to by a machine called the product puller which traps millions of tiny air bubbles into it, which in turn help the sucker to get that sugary hit, and to dissolve the stick of rock.

Watch them at it (phwah phwah), and it is all blissfully

harmonious. A classic stick of rock has three parts to it, the outer pink bit, the inner bubbly bit, and the letters, all of which are assembled under the eyes of master rock-maker David French, who with over twenty years' experience is an absolutely vital member of the company. The really weird bit is to see them all put it together, carrying the whole proto-stick of rock across the room in reassuringly strong arms. I have to admit that I had naively assumed rock was made by some faceless machine, but no. The hand of man is entirely responsible. So think of them the next time you put something pink and hard in *your* mouth!

The origins of rock are slightly obscured in the Lancastrian mists, but it seems that something of the sort was being made in the early nineteenth century. Sir Henry Mayhew, the Victorian diarist and philanthropist, noted that sticks of rock were being hawked on the streets of London. The story goes that he spied someone selling these 'sticks' with letters that ran through from one end to the other, but the business seemed to be doomed, probably because the logos just fell short of commercial snappiness and relevance. DO YOU LOVE SPRATS? was one. LORD MAYOR'S DAY was another. Other versions suggest that it was a Yorkshireman, Ben Bullock of Dewsbury, who thought of the idea in 1887, and it seems likely that he was indeed the first to make rock on a grandiose scale. The truth is that this is one gastronomic mystery that will remain unsolved. We simply don't know. It is also said that the very first words used on a stick of Blackpool rock were WHOA EMMA!, but that too had a limited shelf life, even in those days. The most popular phrase soon became, as it still is, simply BLACKPOOL ROCK.

Blackpool is a place of prodigious appetites. Over 10½ million sticks of rock are sold every year. Some 47½ miles of hot dogs are eaten, along with 2½ million servings of chips, half a million burgers and a million ice-cream cones. But not, as far as I could ascertain, a single portion of Hindle Wakes.

I spent my last night in Blackpool at the circus with a lovely pregnant French lady, *mon amour*, who was transfixed by the enormous volumes of meat pies and chips that were being eaten on the streets, if not so much by the show's intricate plots, the loud-crashing clowning and the piles of Chinese girls riding cycles round and round in circles. The circus is built in the same style as the Grand Ballroom — technically Victorian rococo, I think — and is round and amphitheatrical. This was where the great Cairoli clowned. His successor, if not perhaps great, was just as spooky. I've always had a problem with clowns. They scare me.

But the finale was worth waiting for. The wide-eyed kids waving their flashing football rattles and the women peeking through hijabs watched amazed as the whole arena filled up with water in seconds. Water gushed from everywhere onto the polished wooden floor, and the troupe took to their rafts, a collection of wobbling cylinders dressed in wedding-cake white. A vast man with strong legs and a look of Eastern Europe about him spun a smiling raven-haired beauty round and round on roller skates. It made you want to vomit with motion sickness. The band played louder and louder, the ring-master had indeed mastered his ring, and it was all orgiastically climactic and just so Blackpool.

Later, we shoehorned ourselves once more into yet another B&B, waited for the sun to rise, and as regularly as the cock crowed to be asked, 'Full English, love? Tea or coffee?' And then off up the coast to look for a potted shrimp or two.

MORECAMBE BAY

Potted Shrimps and Cockles

I SET MYSELF A MINI-QUEST: WHILE TRAVELLING THE LENGTH AND breadth of Morecambe, could I see, taste or hear anything that would confirm to me that this is the heartland of the potted shrimp? Is there due respect paid to this delicate crustacean?

It wasn't looking promising. 'No, we can't sell 'em here, they're too dear,' I was told in many ways over and over again. Morecambe is now beyond fading fast. Once called the Naples of the North, the Winter Gardens are now in full hibernation, though it has found a new and rather sedate persona, as a nice quiet town. Perhaps it always was.

I stopped for a cup of tea in a gorgeous time-warped caff called Brucciani's, right on the seafront, and gawped at the enormous mass of sand in front of me. I had been drawn in by a sign for sarsaparilla, an old English tonic that has slipped away from our consciousness, along with dandelion and burdock and other such gems. But the caff was . . . well, if not exactly full, at least busy with pearl-headed old ladies instructing

37

their grandchildren about the meaning of life, and what dandelion and burdock was really like.

'Try it with lemonade, Chelsea love. It's like Coke really. You like that now, don't you, love? Go on, try it.'

To no avail. Chelsea stuck to her guns, sneered at her nan, and sucked on her ice cream.

Maybe if she'd tried to be truthful, things would have gone better: 'Now take some, Chelsea love, go on. It's an ancient and widely used cure for syphilis made from the extract of the root of a bush of the genus *Smilax* widely found in Central America and the Caribbean.'

'What's syphilis, Nan?'

'It's a town in ancient Greece. Now shut up and drink your sarsaparilla.'

These drinks have their roots firmly in the same Temperance movement that fostered Blackpool's Working Men's Clubs and flourished in Victorian times, when the demon drink was blamed for virtually all of the country's ills. For a really bizarre day out you could do no better than visit Britain's one remaining temperance bar, in the Lancashire village of Rawtenstall. It is run by the Herbal Health company, which still makes sarsaparilla.

At Brucciani's, the real house speciality was their ice cream, as befitted a family of Italian émigrés who had run the place since the Second World War. In fact, so proud of their *gelati* had they become that they had on show in a glass cabinet a framed gallery of awards. I felt proud to sup within the hallowed walls of the Winner of the Continuous Freezer Class Prize 1998.

Brucciani's first opened its doors in 1939, and has kept the feel of a wartime milk bar, which is exactly what it once was. Wooden panels and formica tables give it an extraordinary look, a glorious limp epitaph to a forgotten era. I loved it. You could see the family resemblance between the mamma, who ran the caff, and the papà who doled out the *gelati*. The son, soon to take over by the looks of things, sat at the table, still firmly attached to his Italian roots, eating beans on toast.

But there was not a potted shrimp to be seen. In fact I could not find one shrimp in a single pot along the length and breadth of the seafront. I needed that sarsaparilla. To everyone else apart from the Morecambe Bay seafront traders, potted shrimps would seem to have been a very natural choice to entice the hungry tourist. But the cheap food ethic rules, here as almost everywhere else. Potting was once the sort of thing practised to preserve food, and had little to do with garden sheds. It involved covering something edible, usually cooked fish or meat, with a thick layer of – clarified – butter. Add a few spices, whose exact formula will always, of course, be secret, and there you have it. Potted beef and crab, and potted shrimps up here in the north-west, have been made for hundreds of years, and were one of the delights of a fine high tea, the natural predecessor of those rank fish pastes that were once made in thick glass urine sample bottles. Apart from a no doubt happy few industriously potting fresh produce in the privacy of their own kitchens, potted foods seem to have gone the way of the dodo, with one exception: the elusive potted shrimp.

But what is this thing we call the shrimp? Why does it merit such attention? It is a diminutive crustacean with an armour-plated exterior and eight pairs of legs that goes by the delightful Latin name *Crangon crangon*. You might expect a crangon to be a mad, Earth-threatening alien with multiple arms and awful halitosis, but it is in reality much smaller, though it does at least have lots of legs. The shrimp loves the shallow sandy waters of Morecambe Bay, and loves also to tuck into the rotting corpses of other less fortunate fish and shellfish that reach the end of their particular time on the planet before they do. Crustaceans are marine scavengers, and they taste all the better for it.

Crangon are not entirely alone. There used to be a thriving population of what the locals called sprawn, or the pink shrimp, *Pandalus montagui*, but these are much harder to find nowadays and are rarely caught. They called for heavier fishing equipment that was dangerously cumbersome on the shifting sands of the bay. In fact, Morecambe Bay is a rich and elaborate biosphere. Flounders flounder, crab and lobster scavenge, and even the odd salmon swims by. Flat fish, the glorious turbot, and sole can be caught, though rarely now. But perhaps the richest fishery of all is for the common cockle, *Cerastoderma edule*.

Now Morecambe Bay may be beautiful, and you may feel uplifted when you see the laughing sculpture of Eric Morecambe on the seafront, but it is a treacherous, scary place. To a newshound, and perhaps now to others, it brings to mind the gruesome tragedy of the drowned Chinese cockle pickers. It was thought that there were twenty-three of them who died in this awful, cold and lonely place one winter's day in 2004, speaking words that no-one heard, and that few would have understood anyway. And there are, I assume, people out there, still alive, whose consciences must be eternally troubled, the gangmasters and the traders who sent them to this Mephistophelean end. Some of them were said to have called home on their mobiles and pleaded for help, to no avail. I cannot eat a cockle with a clear conscience these days. And will somebody please tell me why this fishery still apparently needs no licence and no safety equipment when the whole industry is said to be overwhelmed by bureaucracy and petty rules I thought were designed to avoid exactly this sort of disaster? It was three weeks before anyone from the government visited the site, and six months later an even worse tragedy was narrowly avoided when two tractors of warring gangs crashed into each other miles out on the sand. They, at least, were rescued.

There are people who live in Morecambe who understand the bay and its complex, shifting sands, who can read the runes, who know where the quicksands begin and where the best cockles are to be found. These are the people common sense suggests should be allowed to fish in the bay, just as they and their ancestors have always done. It should never have been a free-for-all.

Flookburgh is a small village, a dot on the map right on the northern end of Morecambe Bay, at the tip of the Cartmel Peninsula. The Lake District is to the north, and from the west come glorious sunsets, and the smell of industrial decay from Barrow-in-Furness. Morecambe is just across the sands to the south, and before the railway came, local people escorted travellers right over the sands to Lancaster. They knew them intimately. These days, sheep happily nibble on the marsh grass and skitter across the samphire, unaware that the local land-lord is fattening them up to be sold as delectable saltmarsh lamb.

Flookburgh is a strange little place, full of tanned old codgers chewing the fat, weathered and welcoming at that, but it was here that I finally found someone who was prepared to admit not only to selling potted shrimps, but to making them, and even to fishing them too. Herbert Benson was born in Flookburgh. I didn't ask him when, but I should think it was over seventy years ago.

'I didn't go to school you know,' he told me, almost proudly. He had been ill for much of his childhood, but seemed the picture of good health when I met him, but for having only half a right hand. He was brought up cockling, and shrimping, but as he told me more than once, 'I didn't want our Frank to go shrimping at first. There's not a lot of money in it to be honest.'

He took me to the back of his garden and opened up an immaculate shrimp-picking hut, all EU'd and clean, and showed me the last remaining shrimps from that morning's fishing. And the butter. The recipe, naturally, is secret. It's one of the most challenging things when writing a book about British food. It's difficult enough to find these ancient specialities, but when you do you can be sure you'll get the old reply, 'Well, I can't tell you how it's made. It's our trade secret you see!'

But this much you can say. Firstly, the shrimps are caught. No secret there. The idea is to drag a net from a beam, and that's it. In the old days the bay fishermen used horses and shallow-draught boats called noddies, but Herbert had another way: 'We used an old Austin 12 chassis. Worked like a dream! But it has got to be an Austin 12.' Whether Austin or beast, you drag the net along the sandy bottom, and as the shrimp jump away they should land in the net. The horses always found it tricky to pull the net against the tide, so they were worked downstream on the ebb.

Shrimping is a summer fishery, but the year hadn't been particularly good for the Bensons. Herbert's nimble-fingered daughter passed by. 'You should see her work. She picks like clockwork.'

When there are enough shrimp to cook, they are brought up to the shed. 'You 'ave to cook 'em three times, you see. First cooking kills 'em up straight. Then you boil them again. Let them cool, and boil them again. That's one secret anyway!' By the time you've done this, the shrimps will have a lovely streaked bronze colour, and will smell sweetly of salt and shell. And then they are off to be picked by the most nimble-fingered members of the family. Once that's done, the shrimps are placed in a minuscule cardboard pot and the melted butter, with its secret array of herbs and spices, is poured over the top. And away you go.

Potted shrimps

Serves 4

225g shelled cooked shrimps
85g salted butter
1 large or 2 small blades of mace
¼ tsp cayenne pepper
pinch of ground ginger

Melt the butter over a low heat. Add the remaining ingredients, and heat slowly. When hot, take out the mace and divide the prawns between four small ramekins, or pour them into a large bowl. Leave to cool and set. Cover with a little clarified butter. Leave to cool again, and serve with brown bread or toast.

from *Fish* by William Black and Sophie Grigson (Headline, 1998)

I bought a few pots and saved them to daub onto a slice of toast – the one and only way, I think, to appreciate potted Morecambe Bay shrimps.

'I used to eat shrimps whole when I lived in France,' I told Herbert, I suppose in the vain hope that he didn't think I was some scumbag reporter delving into all the tragedy.

'We 'ad some Chinese up 'ere t'other day. They ate the whole bloody thing too, legs an' all! I wouldn't.'

OK, what about the cockles then, for however much pussy-footing I was doing I knew the reality was that the shrimp fishery was tiny and shrinking. It was the cockles that made money around here, and Herbert told me his views in no uncertain manner.

'Well, 'ow would *you* feel if someone came along and took the cockles from under your nose? I mean, anyone can fish up 'ere. There's no controls, nothing. 'Ow do you think we feel?'

Point taken, Herbert. But how did the fishery actually work? It seemed so totally against all that I knew about fishing, where everything down to the very underpants you wear seemed to be so closely enmeshed in legislation.

'Well, this is what you'll need. First thing, a lot of local knowledge. And second thing, a jumbo.'

'A jumbo what?' I asked, slightly surprised at the use of this rather Kiplingesque word.

'Come on, I'll show you. And you can see my riddle too if you want, or you'll never understand it.'

Things were looking up.

A jumbo is a wooden board with two handles at hip height that you place square on top of the sands. You stand on it, then wriggle a little from side to side, imitating the action of the sea birds that stand on one foot and then the other, tapping the sand's surface until the cockles are drawn to the top. The jumbo then moves on, and in move the pickers, who rake and sift the sand to select the best-sized cockles. And so to the riddle. A sieve, I would call it. This riddle was actually an old bread tray with a wire mesh; the undersized cockles fall through to be plucked another day. So, pick up your jumbo, grab your riddle, it's cockle time!

On the vast wilderness of sand that runs around the bay lie millions upon millions of these fat, juicy shellfish. Estimates suggest that there can be up to 10,000 per square metre, a golden harvest of sorts that can be plucked from the sands by absolutely anyone. The value of the cockle beds is said to be around £6 million – not a bad amount for a shellfish that has been picked and harvested from the bay for generations. At least something from the sea seems to be sustainable. But for how long?

Cockles are one of the few means that people who live around the bay have to earn a regular income. Shrimps are fickle. Fish are even fickler. Tourists are seasonal. So the bay lives off being a workable, bankable reserve of shellfish.

'I remember sending thousands of bags of cockles to Manchester and Leeds when I was young,' Herbert reminisced. 'We used to put 'em on the train and off they went. We stopped in the end when the cockles got scarcer, and anyway, some of 'em always paid short. Never could get the money out o' one o' them fellas. Right pain 'e was!'

The cockle was for a long time the mainstay of the shellfish stalls that traded outside pubs and on the seafront in hundreds of British towns and cities. And just as so much in this country is class bound, so are shellfish. Whelks and cockles are working-class shellfish. Suitable for that old favourite of British food preservation, pickling, they have remained attached (conceptually at least) to the shellfish stall. But you will struggle to find any appearing on restaurant menus in Britain.

By now Herbert was getting restless. 'Well, if you come back later, you can talk to our Frank,' he said. 'Anyway, do you like tomatoes?'

A great non sequitur, I thought.

I followed Herbert up the garden path.

'This is where I spend most of my time these days,' he announced, opening the door of a huge glasshouse full of steaming, thriving tomato plants. The atmosphere was positively fetid, but the tomatoes looked fine.

'I spend too much time up 'ere really.' He stooped to pluck a strawberry. 'Give this to your missus!'

And I did. I also took some of Herbert's tomatoes, which rolled around in the car for the next few days as I set off north to talk of drug-crazed poets and gingerbread.

I never did get to meet Our Frank.

5

THE LAKES

Gingerbread, Sticky Toffee Pudding and Mint Cake

'I'LL JUST GO AND PUT T'KETTLE ON, THEN.'

There was a sploosh of water, a clink of a teapot and more stilted Cumbrian conversation, and I wondered why on earth they had to be quite so voluble about making a cup of tea. I had lined up with a Babylonian mix of people to buy my very own Grasmere gingerbread, but filled with a profound ennui, went off to check out the Wordsworths in the local churchyard. Yes, they were still there. So I returned to join the queue, and became absorbed by this scene of charming domesticity, and the warm, gentle, biscuity smell. Until I suddenly realized they were at it all over again.

'I'll just go and put t'kettle on, then.'

I assumed they were just everyday obsessive rural folk, until it dawned on me that it was one of those new-fangled electronic recording machines that Sarah Nelson would never have dreamed of allowing into her kitchen. Sarah was a canny Cumbrian lady who spent most of her eighty-eight years in service near Ullswater, eventually rising to the position of cook to the impeccably aristocratic Lady Farquhar. On the recommendation of a wise French chef, she was encouraged to set up a business selling her gingerbread to passing travellers and locals, and she bought a small house near the church from which, astonishingly it has to be said, you can still buy the stuff, cooked according to the same (secret) recipe that she perfected.

But the curious thing about this gingerbread is that it isn't really ginger *bread* at all. All around the country gingerbread tends to mean a dark, rich cake, made with molasses and treacle, and a sprinkling of ground ginger. Ginger has long been a popular panacea. It was thought to promote sweating, and to help ward off malaria and the plague, which guaranteed it certain popularity. Gingerbread was once hawked on the streets of urban Britain and sold at local fairs. During the seventeenth and eighteenth centuries it became increasingly elaborate, gilded with gold leaf, and patterned by carved wooden moulds. The tradition lives on in the British gingerbread men. But up here in the Lakes it has lost its cakeyness, and more closely resembles a biscuit. I asked the young heritage-dressed lady the unmentionable question.

'Excuse me, I'm writing this book on regional food and wanted to include a recipe for your gingerbread. Would it be possible to—'

She stopped me dead. The whole queue fell silent. I was the man who had broached the unbroachable, the man who had had the audacity to attempt to recreate this unique Lakeland speciality. Shame and damnation would fall upon me.

'No, we can't give out the recipe, you know.'

'Sorry. I've been away from home for a long time. I forgot.'

I bought some instead, and scuttled back to the car. Some for the journey, and some for the French relations, who refused to believe that anything edible came out of Britain at all.

I unwrapped the little packet, and nibbled. It was good. It was very good. OK, it was very very very good, with a lovely gingerosity about it, a firm yet soft crunchiness, and a multitude of crumbs that just waited to get into every nook and cranny of the car, to remind me for ever of Sarah Nelson. I even fell in love with the packaging, a psychological masterpiece, a heritage symphony in greaseproof paper with 'Sarah Nelson's Celebrated Gingerbread' neatly embossed in blue. I could almost hear the burbling streams and the tinkling of cow bells.

The cynic within was convinced that the Lake District was a tourist trap for people with rucksacks and sensible shoes, devotees of Kendal Mint Cake, and lovers of a quiet and Christian life. It didn't really get my pulse throbbing, and as I climbed up from Flookburgh, I nodded respectfully towards the lamb nibbling the salty marsh grass and thought, 'Yum!'

Then, with an almost delirious dawning, I suddenly realized that this was all extraordinarily beautiful. The gentle twisting, the pathological undulation, gave the drive an almost Blackpudlian thrill; the dappled woods, the lichen-covered gates, and of course those sheep. You begin to notice the subtle ovine differences when travelling around the country. I vowed to buy a sheep identification book to help me baa the baa. You may remember *I Spy* books, and motoring holidays, a worthy and rather middle-class thing to do, something our family practised with an almost manic enthusiasm. I needed an *I Spy* for sheep.

Lakeland has long been a conceptual battleground between the upper and middle classes, and it all began with the word of Wordsworth seeping out, for he, though born and bred in Cumbria, in the town of Cockermouth, he it was who began to write of the sheer heartstopping beauty of the Lake District, of its daffodils, of course, and its wild hills and dales. The Lakes gave us a notion that here was heaven on earth, a little piece of pastoral bliss on our backdoor, which appealed to all who sought comfort from beauty. So the Romantics gave life to a strange conflict, for as more people came to witness this special part of England for themselves, their arrival threatened the very beauty they had come to see. A classic but not entirely untypical paradox.

The railway arrived in Windermere in 1847, bringing with it rich industrialists with their families, and worshippers of poetry and nature who were bitten by the bug of this raw and glorious nature. Many were even inspired to write a verse or two, and enter the higher plane. William Wordsworth spent some of his most productive years writing in the ravishing little Grasmere cottage we know as Dove Cottage. In fact, it was originally a pub called the Dove and Olive Branch, and it can still be seen, touched and inhaled, close to the northern shore of Grasmere.

Come the French Revolution, off he went, walking for hundreds of miles around the French countryside. He was apparently warmly welcomed, and returned enthused by the idea of revolution. After a brief sojourn in Somerset, he returned to his native Lakes and set up home with his sister, Dorothy. Now, she seems a curious character to us these days. She was clearly besotted with her brother and swooned in his absence, but her intentions were, one must assume, entirely honourable. She provided him with a crutch to lean on, and helped to run the house that was by all accounts a busy and welcoming place.

Their most frequent visitor was Samuel Taylor Coleridge. This thick-lipped, hyper-energetic man was also a fine poet in his own right but he too came under the spell of Wordsworth and devoted much time and energy to developing the friendship by doing such sociable things as dropping in unannounced at one o'clock in the morning, after a hard night's fell walking, to discuss poetry. He must have been the ideal guest. And to make the night go fantastically, he took a copious amount of drugs. Opium was the drug of choice in those days, and although Wordsworth did not apparently indulge, Coleridge most definitely did. As did many others, for in its alcoholic version, laudanum was part and parcel of the doctor's medicine chest, and was freely prescribed. Initially Coleridge seemed to suffer from little more than aches and pains, but gradually he became an addict, and it was under the influence of opium that he wrote his infamous verbal outpouring *Kubla Khan; a Vision in a Dream*.

Wordsworth eventually became a respected establishment figure, and moved to a larger house at Ambleside, on the northern edge of Lake Windermere. But, cometh the train, cometh the man . . . and the woman and the granny and the whole family on an educational holiday, so that the Lakes were far removed from the aggressive masculinity of the seaside resorts. By 1910, the Windermere Express could deliver tired industrialists from their smoggy urban factories in Lancashire and bring them to the peace and quiet of the Lakes. Sarah Nelson's business boomed, profiting from all these passing tourists, though history doesn't relate whether the Wordsworths ever bought any of her gingerbread.

Windermere itself, however, suffered in the process of development, though not terminally. The water that was once described as a cesspool has been cleaned up, but there is still a blissful serenity about the lakes. Steamers still steam. Fish still swim, but only just.

One of the lake's great delicacies is a fish known variously as the char, the charr, or even the Arctic char. To be precise, it is a brook trout, *Salvinus alpinus*, a fish that once migrated from salt to fresh water but was trapped by the receding waters after the last ice age. They live on in a few obscure lakes in Europe, but only where the water is deep and cold. Lake Geneva reaches depths of almost a thousand metres and hosts a population, and you could even eat a fish or two there until recently.

Windermere fish were traditionally potted, just as the Flookburgh shrimp was. But being Windermere, and being ever so slightly posh, they used ceramic dishes to pot their fish that were apparently rather beautiful. Thus packed, they were despatched around the country by carrier to expectant gourmets who developed a real enthusiasm for this obscure delicacy.

> At the King's Arms one Mrs Rowlandsons she does pott up the char fish the best of any in the country. I was curious to have some and so bespoke some of her, and also was as curious to see the great water which is the only place that fish is to be found in . . . the water . . . is very clear and full of good fish, but the charr fish being out of season could not be easily taken so I saw none alive . . . the season of the charr fish is between Michaelmas and Christmas, at that time I have had of them which they pott with sweet spices . . . if they are inseason their taste is very rich and fat tho' not as strong or clogging as lampreys are, but it is fatt and rich as food.
>
> from *Through England on a side saddle* by Celia Fiennes (1888; a post-humously published account of her journeys through England at the end of the seventeenth and the beginning of the eighteenth centuries)

Needless to say, by the middle of the nineteenth century potted char became almost unheard of, suffering from the fateful combination of raw sewage and overfishing. It seems that potting superseded the seventeenth-century habit of baking absolutely enormous 'charr pyes', weighing a mighty twenty to thirty kilograms, that were also delivered to keen gourmets in London and Lancashire. Its very rarity established it among the dishes that only the wealthiest enthusiast would ever taste. The pie wasn't always completely edible, however, and in this case the crust was used to the same effect as the later pots, to protect the cooked fish from spoiling.

These days char is appearing once again, but the fish are

mostly farmed, reared on land-locked pens far away from any lake. The last thing any remaining wild char needs to deal with is becoming overly familiar with a farmed fish, my dear. Not the done thing at all. It's all down to genetic purity and biodiversity, you see.

But not all is dead and buried up here. Cumbria has a particularly defiant food culture. The whole area was so traumatized by the last foot and mouth epidemic that they seem to have vowed a collective vow and hunkered down to do what they do best – diversify, and celebrate that diversity. It is a particularly rich part of the country as far as food is concerned. There is the exquisite Herdwick lamb, and mutton. Fish is freshly trucked up from the coast, and it is all served in goodly dollops, and cooked with real skill.

Sticky toffee pudding has been cooked at the Cartmel Village Shop for years now and can be bought by anyone in the UK, online. This will call for a little forward planning, but what a pudding it is. Regal and sickly sweet, you feel you could almost make it yourself. Well, you can. If I can, you can. And I did.

A few years ago – well, forty odd, which is, I suppose, a little more than a few – a Cumbrian farmer by the name of Alan Rayner thought he'd start a business selling plastic bags to other farmers so that they could wrap up their chickens. Dead chickens, that is. Nothing particularly world-shattering there, but the business thrived and expanded and the Rayners decided to move into mail order. Their range expanded too. They acutely reasoned that plastic bags for chickens had a fairly limited market, so they began to sell plastic boxes, and even freezer bags. The world was their oyster.

The company was called Lakeland Plastics, and it became deeply involved in the utopian dream of the good housekeeper, the supplier of those stacking boxes and salad servers without which life became almost unbearable. Egg timers, cake tins and tea towels poured through their doors by the thousand with mad monotony. They jettisoned the Plastics and became Lakeland Limited, and now have an extraordinary twenty-six stores nationwide with a range of over four thousand goods. Business is booming, for Brits just love plastic. And to cement their success, they have built a gloriously modern and entirely non-plastic head office just next to the train station at Windermere. It is full of the loveliest plastic things imaginable. The top seller at the moment is a shower spray and Australian liquorice (the latter has a plastic wrap, so it's OK).

Now this may seem all very nice and inspiring, a lesson to all you budding entrepreneurs out there, but what really drew me here was an invitation to have lunch in the café. Maybe you're thinking, that can't exactly be Le Gavroche. But that's just it. It almost is. The café is run by a Roux-trained chef, Stephen Doherty, and his wife, Marjorie. Stephen in his London days used to be one of those patient few who waited for my van to turn up fresh from the French food market, and he would, unless particularly stressed, offer me a coffee, even lunch if I timed it right, and rootle about in my van until he found something he liked. Ah, those were the days, when I used to deal in immaculate boxes of French fish, vegetables, mushrooms, even the odd Bresse chicken – never wrapped in plastic, by the way – and hawk them around London's finest restaurants.

I learned a lot about the stressful, energy-sapping life of a chef, and had nothing but respect for their exceedingly hard life. So, fast forward ten years or so and it was quite exciting to meet up with Stephen after so long, a man who now had his own mini empire, the Lakeland Café, and just up the road at Crosthwaite the Punch Bowl Inn, a thick, white-walled village pub that offers the most exquisite food, and even rooms when you feel you can go hiking no longer.

The pub is a particularly fine one. It buzzes. They offer local food, but not entirely for local people. There is often a tension between villages and pubs that may seem to be overly ambitious. But they have found a strong following who appreciate their carefully constructed menu, and the quality of the food on offer, though it only works because it is not, by any standards, expensive. And the food is glorious.

But, the café is exceptional. It seems to have done the one thing I always thought was impossible in Britain. In other words, they offer good, cheap food that is not just well cooked, but brilliantly cooked. And in quantities that are so mind-numbing you almost need an abacus to count the hordes. Silver-haired ladies and their uneasy husbands settled comfortably down to great plates of fish, cooked *à point*, that flew out of the kitchen. The great Cumbrian classic, sticky toffee pudding, followed plates of sorbets. Some just came and sipped tea.

It was, in fact, a most unlikely setting. How many times have you sat in the café of a department store and eaten something totally dry and relentlessly dull? Or a motorway caff, and spent pounds on a rubbery cake and a cup of coffee? Well, mass catering can succeed. Or at least it does here in Windermere. So, forget the country-house splendour of Miller Howe, and the frou-frou of Lakeland views. Get on down with an empty stomach to the café at Lakeland Limited and see how it can be done!

Even though this is a place where you can eat food that has been produced locally, it neatly expresses the contemporary reality of eating in Britain. The fish is trucked up from the nearest port, rather than from halfway around the globe. Estimable, delicious Herdwick hill lamb bleats but a few kilometres away. Doherty has a whole network of faithful suppliers that keep the Lakeland Café, and his pub, going through the year. The sticky toffee pudding sits quite happily alongside linguine and pesto, tuna niçoise next to pea and ham soup, and so on. Which is all profoundly typical. British food is, and perhaps always has been, a curious hodgepodge.

We absorb rather than create. Pasta is now as British as chicken tikka massala. Italy and France have always found such cultural promiscuity almost sinful, but here we are virtually shameless.

Cumbria suffered an almost critical blow during the foot and mouth crisis, but it has recovered; in stereotypically British fashion it has pulled itself up by its collective bootstraps and recreated a vibrant regional gastronomy. But it is a revival of the classic we've-got-the-best-ingredients kind. Surely the next logical step has to be to cook some of those odd little dishes of ours?

If marketing skills have triumphed and made a plastic bag company morph into something rather more exciting, sometimes commercial joy just falls from the sky. As the intrepid mountaineering duo of Edmund Hillary and Tenzing Norgay reached the summit of Chomolungma, or as we call it Mount Everest, on 29 May 1953, with energy levels in need of a sturdy boost Hillary slipped his hand into his pocket and pulled out a tablet of Kendal Mint Cake. History doesn't relate whether Tenzing took a bite, but Hillary most certainly did, and the rest is history.

From that moment on ramblers and mountaineers took to the peaks in their thousands with the neat rectangular outline not of a mobile phone in their pocket, but a tablet of the finest mint cake, made exclusively in the dreamy little Cumbrian market town of Kendal. But does this all not sound frightfully British? Do you not have a vision of these two altitude warriors sitting down on the peak, lighting a fag, brewing a bevvy and saying, 'My, what a view!' and then almost automatically reaching for the mint cake, before packing up their picnic hamper and tumbling down the hill? In fact, Hillary's words were recorded for posterity, and have since been much quoted: 'We sat down on the snow and looked at the country far below us . . . we nibbled Kendal Mint Cake.' Sheer poetry.

But this mighty mountain does not suffer fools gladly. I was fascinated to read that maybe Hillary and Tenzing weren't the first to conquer the mountain after all. In 1924, a Kendal man, Howard Somervell, managed to climb close to the summit, without oxygen. He gave up, but as he began his descent he crossed the path of two more English mountaineers, George Mallory from Cheshire and Sandy Irvine from Birkenhead. He offered them his camera to record the conquest. They were seen disappearing into the clouds just a few hundred feet from the summit, but nothing more was heard from either of them. Mallory's body was found in 1999, but as yet it has proved impossible to know for certain whether these two conquered the mountain. Intriguing.

You probably know by now that Kendal Mint Cake isn't actually a lightly crumbed, mint-flavoured Victoria sponge to be nibbled at tea time, but a thwacking, clumsy, intense burst of sugary energy that is ideal for the mountaineer, compact and calorific but hardly delicate. The story of its invention takes us into the realms of those great moments of happenstance. Fleming and the penicillin on rotten bread. The Curies and radioactivity. Logie Baird and the television. Mr Joseph Wiper and Kendal Mint Cake.

Tucked into the mint cake file in Kendal Library, I was thrilled to find a letter from the great man's descendants who had decided to put pen to paper – actually, finger to typewriter – to scotch the vicious, damning rumour that someone else was responsible for creating mint cake. It seems it was all an accident. One Lakeland morning in 1868, Mr Wiper was busy making some sweets when the mixture spilled onto the floor and quickly hardened. These days it is highly unlikely that somebody would have stooped down and tasted this solidifying sugary mass on the floor, but in the nineteenth century men were really men and didn't fear the health police so deeply. He took a bite, and liked what he tasted. Kendal Mint Cake was born.

The art is said to be in knowing exactly when to pour the mix, so that it is neither too soft nor too hard. Other than that, mint cake is not one of the world's more elaborate culinary creations.

Kendal Mint Cake

350g cane sugar
200g glucose powder
1 tsp peppermint essence
150ml milk

Boil the sugar, glucose and milk to 116°C, the soft ball stage.
Take from the heat and add the peppermint, then beat thoroughly until it is smooth and about to set. Pour into an oiled
tin to a depth of 0.5 cm, and mark into large squares just
before it sets. Cool and cut.

from *The Taste of the Lake District* by Theodora Fitzgibbon (Pan Books, 1980)

There are but three mint cake producers left in Kendal
these days. I called them to see if I could witness the creation
of this ever-popular slab of sweetness. The first was too busy
and the second was deeply engaged in making boiled sweets,
but I was happily ushered into the third, Wilson's, to see how
they were doing in the sticky world of mint cake. The head of
the firm was away sourcing mint in Marbella, so the company
was being run in his absence by his children, Tom and Felicity.
And, yes, they knew all about the mint cake, and told me with
enthusiasm how much they loved it (with slightly gritted
teeth), and a little about the company.

'We still make it according to the original recipe,' Tom
said. 'We all do. There's not a lot of difference between the
three of us. It's quite a friendly business really.'

But sales of mint cake have, let's say, plateau'd. It might
strike you as odd that while sticky toffee pudding has
conquered the world, mint cake seems to have retained a
rather quaint, parochial market. The reason is, I suspect, to be
found in our unquestioned love of the pudding as the formal
rounding-off of any good meal, out or in – an attribute that is

most definitely one of the defining characteristics of English, though not necessarily British, cooking. I suspect that mint cake, while it may appeal to many for sentimental or mountaineering reasons, is just too cloying, and thoroughly unsubtle. Very like sticky toffee pudding, actually. Hmm . . .

Certainly, new markets were needed to keep the Wilsons busy, and they showed me with some pride the new chocolate production line they had bought from a defunct *chocolatier* in Scotland. Businesses like to be inventive, and Wilson's took a long hard look at where they wanted to go and decided to tap our infinite love of yuk, and sauce. So now, while mint cake languishes at about 8 per cent of sales, they have created a vibrant market for chocolate maggots, chocolate snotty noses and cream-filled chocolate willies. It's providing stiff opposition. This is the new millennium after all, and no holds are barred. The chocolate willies sell in Ann Summers, and the day they are moulded provides the workforce with endless mirth. I wonder if Joseph Wiper would have approved.

6

NORTHUMBRIA
Roast Beef and Mead

THE SCENE COULDN'T HAVE BEEN MORE BUCOLIC. PIGEONS COOED
in a sweet-smelling Northumbrian wood, wild raspberries grew
in the dappled shade. There was even the odd wild strawberry,
and a whole array of peculiar wild mushrooms that would
either drive you mad or kill you. In the tiny, ancient church
of Chillingham you can see the stupefyingly beautiful fifteenth-
century tomb of two ancient landowners, Sir Robert Grey and
his wife, he moustachioed and prim in death, she clean shaven,
demure and classically wifely.

Yet despite all this pastoral contentedness, less than a mile
away lay a herd of the world's most vicious cattle, horned and
hardy, and utterly unique. The Chillingham herd of wild cattle
has somehow managed to survive the Roman invasion, the
dissolution of the monasteries, Mrs Thatcher's regime and even
foot and mouth, but only just. Their bleakest moment came in
1947, when post-war Britain shivered and froze to such a
degree that the fields were covered in snow so thick the cattle

couldn't get at the grass. The group sensibly made for the stream on the Chillingham estate, but became trapped in the ice. Extinction loomed, but thirteen head survived. Their descendants now exist carefully enclosed on the estate and are, it is said, the last remaining cattle of their kind.

Britain is supposed to be the land of divine roast beef, so the idea of seeing the ancestral relative, ur-cow, appealed. But I have to admit that I have always had my doubts about cattle. Strange stories abound about their unpredictability. Never wear red when walking by, we are told. Never run. Never say horseradish in a cow field either. Cattle have a way of fixing you with their oh so sweet brown eyes framed by those long lashes. Try walking a dog through a field of cows. *They* know; dogs are no fools. I suspect that cows are psychic. But where does all the energy come from? Can it really be just from grass? Grass certainly doesn't have that effect on people. Of course, our love of roast beef was never going to endear us to them. The French have foolishly called us *les rosbifs*. This is taught to every cow at school. They know what we feel about them, how we almost lick our lips when we pass by a fine specimen. They can tell if a human being is fond of Yorkshire pudding from three hundred metres.

So there I was in Chillingham, off to meet the closest living relation to the real ur-beast, the wild ox or aurochs, extinct now but only surprisingly recently. The last *Bos taurus primigenius* breathed its ultimate breath in the royal forests of Jaktorów in the Mazowse region of Poland in 1627. The Polish king had long exercised the royal privilege of being the sole person permitted to hunt the aurochs, so it survived in the vast forests that had once been the animal's natural habitat. Until, that is, man came along and destroyed it all. But it wasn't just the gradual elimination of the forest that caused the beast such difficulty, for it seems from contemporary accounts that the aurochs were nervy creatures, and when the locals grazed their domestic animals on the same lands, the aurochs simply stayed away – and starved as a result. And then there was the disease that festered in the local cattle population, for which the aurochs seemed to have had little resistance. So the poor beast slipped into extinction, largely unnoticed, and unlamented.

But its image lives on. It seems to be the self-same creature depicted in the extraordinary ancient cave paintings at Lascaux, in France. Thousands of years ago, the aurochs must have been a highly prized animal, and one whose eventual domestication was the origin of that quintessential farmyard creature, the cow, and the beginning also of our great culinary speciality, the cheese slice and the hamburger. In 1417, the King of Poland sent a freshly killed specimen to Henry V in England, where it caused a sensation. Descriptions tell of its broad black body, short tail and horns.

Given that the Chillingham cattle are white and the aurochs was apparently black, a degree of domestication appears to have occurred. So the story that they are the last remaining remnant of the wild ox population possibly needs to be revisited. Nevertheless, some experts reckon that the Chillingham herd is indeed derived from an earlier form of cow that once existed in medieval England. Whatever the truth, they have remained largely untouched since the mid-thirteenth century when Henry III allowed the castle to be 'castellated and crenellated', and the cattle were surrounded for the first time by a sturdy brick wall.

When the Ninth Earl of Tankerville died in 1980, it was decided that the estate, cattle included, should be sold. A family connection that went back into the Middle Ages was thus broken, and the future began to look bleak. But a white knight came along to save the cattle from an uncertain fate in the form of fellow Northumbrian the Duke of Northumberland, a man not short of a bob or two, who owned the vast castle at Alnwick (pronounced, for the unwary, Ann-ik). When he learned of their plight, he teamed up with a benevolent philanthropist, bought the land and the cattle and gifted them a 999-year lease, which may just outlive the shelf life of this book.

Happily, there are now fifty-five of these odd wild cattle left, and the future looks brighter than it has been for some time. However, there is always the spectre of foot and mouth looming. In 1967, it almost crossed into the park. Sheep were dying in large numbers without the estate walls, but luck and determination saw them through. And in the latest outbreak, in 2001/2, again the Chillingham herd just avoided extinction through compulsory slaughter. In the surrounding valleys vast bovine funeral pyres lit up the skies. Wise voices successfully encouraged the duke to keep a secret reserve of wild cattle in Scotland, in case the Chillingham herd becomes infected next time round. As they surely will be.

In a way, the Chillingham cattle are entirely pointless. They are not really wild at all, but have simply been left alone. They are grossly inbred, and are in fact scientifically considered to be genetically identical. In other words, they are clones. This struck me as a little ironic, for I seem to recall that the idea that we should clone animals was greeted with one of our occasional soul-searching sessions. In a way it was a relief that poor old Dolly the sheep passed away with a severe case of arthritis. The Chillingham herd, however, soldier on.

You can take your life in your own hands and go and visit these bovine warriors, and be guided around their fiefdom by the warden, a rubicund exile from the army and the city of Gloucester who goes by the name of Mr Austin Widdows. He has spent the last thirteen years looking after these beasts, and talking the talk in a loud and resonant patter. You feel the cattle themselves could by now moo it all backwards.

We were told to assemble by the hut. After walking through a field of the lamest-looking sheep I had seen for a long time, Austin arrived, then set off into the green yonder, saying, 'Oi'll just go and see if oi can find 'em. They shouldn't be too far away in this heat.' At the time, you see, while the south of Britain was basking in a 32°C heatwave, the thermometer in Northumbria was pushing 21°C.

I whiled away the minutes looking at the letters and photos pinned up on the wall of the hut. One of the former was from a pre-Soviet-era director of a Russian museum, a contemporary bleat of the aristocratic kind asking his lordship if at all possible for a stuffed animal or at least a drawing or two. Another was from Charles Darwin, who started off by apologizing that his lordship's letter had been opened by his son, who was rather keen on collecting stamps. It has never ceased to amaze me just how obsequious and deferential everyone was to the aristocracy in those days. Blimey. You wouldn't get that now. You could even call the Queen Mrs W and live.

The most telling exhibit of all was a photo of the renowned royal gourmet the Prince of Wales, later crowned King Edward VII, who was photographed having shot one of these incredibly rare beasts ('as rare as a panda, really, you know,' Austin told us later). As the caption told us, 'The Prince of Wales was granted the privilege of shooting a bull.' And not just any bull, mind, but the dominant king bull. This would definitely not endear the royal family to their loyal subjects these days. The herd, you see, has over the centuries developed a complex and brutal form of behaviour that rather reminds one of the antics of a pack of lions. It is called the kingship system, and involves a short and presumably rather stressful reign by a bull who has to be ready to accept a challenge from another bull at any time of the day or night. The winner of the fight reigns supreme. They were presumably forced to undergo a sharp session of combat to re-establish order after this particular royal visit. (Sadly, history doesn't relate whether His Royal Highness carted the carcass off to the local butcher for preparation. Probably not. It was enough just to shoot one more incredibly rare animal in a precarious environment.)

Austin returned. 'They're just over there,' he announced, 'so if you'd like to follow me . . .'

Off we all strode.

'Now, can you all pay attention, please. Before we get any closer, please do remember that these are wild animals, and can become aggressive, so just keep your distance and we should be all right. But do not, I repeat do *not*, leave the group. We don't want them to pick you out and gore you, now do we?'

We all laughed nervously.

'And one other thing. I would appreciate it if you could leave your questions till later. If anyone interrupts I tend to forget what I've said, and you'll usually find I have answered most of the questions anyway.'

Then, just over the brow of the hill, we caught sight of the herd, munching gently together in a tightly formed group. They eyed us with that soul-searching look I was expecting. Tails swishing, they settled down to Austin's little talk, playing the game.

'In about 1260, Chillingham Park was enclosed by a great stone wall, but before that the cattle, exactly the same as you see here, roamed free in the forests as far north as the Forth of Clyde. They were probably brought over by the Normans. The herd is pure and inbred, which is odd in that you would expect it to be full of weakness, deformity and madness, but as you can see, that is not the case with this herd.'

The beasts stirred uneasily.

'Now, how do they avoid this? Well, they have evolved the king bull system. Heifers and bulls reach sexual maturity at different ages, so there is no direct breeding within the same year group. Any mutations simply don't survive. You'll notice that some of the cattle have foxy red ears, and this distinguishes them from the white park cattle that have black ears and are generally bigger, and are bred for beef. These cattle are not eaten, and if one does die, the body is used for research purposes.'

Austin gave me a sidelong glance at this point, remembering that I was interested in eating them.

'So, may I remind you that we don't actually eat these cattle at all.'

Meanwhile, the herd had looked up, and were staring at me. They didn't like that last bit at all.

'We'd better take a few steps back now,' Austin said. 'As you can see, the herd is getting closer. Just follow me.'

We chose to obey. And if any of us felt like scoffing at the apparent necessity of retreating before a group of cows, Austin began to tell us of the brutal dynamics of life in the Chillingham herd.

'When a calf is about to be born, the cow will leave the herd, find a quiet spot, and calve. She'll be very protective and aggressive at this stage, but when she is ready she will introduce the calf to the herd. Now, it can be that if they sense it is weak, or if there's something wrong with it, then the calf will be killed. Just as they do with any of the weaker animals. That's how they preserve the characteristics of the herd. A lot of their behaviour seems to be a relic of the time when wolves wandered the forests. They are still very wary of foxes. If one is around and it sends out a cry of alarm, the herd will react and stampede. Likewise, they won't let any animal that has been touched by a human into the herd. They'll kill that too. So none of these cattle has ever been touched at all. The dominant bull will see to that.'

With tales of instinctive killings ringing in our ears, the herd came closer once again, jangling our nerves.

'I think we'll just have to step back a bit more.' The ever wise warden had our best interests at heart.

With a population that hovers between fifty and sixty, the Chillingham herd is hardly numerically significant, but does it, I wondered, have any significance at all?

'They have quite a lot of properties that any cattle breeder would give their eye teeth for,' Austin replied. 'Look how they eat thistles, for example. I've watched them doing this. They seem to get their tongue around the plant and just pull it out, before the plants set seed. When the frosts start they even eat the roots too. Now that's a useful trait for a cattle farmer. But as soon as man interferes you get problems. Leave them to themselves and they are doing fine. There must be a lesson there!'

With their strength and aggression, the Chillingham herd is in a way the complete antithesis of what modern farming has created – an overmuscled, over-lactating beast that is often surprisingly delicate and susceptible to all sorts of ailments. But then, where would we be without our beef, and without the mountains of milk the distant cousins of this weird cow produce? What would the French call us then?

The association between the English and their roast beef is so long standing that it's difficult to know where to begin. A pastoral country that is so well suited to growing grass inevitably relied on the descendants of those wild and angry bulls, and constantly sought to improve the yields and the temperament of domesticated cattle. Beef is as English as ale; indeed, the two are excellent culinary soul mates. We can still sense the aroma of succulent sides of beef roasting in front of the cookshop fires in medieval London, the dredged carcasses sizzling and crisp-skinned, and imagine that traders arriving in the city would have been delighted by such abundance. Charles II, it is said, 'on loin of beef did dine; he held his sword, pleas'd o'er the meat; arise thou famed sir loin' (*A Cooks Oracle*, William Kitchener, 1821).

The love of beef has given the English in particular the clearest of identities, and is an almost inescapable fundamental of British cooking. Just as fundamental is the constant emphasis on their fondness of plain and simple food. The assumption is that this land provides beasts so utterly near perfection that it would almost be an insult to add and to fancify, to elaborate and encourage the excessive use of sauces to conceal the mighty succulence beneath. This gives cooks and writers a constant opportunity to contrast this simplicity with the French way of doing things. It is quite extraordinary just how often this theme comes up. Even as far back as 1747 one R. Campbell was moaning in the *London Tradesman*, 'In the days of good Queen Elizabeth, when mighty roast beef was the Englishman's food, our cookery was plain and simple as our manners. But we have of late years refined ourselves out of that single taste and conformed our palates to meats, and drinks dressed after the French fashion. The natural taste of fish or flesh is becoming nonsense to our fashionable stomach.'

The round and rubicund Englishman stands as a stark contrast to the devious foreigner, thin and mean of complexion, the clearest antithesis to the pot-bellied John Bull. And to complement such God-blessed perfection, the English have loudly boasted that their cooking is also simplicity itself, exemplified in the passion for roasting (and eating) meat. The very way an ideal dinner is presented carries this message through from generation to generation. We eat meat and two veg, slices of roast meat originally, adorned with little more than boiled vegetables, and covered with a thin layer of gravy.

It became the aim, whether implicit or explicit, of every family to sit down to dinner to identically dressed plates. Sunday was the one day in the week when the family might worship their God, assemble for a classic Sunday roast dinner, and watch with love and adoration as the master of the house exercised his great skill in carving the Sunday joint. It was expected that a successful family man knew how to carve, an ancient skill that seems to have been lost on my and all subsequent generations. The last people to embrace this myth seem to have been the post-war parents who strove so hard to reinstate 'normality'.

A typical suburban house had a dining room that was used for that special Sunday meal. Dining tables were family heirlooms, as were the sideboards that once concealed chamberpots so that gentlemen caught short could relieve themselves without fear of losing the flow of the conversation. Dining rooms often had a hatchway leading directly to the kitchen so that the cook, i.e. the mother, could quickly supply the food without the need for staff.

It became extremely difficult for working-class families dutifully to pay heed to this social norm, yet the roast dinner was the social beck and call that many tried to obey. When Victorian philanthropists tried to hector the undernourished into eating nutritious gruels and soups, they singularly failed to take this into account. But tinned meats fitted the bill to some extent. These creations of industrial agriculture supplied the demand for meat in any form, and were shipped halfway around the globe in vast quantities. Corned beef, and the inimitable pork luncheon meat – a.k.a. Spam, which as I write is on the verge of another relaunch – became deeply entrenched in Anglo-Saxon taste buds, and were widely available from every corner shop in the land. The colonies provided the country with endless supplies of cheap food, so the British became used to tinned, and later frozen, foods long before anyone else. Such foods were cheaper than anything that could be produced domestically. By 1914, over 80 per cent of what was eaten within the United Kingdom was imported – an astonishing figure when you think about it.

So, if you wonder – and I hope you will from time to time as you continue to make your way through this book – why it is that the British have at times a distinctly cool and distant appreciation of food, why their taste buds seem to have atrophied, and why they seem generally to be uninterested in cooking with fresh ingredients, you may care to reflect on the headlong love affair the country has had with industrialization, and the constant need to reassert Britishness by eating a plate of meat and two veg.

You may also wonder why it is that our beloved beef has become so profoundly dull. It is rare to be bowled over by the beef you buy in Britain these days, by those bright red slabs of carnal nothingness. A few years back I visited a farm in Yorkshire to try to source some Dexter beef to sell into the restaurant trade that at the time was my bread and butter. It was an excellent breed, if a little short in the leg, which was beginning to reappear in a few specialist butchers who were prepared to champion an ancient breed of cattle or two, and to offer meat that was full of fat and taste. I had helped set up the first regular deliveries of rare-breed meat into London and the problem of supply was continually rearing its ugly head. There were simply not enough beasts around to satisfy the demand. But here was a supplier, an energetic Yorkshire-woman, a committed farmer and a passionate beef-eater who was so keen to sell that she took me to the local abattoir and besought me to understand the multitude of problems that arose when it came to getting the best meat to the table.

Problem number one. Not all beef cattle are fed on grass, their natural diet. They can be intensively reared on cereals or, famously in the days of BSE, recycled sheep brain, which is about as far removed from a natural diet as you can get. Secondly, breeds were becoming so overbred and overmuscled that carcasses were losing their classic conformity, and the market was constantly being led by the dread of seeing any fat on the meat. In the old days a slab of British beef may well have been studded with fat, which is an absolutely crucial source of taste in meat, but most consumers now recoil in horror at the thought of eating any fat at all. Thirdly, as I was shown among the hanging carcasses, meat is simply not hung long enough any more. At this commercial abattoir they looked at us as if we had just asked to drink fresh blood when we wondered whether the beef could be hung for three weeks. No way, we were told; three days was the maximum. And I learned with genuine surprise that there was even a machine that passed a huge electric charge through a carcass – a quick and cheaper alternative, apparently, to tenderizing meat through the time-honoured but sadly uneconomical method of hanging. Which is why good beef costs more. Perhaps this will make you less surprised that your steak is so often tasteless.

Not many miles away from the savage inbred cattle of Chillingham runs what many believe to be the wildest and most beautiful part of the English coast. This was a must-see as far as I was concerned. I am drawn by wildness and wilderness like a behemoth to a flame. And for some inexplicable reason I was even more drawn to a strange little port called Seahouses – or Se'oozes in local speak, a curious transitory mix of Geordie and Scottish.

It has a culinary claim to fame too, for it was here that a Mr John Woodger first dreamed up the idea of doing something radical and new to a herring, other than pickling or salting it that is, and invented the kipper. Actually, as is so often the case, he profited from an accident. One day a load of herring was lost in a fire, and the doom merchants cried, 'Aye aye, we must chuck 'em all oot!' But someone took a crazy reckless risk, took a nibble, liked the taste, and the kipper was born. Great story, though perhaps something of a red herring.

One of the things about this region of England that really got my cultural juices flowing was the story of Lindisfarne, an island off the Northumbrian coast just a few miles to the north of Seahouses, and the creation of the truly scintillating eighth-century illustrated manuscript known as the Lindisfarne Gospels. Experts seem to think it was Bishop Eadfrith of Lindisfarne who spent his life working on this extraordinary document, alongside the Northumbrian scholar we know simply as the Venerable Bede.

The importance of the Gospels is this: they are among the first Christian documents that are wholly English in origin, and they helped to give a Christian identity to a country that needed a clear direction, having lost its way during the endless internecine wars in the absence of the colonial masters the

Romans, who had simply upped sticks and left in the fifth century.

And if your mind doesn't immediately cry out 'Gospels!' or '1970s folk music!' when you hear the word Lindisfarne, it may just say 'Mead!' Mine did anyway. But I have to admit I had naively assumed that here was one of the country's most venerable drinks still being made by monks in hessian to background music of Gregorian chants. Wrong again. In yet another brilliant marketing ploy a few decades ago, a Cumbrian émigré by the name of James Michael Hackett decided to expand his passion for making home-made wine into mead. And Lindisfarne seemed the perfect location. It has been a rip-roaring success, and his son, Michael, still runs the business from the island.

'My father had this brilliant idea,' Michael told me. 'He was quite far-sighted really. But we sort of reinvented something to be honest. In the early days our saviour was these medieval banquets that started back in the 1960s. They took about fifty per cent of all our production.'

He showed me round the warehouse, warning me, 'There's not really much to see.' He was right. No bubbling barrels, or babbling monks. Just huge stainless-steel vats full of fermenting mead.

And then, more disillusion. Local honey, however good, was never used.

'The moisture content is all wrong. To get a consistent level, we need about twenty to twenty-four per cent. We buy all our honey in from abroad, and test each batch.'

So this most ancient of British drinks is made in this ancient British place with grape must from Cyprus and honey that is as likely to come from Argentina as it is from Tanzania, Mexico or Belize. Apparently there is an odd underworld of honey agents around the world who deal in this sticky super-food by the ton, and help direct the buyer towards the best deals around. It's all very global, you know.

Into my mind popped tales of mead benches and riotous storytelling which flourished during the Dark Ages and beyond (preconceptions that had yet to be honed by my visit to a reconstructed Anglo-Saxon village in Norfolk), and I wondered what on earth could have happened to mead, at that time in our island's history an almost society-defining drink.

'I think it's all down to the Normans,' Michael told me. 'As soon as they came along they brought with them a wine culture that eventually helped push mead into virtual oblivion. Well, not quite oblivion. We still make it, anyway. Have you tried any yet?'

Yes, I had, but gift horses and all that made me say, 'No, I never have.' He handed me a bottle.

With a colour of straw, or a medical sample depending on your sensibility, mead is a pleasant enough drink, but I cannot think when you would really feel the need to drink it. Possibly at a medieval banquet. It isn't stocked by supermarkets, and it doesn't sell well in Britain in any case. Indeed, it has all but disappeared over our gastronomic horizon.

So this was Northumbria. With a cow that we never eat, a kipper that was invented by mistake, and an ancient drink that usurped its location. What a strange culinary landscape we have. But stranger things still were to be seen over the border in Yorkshire.

EGTON BRIDGE

Gooseberries

'THEY'RE QUITE HAIRY, AREN'T THEY? OH, THEY'RE GORGEOUS!'
Words spoken as I stepped out of the car fully clothed. I
was in Egton Bridge, in North Yorkshire, on the second day
of August 2004. I know that because I had deliberately driven
to this minuscule village, only a few metres long, just off the
North Yorkshire Moors so that I could attend the world's
oldest giant gooseberry show. It was a Tuesday, the first of the
month. As tradition dictates. There were no tears, and no
histrionics. No paparazzi either; just me, a reporter from the
local paper, and a dedicated band of enthusiasts for whom
August means but one thing: the Egton Bridge Old Gooseberry
Society's Annual Show. Oh, and there were the gooseberries
as well.

This annual get-together – the Gooseberry Oscars in all but
name – prompts Egton Bridge to spring to life. Stretch limos.
Ray Bans. Gawping crowds greet the monster berries as they
arrive in the loving hands of their growers. Well, perhaps it's

not quite that awe-inspiring, but there is definite tension in the air. There is the Champion Berry Cup to win after all.

Now I am sure you will all be familiar with a gooseberry, a mildly hairy fruit that can be tart or sweet depending on the variety and can be made into crumbles, fools and other classic British puddings and desserts, but you may be less familiar with the cult of gooseberry growing. I have a bush on my allotment that gets absolutely no attention at all, and crops as heavily and as regularly as a man on bran. Its fruit are . . . well, let's say modest in size, but I have always thought them to be quite adequate. But now I know better, and I look at the bush somewhat differently. I have plans. Yes, it's true, guys: size really does matter, at least here in Egton Bridge. Indeed, it's absolutely crucial, for the whole idea of the competition is to grow the biggest, fattest berry of all time.

But what class to choose? Well, first of all, despite your personal history, new entrants and those who have never won a prize are all put into the maiden class. All you have to do is pay your annual sub at Easter, and get growing. The choice is yours. You could go for a red or a yellow, a white or a green berry. Or, you old devil, you could even choose the hyper-tricky twin section, where two berries are presented with conjoined stalks. And no microsurgeon is allowed near them. They absolutely must be clearly linked, or else disqualification beckons. The only other thing to be careful of is to keep their skin whole. Not a single cut is permitted on a show gooseberry. And definitely no bleeding or wounded berries, thank you.

At ten o'clock in the morning a stream of cars, and 4×4s for the bigger gooseberries, began to arrive.

'Oh, 'allo there. Luvly to see you. You're looking well.' (You'll need to think North Yorkshire accent here by the way.)

With all the usual pleasantries out of the way I hoped the conversation would turn towards the profound. I needed the aggression of a John Humphries. ''Ow big are yours, then?

And 'ow the 'ell do you get them that big?' But there are some things you just don't ask a decent gooseberry grower. Like, what's your secret? And, 'ow big are yours? So everyone just clung to the pleasantries, and walked into the school hall, holding their precious berries tightly to their chests.

Come war, pestilence, starvation or floods, the gooseberry growing just keeps on going. Actually, not pestilence, come to think of it. The year 2001 was the one and only time in two centuries that the show had to be cancelled. And all because of foot and mouth, which managed to do to British agriculture what the Romans did to the Sabine women.

The show is held in the old school, but the real business takes place well away from the hoi polloi in a small back room. I was ushered through, desperately seeking Mr Gooseberry, the guv'nor, Eric Preston.

''Ow do!' he said. 'You're that writer chappie from Oxford, aren't yer? Well, we should be able to talk later.'

Wow! I had spoken to the chairman. The chairman had spoken. But, just as Esau was a hairy man, Eric was a busy man. So I left him to stroke his chin over the perplexing matters at hand.

Four even more serious men sat around a perfectly normal-looking table gazing at an ancient pair of scales. It could have been a ouija board. They were the weighmen.

'We've been using 'em since 1937,' said one. 'Luvly, aren't they?'

Indeed they were. Apothecary's scales, gleaming and brassy, which wobbled meaningfully as each gooseberry was placed on them. Tradition has it that there be a feather nearby to stop said wobbling. Nothing else will do.

What happens is remarkably elaborate. A contestant enters, and all eyes turn. He — almost all the competitors are men — brings with him his gooseberries, cosseted in cotton wool, and registers with the clerk. He — the clerk, you see, is also a he — then hands the berries on to be kept under careful watch until the judges are ready. There can be no question of trickery or legerdemain.

Then the discussion begins. Now that's a Lord Derby. This is a Woodpecker. They all know. Almost always, anyway. They occasionally seem to have a bit of trouble with the concept of colour, though.

'That's a green berry, intit?'

'No, it's a yeller!'

And so on. It was very light-hearted. I just prayed they weren't all colour blind.

The wise men spent four hours clustered next to the scales, cogitating over weights and twitching the feather. My mind wandered back to the days of harmless drugs and five-quid deals. Expert eyes drew the correct weights, placed them on the scale, then gently lowered the gooseberry onto the other side of the balance. The needle moves, the weight is read out, and the figure is written into the *boook*. And there's none of this newfangled metric nonsense, none of this pounds and ounces nonsense either: the berries are weighed in drams and grains. Or dwts and grns.

I cheekily asked how many grains there were in a dram.

'There's sixteen drams in an ounce. We know that cos of the two-ounce berries. Now, 'ow many grains in a dram?'

'Thirty-two?'

'No no no, it's twenty-eight.'

He was right. It is.

I also asked why on earth they use such a completely defunct system.

'Well, it's avoir dew poyz,' came the answer. And anyway, it's what they have always used.

It's blindingly obvious to all and sundry that weighing gooseberries could just as well be done on a natty pair of digital scales in seconds, but the gooseberry elders are adamant, and rightly so, that this is just not what the gooseberry show is all about. It's all to do with tradition. Rural life and gooseberries are easy bedfellows. In the nineteenth century there were gooseberry shows all over the north of England; today there are but two: one at Egton Bridge, and the other at the appositely named village of Goostrey in Cheshire. But, while Egton Bridge welcomes all comers and has members all over the world – indeed, they have a fully paid-up gooseberry enthusiast from Hawaii – the Cheshire lot don't allow anyone in from outside at all.

'They do things funny down there,' I was told.

But when they come to Egton Bridge, that's different. They are welcomed into the fold like long-lost buddies. They are, it has to be said, a very friendly lot at Egton Bridge.

'O, good t'see you!'

The weighmen smiled as a man from Cheshire walked in, a wit at that: 'This is my chest. This is my hair. I am the one with the string vest and the chest hair. I'm the one from Cheshire!' They all laughed politely. At least they understood him. I had to switch accents to avoid too much 'Sorry?' as they struggled to interpret my southern accent. It was class not clarse up here.

Come eleven o'clock and the team was in full weighing mode. Cars were still drawing up, drivers getting out into the damp moorland air with even more parcels and egg boxes, their fat, juicy berries mollycoddled inside.

I was an embedded reporter by that stage, in the thick of it, standing by the arm of my special gooseberry friend Julia Brierly, whom I'd first seen sitting at the end of the weighing table – one of the committee's rarer finds. She'd smiled at me and chatted away when the tension had seemed just too unbearable for the men. Julia quickly became my confidante. Not so long ago the world of the gooseberry had been rocked to the core by Julia's massive pair of twin gooseberries, which hold the record to this day. And this she achieved after only a few years' competing.

'That's Mr Holt,' she whispered to me, 'the man from Cheshire. He always has some big berries!'

Mr Holt brought his gooseberries to the table in a beautiful, well-worn, varnished wooden box specifically designed for berry transport, I suspected, with a few gentle blobs of molten wax on the lid. Indeed they were big. Were there gooseberry covens over in Cheshire, I wondered?

One gooseberry in particular caught the attention. The judges usually knew immediately what type of berry each consignment comprised, even if the colour occasionally confused them. 'Now that's a fine-looking Woodpecker,' was said for a yellow gooseberry; 'Ooh, look at that Lloyd George, Eric. That's a beauty, that is,' another cooed while fondling a fat, juicy red berry. And what glorious names they had. Firbob, Lord Derby, Surprise, Mr Chairman, Transparent – all venerable varieties little used now. But one particular berry had them all wondering, despite their collective wisdom.

'Well, I'm not too sure about this one. It looks like a Bank View. Aye. Is that right, Mr Holt?'

The man from Cheshire came bounding over, chest hair pinging from his vest, and confirmed that it was just that, a Bank View.

There used to be literally hundreds of varieties of gooseberries, and by the end of the nineteenth century a Gooseberry Growers Register was in existence. Records from Petworth House down in deepest Sussex show that they once cultivated over a hundred varieties in their fruit gardens. And even then they had evocative, patriotic names: Nelson's Waves, Wellington's Glory, Hero of the Nile . . .

By twelve o'clock things were beginning to calm down a little. Brows unfurrowed. The weighing had finished for the moment, and the dedicated foursome set off for the pub. Meanwhile, the school hall was beginning to fill with plates full of neat little gaggles of gooseberries, numbered and ticketed, with names and weights on the labels. And to keep everyone off dangerous tenterhooks the prizes also began to emerge, to be laid alongside the berries. Julia won a garden fork.

Old acquaintances continued to greet one another with the warmth of a gooseberry crumble. In fact everyone seemed to be a little on the old side, so it seemed understandable that there was some concern about the future of gooseberry shows.

Later on in the afternoon I managed to squeeze in a *tête-à-tête* with one of the show's longest-serving growers, Mr Brian Nellist, who has been exhibiting his gooseberries since 1951. I was secretly weighing up the idea of becoming an exhibitor myself and asked him where you can get the stock. I'd been told there was a nursery down the road.

'You could cross my palm with silver,' he told me, as keen as mustard to spread the growing stock around the globe.

'But how do you actually grow them?' I pressed. 'I mean, my gooseberries would get absolutely nowhere.'

'Well, you have to build a pen first.'

Marvellous idea, that. Just in case the gooseberries want to escape?

'And pruning's important. Keep the bush open like an ice-cream cone.'

There is a specific technique to pruning, which I hadn't quite mastered, for in order to get the berry as big as possible you should ruthlessly prune out every other berry on the branch. It is the survival of the fittest to get the fattest.

Then I told him about the mare's tail on my allotment, which caused a lot of tut-tutting.

'Terrible stuff, that is. You just can't get rid of it. Spray it and it comes back after a year or two.'

It seemed as if he was about to advise me to emigrate.

One of the growers then came up with a brilliant idea for me to conquer the awful reality of this tall, slender plant-pest: 'Why don't you dig out the ground and then put the bushes in forty-gallon drums with the ends cut off. That should beat the mare's tail.'

'And fill it with what?'

'Now that would be telling, mind! That's the secret! Just

get your hands on some good manure, and keep it covered. But don't let all that goodness wash away.'

Mr Nellist briefly resumed his own cultivation hints, then turned wistful. 'It's sad you don't see much young folk 'ere any more. We need to attract them or there'll not be a great future for the show. It's been part of life 'ere for over two hundred years after all.'

The Victorians were the first to create a real enthusiasm for growing things big. It was almost entirely a working-class occupation. The aristocrats expended, or rather their staff expended, equal amounts of energy on getting the first and rarest fruits to the table – pineapples for Christmas, and musk melons, delectable table grapes, peaches, even apricots. But among the towns and cities of the industrial north, the indigenous gooseberry thrived without the need for anything other than a plot of good fertile soil. Men found solace in their allotments and there developed a whole subculture of giant this and that which hasn't entirely died out. To keep the gooseberry growers from boredom at the end of the season, many seemed to have developed a particular fondness for delphiniums. Others for auricula, but again it was size and conformity that were crucial. They seemed a happy group of Yorkshiremen, rural people, farmers, retired gamekeepers, full of that innate modesty of the Englishman.

Then I suddenly remembered. Gooseberries. Food. Fool! The gooseberry appears at an auspicious time, just as the strawberries are finishing and the raspberries haven't quite begun. Every June, I trudge up to the allotment and strip my bushes, in the process gashing my hands on the thorns, and sit around the table boring everyone with gooseberry tales of years gone by. Gooseberries make the most exquisite jam. They are high in pectin, so the jam sets easily. And in one of those classic culinary combinations, just as the berries are ripening, the elder should still be in flower, and its floral muskiness complements the gooseberry brilliantly. All you need is a flowering head or two of elder wrapped in muslin to boil with the gooseberries to add a subtle nuance that will have the family in raptures.

I asked Julia if she ever actually ate the gooseberries, for I had begun to suspect from the number of men involved that they may never be eaten at all, just grown big and gawped at. Julia put me straight on that one.

'Ooh yes! None go to waste. I'll give you a recipe if you like. This is 'ow I cook them. Stew the berries – whatever you've got really. Cut them up if they're too big, and then put some crumble mix on top, sprinkle it with demerara sugar, and put it under the grill.'

Just the sort of recipe I like.

Some of the men were less forthcoming. 'Oh no, we don't *eat* them!' – this from an ex-champion, who almost seemed shocked at such a question. Brian Nellist did, though, and he loved them.

We then touched on the thorny issue of chemicals. Though to be honest, it wasn't a thorny issue to anyone else.

'Well, you have to spray 'em,' Brian said. 'I do 'em every two weeks or so, just to get rid of the mildew.'

'They were saying they spray their gooseberries,' I confided to Julia. 'Is that the only way you can control the mildew?'

I felt she wanted to take me by the hand, look me in the eyes and tell me straight. 'Now I know you're not from round 'ere,' she began, 'but you seem a nice enough chap. There's something you should know. Listen carefully. Mildew was introduced into this country by the Americans in 1905. Since then we've struggled. Spraying is the only option with these varieties.' Yet she didn't. 'Funny, that,' she mused. 'My mum said that in the old days they used to put the bushes by the outside privy and when you'd finished you'd pour the pot over the bushes. *They* never 'ad no mildew! I didn't use to spray mine, but I did this year. It's been that damp.'

The afternoon wore on, and I slipped off for some tea.

There were slices of home-made tea bread, and Yorkshire parkin (a thick, gingerbread-type tea bread), lovely freshly made sandwiches, home-made biscuits . . . ooh, it was all luvly luvly luvly. But to be honest, after five hours' talking gooseberries I felt I wanted closure. I told Julia I was thinking of setting off across the moor — one of the bleakest parts of the country I have ever seen, I have to say.

'You can't leave now!' She looked positively shocked. 'You'll miss the Stape Band!'

So I set off for a brief conceptual break to Whitby a few miles down the road, promising that I would return to see the Stape boys perform.

I wished I had stayed. Whitby was heaving, stuffed full of people eating fish and chips, and children in Eng-er-land football strips. I parked on the grass (not grarse, remember), watched a game of bowls, thought about Walter Ralegh and had a cigarette. Fish and chips is another classic domestic dish whose fitness to be enjoyed by all and sundry is now being threatened by our innate conservatism. There exists an intranational divide between the Scots, who prefer haddock, and the English, who prefer cod. Indeed, so popular has cod become, and so poorly have the North Sea fish stocks been managed, that the raw material is fast becoming too expensive to be served as the classic everyday food. There are decent alternatives, such as coley and pollock, relatively abundant fish, but few Brits would be happy asking at the counter for two large pollocks. Fish and chips is now losing out rapidly to other fast foods such as the burger, the kebab and the pizza. In Scotland, haddock stocks are more plentiful, indeed so much so that there is a campaign afoot to try to get us to eat more of the stuff.

Before long the siren call of the Stape Band drew me back to Egton Bridge. I arrived just as the musicians were pulling out their trumpets and horns from the mini van, went and had yet another cup of tea, and sat and watched. That's what everyone else was doing. It was all lovely background music; not a hint of dancing. You don't dance to brass bands as far as I know.

I couldn't help but reflect on how totally and completely unlike Italy this all was. There was absolutely no culinary curiosity at all. No passionate fondling (of the berries), no discussion about the minutiae of making gooseberry fool, or the best way to make gooseberry jams and jellies. There was not one single pot of gooseberry jam for sale, no gooseberry and prosciutto, nothing even vaguely edible that related to *Ribes grossularia* at all. Would it be ethical, I wondered, to introduce the tiniest touch of cooking into this wise but unworldly event in this lovely Yorkshire village? Or why not apply to the National Lottery and open a gooseberry museum? It was all about the quiet art of producing berries, defying nature, and cultivating that serious, slightly wacky amateurism so beloved of the British.

Traditions are clung on to almost desperately, in the face of a very real sense that something has to be done to keep this quirky event from dying on its feet. While the urban gooseberry growers have moved on to chrysanthemums or died, or bought motorhomes and died, the rural North Yorkshire village of Egton Bridge is valiantly holding on to a gentle civility that is rare but was once what the British were supposed to be famous for. Doomed and irrelevant? Perhaps, but my gentle, bucolic day in Egton Bridge reminded me of that dream of England the English hold so dear to their hearts – the green and pleasant bit, that is, not the militaristic fascism of St George and his white van. And on the day that Blackpool was outed as having one of the highest teenage pregnancy rates in the country, and on the day that our obsession with the sexual shenanigans of a Swede led the hallowed Football Association to implode, it made me earnestly hope that the show manages to survive.

*

Etymologists among you will no doubt have been champing at the bit for a while now. What has this magnificent but eclectic fruit got to do with the large bird of renowned aggression, the goose? The *OED* goes for the classic schema: we used to make a sharp sauce with them and eat it with goose. But there is another idea, originally put forward by George W. Johnson in his groundbreaking work *The Cucumber and the Gooseberry*, that suggests the word might well have come from the Dutch word for cross, *kruis*, combined with the Dutch for berry, which as you will all know is *bes*. That gives you *kruisbes*. But somehow I wonder at the accuracy of this explanation. Why, then, do we not just call them cruiseberries?

The gooseberry seems to be the fruit equivalent of the parsnip in a way. No other nation seems to eat it. The French have absolutely no idea about either and call the gooseberry, rather insultingly, the *groseille à macquereau*, or mackerel redcurrant. But then they have never really understood the full joys of the crumble. And certainly not the gooseberry fool, the very best way to eat this spiky super fruit.

Gooseberry fool

Serves 6–8

700 to 800g gooseberries, topped and tailed
300g strained Greek yoghurt, or single cream, or a
mixture of both
100g caster sugar

Heat the gooseberries and the sugar over a moderate heat, boil gently for five minutes, then mash. If you like a thicker fool, keep some berries back and add later. Allow to cool. Add cream or yoghurt and serve.

HARROGATE

Tea and Fat Rascals

THE ONE THING YOU WON'T BE ABLE TO BUY WHEN YOU COME to Harrogate is the town's famous bottled spring water. There is but one tap left now, as unloved and desolate as a tap can be. It disconsolately dribbles spring water at the back of the Old Pump Room. I know this because it was pointed out to me, *sotto voce*. I was a little perplexed, for Harrogate seems to have completely laid its spa persona to rest. I had to ask inside if it was even possible to take the waters.

'We don't actually have a working spring here any more, but you can see a lot about the past in the museum, if you'd like to buy a ticket.'

My museum budget was skyrocketing. I resisted the invitation.

'Thanks, but I was really just trying to find out if you can still take the waters. Where have all the curistas gone?'

'If you buy a ticket it should tell you all that, I think you'll find.'

So I did. But it didn't.

Back to the reception desk.

'I'm still not sure what I can see *now*. Sorry, maybe I am being dim.'

'Harrogate isn't really a spa town any more,' the receptionist explained. 'It hasn't been since the NHS stopped sending anyone here to be cured. I suppose we are a conference town nowadays.'

'So what's happened to all the old springs?'

'Well, this is the Old Pump Room, as you can see. But I'm not too sure about the Assembly Rooms; I think they have become a restaurant. Then there are the Winter Gardens. They have been developed too. So, yes, you're right, there's not much left really.' The receptionist concluded his short piece as if he had stumbled across an evangelical truth. 'But if you like,' he added, lifting a carafe of gently bubbling water off a natty little doily, 'you can try this.'

I took a sip. It was utterly wretched. Sulphurous, and eggy. If this was good for you, I wanted to be ill. I asked if I could buy a bottle, thinking it would make the ideal Christmas gift.

'Well, no. It's quite impossible, I'm afraid. Health regulations and all that. You could help yourself to some out the back, though.' This last was said in an almost conspiratorial whisper.

The only reason why there is a tap outside is due to some arcane ordinance that was meant to allow the poor to enjoy the same waters as the rich, at any time of the day or night. You too can still, if you wish, drive up and fill your jerrycan free of charge (remember road miles, though – no ecological embarrassments, please). But you will find no line of joyous travellers there, just a grotty old electric switch that arouses the tap to a fitful spluttering.

Yet Harrogate lived off its reputation as one of the country's finest spa towns for nearly four hundred years. In 1571 William Slingsby discovered a spring in what was then a royal forest that was particularly rich in minerals. So people began to visit to drink the health-giving waters, no doubt spreading any communicable diseases they had in the process. In time the spring was referred to as the English Spaw, named after the town in Belgium from which we derive our word spa. Drinking copious amounts of mineral water was thought to be a great curative for many of the contemporary ailments no physician could cure. Which was almost all of them. The government was also keen to promote domestic springs, since foreign spas were thought to be dens of Catholic plotting and general iniquity. Over time, Harrogate became a suave Georgian town to which people travelled from afar to 'take the waters'. A neat phrase, for it could mean either drinking or bathing, and the physicians of Europe were at great pains to encourage both. And profited enormously as a result.

> At your first coming hither you shall meet with a troublesome delight, an importunity among the women here almost as eager as that of the water-men of London, who shall be your servant to fill water to you when you go to the wells, or bring it to your lodging when you do not. And this clamour we were fain to endure because we were not resolved to drink the water, this evening the next morning – for they got into our chambers before we got out of our beds – with pots of water one cries out 'I am pretty Betty, let me serve you'; another cries 'Kate and Coz Dol, do we let tend you', but to tell you the truth they fell short of that, for their faces did shine like bacon rine.
>
> from *A Journey into the North with my friend Mr Washborne* by Thomas Baskerville (1658)

From the late seventeenth century British spa towns positively boomed, and they became an intricate part of British society, particularly when Queen Anne took the waters in 1702. All the sycophants and the idle members of 'society' felt they just had to spend part of their arduous year at a spa town.

Or, as another writer put it, it was where the 'plutocracy mingled'.

Such mingling involved a great deal of organization, and for a while the resorts were ruled over by a master of ceremonies. The most famous of these was Richard 'Beau' Nash, who made a fortune in the eighteenth century by becoming the man who ran Bath. But Harrogate always thought of itself as less elitist than Bath, so it constructed a Royal Pump Room, the Winter Gardens and an opera house to show just how true this was. Oh, and the tap for the poor outside the Pump Room.

Springs were found all over the place. Some had sweet water, others were particularly sulphurous. Every year regulars arrived with the summer, ostensibly to take the waters but also to catch up on the gossip of the day, listen to music, consult the physicians (who were happy to milk them dry) and drink nice cups of tea all the while. Lazy rich people were constantly reminded of the joys of indolence and wealth, and the town thrived on it.

There was a recommended daily intake of water for each and every one, and a strict regimen of exercise was suggested, again by the physicians. Over time the cures became more complex. The one that particularly appealed to me was the peat bath, for cases of 'chronic pelvic disorders of an in-flammatory nature'. Patients were encouraged to bathe in fifty-gallon baths of hot peat to cleanse themselves of their pelvic sins.

What better, I thought, what better in this genteel and harmonious place than to sit and sip tea, as the spa regulars once did; to talk tannin and address what is one of Britain's most irrevocable addictions – tea drinking?

Tea was once purely a society drink, vastly expensive and utterly elitist, quite beyond the pockets of the average family. But times changed. In the 1820s, tea began to be planted in the Indian subcontinent, where it grew well. Which was hardly surprising really, for the plant already grew wild in Assam.

The tea trade with China had become so unbalanced that the East India Company took to bartering tea for opium grown in India, shipping it across to China in tea clippers. British tea drinkers carried on oblivious to all this perfidy, and with increasing supplies coming from India and Sri Lanka, prices dropped and the social pattern to tea drinking began to change. By the middle of the nineteenth century it was becoming affordable, and increasingly popular among the working classes. Tea stifled hunger, slaked thirst and invigorated flagging spirits. The tea break – an opportunity to re-energize yourself with endless cups of warm, milky, sweetened brew (and to have a chat and a fag at the same time) – eventually became a national institution. (Though not everyone agreed with tea's supposed qualities: nineteenth-century English writer and champion of the poor William Cobbett, in his travelogue *Rural Rides*, labelled tea 'an enfeebler of the frame, an engenderer of effeminacy, a debaucher of youth'. No-one took any notice.)

In some households there was a weekly elaboration on the afternoon cuppa, and it was particularly popular in Yorkshire. This was called high tea, a variation on the theme of aristocratic salon teas, and it would be taken at five o'clock in the afternoon, one hour after the traditional time for a tea break, but before evening church or chapel. It was also a time to demonstrate domestic prowess, and for the skills of home baking to be honed. Everything was placed on the table before the guests arrived, and tea was served from stout round teapots. There would be a tablecloth and even the odd doily to transform the scene. High tea was a peculiarly British invention. Primarily it was an occasion for the family to socialize, and it had about it an almost Mediterranean warmth, though that was often stifled by scandal and stiff collars. But it is the reason why there is a profusion of cakes and tea breads in Yorkshire, the parkins, pikelets and spiced loaves, all of which made their ritual appearance at high tea. Sunday high tea might also see the family eat one of their few affordable luxuries, a can of tinned salmon, or slices of boiled ham. 'Slow walking bread' it was called in Skipton, for no decent citizen would have been buried without ham at their funeral tea. Funeral biscuits were even given to the mourners wrapped in white paper, and decorated with black sealing wax. In Keighley, funeral teas went by the bizarre name of 'arvills', which is thought to come from the old Norse word *arveol* which described a funeral feast for a clan chief.

It wasn't quite the same as tea with the upper classes, who used tall silver teapots, strainers, and ate crustless sandwiches. That was far more effete. They would use the family's best tea service for the occasion, fine bone china cups and saucers. The cups had handles so small that one just had to sip the tea with one's little finger sticking out, which was considered to be a sign of good breeding. At one time there was little difference in the shapes of pots, be they for tea, coffee or even chocolate, but when tea first appeared from China in the first half of the seventeenth century British merchants began to import the odd porcelain teapot too, delicate and fabulously expensive, and importantly not at all heat conductive, so they could be easily handled. The search for the secret of porcelain kept many an ingenious potter in business for decades.

But whoever was taking it, afternoon tea was a drink to be sipped, not slurped. At the other end of the social tea scale the four o'clock cuppa was consumed almost without any sense of social decorum at all, and one could happily dunk a biscuit without fear of ostracization. In recognition of the popularity of dunking, a Yorkshire biscuit has been designed in the shape of a T, an ideal shape for the dedicated dunker, a biscuit that can be soaked and dangled into your tea without fear of crumbling, or of leaving behind those awful slushy deposits at the bottom of the mug.

Afternoon tea in this archetypal Georgian town seemed an excellent way for me to begin, and Harrogate conveniently has a café with a most mellifluous, evocative English name: Betty's (cutting-edge inventors of the aforementioned T biscuit). It was founded by a Swiss émigré in 1919. Betty's has become a local if not a national institution, and I needed to wash away the sulphur from my palate and to indulge myself, to sip a Single Estate Darjeeling and nibble at something effete. A crustless cucumber sandwich, perhaps? A fondant fancy? How about a fat rascal?

Walk into Betty's and you will see that its Swiss roots are still very much in evidence. The air is chocolate-scented. The counters are immaculately clean and it is all run with a practised and professional air. Betty doesn't actually stand at the door and greet you personally – indeed, no-one is 100 per cent sure who she was – but it's a brilliant name. They're canny, the Swiss, and Betty's is certainly busy. Anywhere that has tea and a warm, pungent whiff of cake in the air will always have a place in the British heart. But have you ever actually wondered why it is that we are as a nation more culturally attached to tea than to coffee? Yes, yes, I know the answer may well be no, but I at least found it a little odd, particularly considering our seventeenth-century passion for the coffee house.

I had been asked, or more exactly I had asked myself, to a tea tasting the following day chez Betty's, at their head office. But I thought a bit of practical investigation wouldn't go amiss. Betty's have shown real entrepreneurial flare, and genteelly swallowed up another Harrogate institution, a company that's almost as famous, Taylor's of Harrogate, who were and are tea and coffee merchants of even longer standing than Betty's – Taylor's began business in 1886. So Harrogate now has a little empire of caffeine and cakes whose headquarters can be found on the outskirts of the town.

Walking into Taylor's tea-tasting room the next day, there seemed to be something of the school science laboratory about the place. Tins of tea lay around its edges. Packets from Assam were rushed in by courier, there were secret codes and bubbling brews, and then, in my honour, a line of teacups with tea so thick and muddy with tannin it made my heart pulse and my limbs shake even to think about it.

Ian Brabbin is one of Taylor's tea buyers, and has the arduous duty of travelling the world, seeking bevvy and fostering goodness. His specialities are the teas of India and Africa, and here he was in Yorkshire about to introduce me to the art of tea tasting.

'I thought we'd start by tasting some of our teas, and some of the other ones on the market, so you could see the difference,' he said. 'Now, this one' – he pointed at a brew of ditchwater aspect – 'is one of the cheapest on the market, and as you can see, it looks a little different to the others.'

It did. It had no twinkle to it. The others danced in the light.

'And you can see, if you run your hand through it, that the tea is like fine dust really.'

Moving up the social scale, we passed on to my own favourite, good old PG Tips. Only it wasn't like the good old cup I was used to. Tea professionals taste it double brewed, and it isn't poured from a lovely old teapot either.

You sip, as noisily as you can. You assess. And then, wa-hay, you spit it all out into a giant spittoon that probably has a technical name but I forgot to ask what it was. Ian, of course, could do this with pinpoint correctness, but I kept on dribbling like an old dosser and wiping my chin surreptitiously. Still, I began to sense a growing fascination within me as we moved on to their very own Yorkshire tea, widely drunk in Cornwall.

Which is a blend. As is most of the tea you, or at least I, would drink. The creation of a brand or blend requires a consistent attention to what is going on in the world tea market. Up until 1998 there was an important Tea Auction in London, a sociable place by all accounts, where everyone sat down in the morning for a good old chat over a nice cup of tea. Actually it was slightly more cut and thrust than that, but Taylor's were experienced buyers, and they sentimentally bought the very last lot of tea to be offered on the final day of business. But buying tea, just like blending it, has now become more technical, and scientific. Computers record the exact details of the blend, and allow the buyer to deal directly with the producer, which is a crucial principle in the world of food and drink.

We digressed into a bit of jargon.

'All the teas we've tasted so far are CTC teas, so we'll move on to some leaf teas now if you want.'

And what did CTC mean?

'Cut, tear, curl. To get the quick brew of a tea bag, the tea needs to be rolled and mangled, otherwise it wouldn't work. The tea would be too weak.'

Aha. So, does that mean that tea bags are made with second-rate tea?

'No, not at all. But that's not to say that it is all good either.'

As we had seen.

The next brew was milkless, a dark and alluring colour. We were moving slowly up the scale now, and I took a gulp of one of their best teas.

'If you take a look at this you can see in the tea there are a few golden specks, which is a good sign. It means there are young leaves in there.'

We might all wish to remain in the first flush of youth, but with tea it's the second flush that's the best, a flush being the new season's leaves. In Assam, where there is a spring and a summer, the tender leaves, the top two to three leaves on a stem, are picked and carefully dried. We were tasting a single estate tea, Tippy Assam, which was a complex drink compared to the blend. Complexity seems to be suitable for afternoon tea, for teas drunk with no milk, and reflects a little of the tone of afternoon tea as once it was taken in the upper echelons of society. Tea drinking has its own social duties to perform.

I was surprised by just how old a productive tea bush can be. Tea is a member of the camellia family, *Camellia sinensis*, and can live happily for over twenty years. Given a good mulch and enough light, heat and moisture, tea bushes appear to be relatively problem free but are still incredibly labour intensive for there is simply no way a machine can outdo the skilled tea picker. And hopefully there never will be.

Concerned punters like to know whether they can have their cuppa with an easy conscience. Taylor's are a modern, enlightened company paying more than lip service to the idea of being socially responsible. It is now what consumers expect from their tea, their coffee and their bananas, all part of the triumvirate of Fair Trade which has now seeped into our collective consciousness. But, although we are a prodigious tea-drinking nation, we are not particularly well educated about our teas.

'It's very odd,' Ian remarked, 'and I really don't know why, but some of the best teas are drunk in north Germany.' They are an experimental lot up there in the Bight of Heligoland.

By now the dried leaves, and the brews, were beginning to look distinctly different. I was beginning to pick up on the subtleties – the leaf colour, the tips, and the curls. One dish was full of gorgeously speckled tea leaves with electric-blue cornflower petals. Another exuded the musky blunt sexiness of roses. All Indian. All black.

I asked Ian about Chinese tea.

'To be honest, it's not my area,' he replied, 'but I can tell you about green tea. It comes from exactly the same bush, but what gives black tea its colour is the process of fermentation. This is where the skill of the producer comes in. It's what helps to give the tea its character.'

When the tea is picked, it will be left to ferment for about an hour and a half, depending upon the heat and the humidity, and then dried. The whole lot is then graded, from dust to broken tea, which begins to explain what on earth Broken Orange Pekoe is. Green tea is still the preferred brew of the east. Russians love it, and so do tea drinkers in Islamic countries – the Koran forbids all fermented drinks – but it is mostly drunk heavily sweetened. Which would not be at all the done thing in China or Japan. The Chinese tea trade with Europe and the New World was once enormously important, with tea clippers hastily transporting vast quantities of tea from China to be served in the salons of Europe and the New World. It was expensive and highly prized. Indeed, so valuable were the tea leaves that they were often stored in elaborate tea caddies.

The very last tea we tasted was that good old middle-class favourite, lapsang souchong. A tea that didn't excite Ian as much as it does the good folk of Woking.

'It's just that it's a bit unsubtle, that's all,' he commented.

Lapsang comes from Fujian in China, and tradition has it that an accidental fire gave the tea its smokiness (shades of Seahouses' kipper tale), which far from putting the discerning clients off their tea actually got them all rather excited. So that is how it is still made to this day. Just not your cup of tea, perhaps?

Once we had exhausted our taste buds, and with incredible good fortune, since Betty's and Taylor's are now one spiritual whole, I was escorted across the tarmac to take a look at their bakery, to see how they make their very own tea-accompanying Yorkshire favourites. From the outside the building gave me the impression that Heidi had taken up architecture, with its splashes of wood and wide open windows, flowers, and peo-ple who smiled and greeted you as if they really enjoyed being there. In fact, that's the one overriding thing that struck me about my day at Betty's and Taylor's: people actually smiled at work. They smiled at you in the corridors. It was as if we had stumbled into a mad world of happy British people who had seen the light, and put all their energy into making spiritual cakes.

The bakery was winding down by the time I got there, but cakey smells still emanated from the pristine guts of the building, drifting along corridors and seeping under doors. It was intoxicating. We walked past the huge wood-burning oven, carefully cossetted by two master bakers. 'Bid my bread feed, and my fire warm me!' was inscribed above the oven door. In a tiny annex, someone was consulting a pastel palette of colours for a wedding cake, but the chocolate section was still hard at it. A solid stream of chocolate poured from a tap, filling moulds and shapes, the surplus dripping back to be recycled. In the next room I spied a shelf full of fondant fancies. My heart sang. These finger-sized cakes are simple, really – sponge covered with icing, and topped with a delicate dollop of cream – but they have been ritually abused by years of mass production. How few of us have ever really tasted a fresh, home-made fondant fancy! Pathetically few. And the name! A touch of French, a hint of lewdness, pink icing – ooh, it's almost too much to bear. And that evocative dollop of cream. Class indeed!

Then I was shown another trolley loaded with what looked to me like dumpy tea cakes.

'Oh, they're fat rascals!' I was told. 'We make over a quarter of a million of them a year now. Incredible, isn't it?'

Fat rascals

Makes 15–20

225g plain flour
¼ tsp salt
1 rounded tsp baking powder
65g lard
25g sugar
65g currants
4–5 tbsp milk
egg yolk, beaten

Sift the flour, salt and baking powder together. Rub in the lard until the mixture is like fine breadcrumbs, then stir in the sugar and currants. Add just enough milk to make a soft dough. Roll out onto a floured board to a 2.5cm thickness. Cut into 5cm rounds and place close together on a greased baking tray. Brush with a little beaten egg yolk and bake at 220°C, gas mark 7, for 15 minutes.

from *A Cook's Tour of Britain* by the WI and Michael Smith (Collins Willow, 1984)

I had never heard of fat rascals at all, so I was ushered into the café and given one, toasted and buttered. Its origins are 100 per cent Yorkshire, a version of what was once known as turf cake, which was cooked on a griddle over a peat fire. Britain is in many ways a land of tea and cake, and the thought made me hungry.

DUMFRIES

Grouse and Haggis

FROM YORKSHIRE, I SET OFF TO DUMFRIES, AND BEYOND. MISSION? To check out the state of *Lagopus lagopus scotticus*, the red grouse, the bird that must dread August with a deep and atavistic loathing. Every year the Glorious Twelfth comes around, and if all is ready and the grouse haven't all emigrated, rabid bird slaughterers flock – well, perhaps that is an exaggeration; let's say they arrive in their 4×4s at leisure – to shoot what is considered by many to be the finest of all our game birds. It's tough being a grouse.

A few days before I arrived in Scotland, I trawled the net for information on the grouse. I like to prepare the ground if I can, and surprise my temporary hosts with a sliver or two of knowledge. It's a psychological thing really. Ignorance can be very wearing for the expert. I wondered why my net nanny kept on blocking out anything to do with grouse, particularly the black grouse, until I realized that it had discovered my awful crime: I was looking up articles containing 'black' and 'cock'. I double-locked the door, fearing a call from the social services, and once I'd disabled the nanny the information came rushing down the ether.

The red grouse is a bird that is very particular about where it lives, and about what it eats. It likes nothing better than to nibble at the tender young shoots of heather, and it likes to nest in it too. It may, for all I know, even dream of heather. I had never seen a grouse — alive, that is. I had seen many of them dead, but it's always a little difficult to imagine a stone-cold symmetrical corpse ever flying or breathing, let alone copulating.

And I have to say I didn't immediately associate grouse with Dumfries, a town only fifteen or so miles from the border with England. There seemed no popular connection there at all, but then grouse shooting is hardly a popular pastime. It is a sport for the rich. Indeed, the very rich. Every day on the moor will cost you about £50 per brace, so a day-long shoot on a top grouse moor might cost you and your shooting buddies up to £10,000. Forgive me if you are disappointed that I didn't grab my Holland and Holland and join the fun on the Glorious Twelfth.

It's one of the inevitable problems when writing a book about food that you need people who know their stuff, and who like to talk. In Italy, this was no difficulty at all. Quite the opposite, in fact. You could meet people who held your hand and smouldered with passion and enthusiasm, but the British with their customary reserve can be infinitely more challenging. You make contact, you ask questions, then you pounce and meet. Through the restaurant network, I contacted a game dealer and landowner called Ben Weatherall, and we agreed to meet near Dumfries.

I left Harrogate and all its steady, middle-class charms, and glorious landscape, and made my way north-west to the border, narrowly deciding against a quickie stop in Gretna Green, happier to leave the image of this town to my imagination. I have always had this extraordinarily clear picture of a ravishing young woman laughing in a wedding dress, holding a bunch of white lilies, running alongside a square-jawed hunk who is about to have his cake and eat it. But I don't want to see the reality. I did that in Blackpool.

Nor did I feel immediately drawn to Dumfries. It seemed too dour. So off I went seeking something a little more rural, and I eventually found it. The man running the hotel looked up, and spoke. They do that sometimes. But he did not speak with the Scottish och I was expecting, but in broad Yorkshire. I found myself becoming almost obsessed by the nuances of the English language, by the subtle shifts from, say, Lancastrian to Cumbrian to Scottish. Everywhere lay subtleties and pitfalls. The glottal stop has not as yet been all-conquering.

Come dawn, I was out of my usual backbreaking bed and off to meet the red grouse. And exactly on time, my grouse man came in. Sometimes you meet people who have something so gobsmackingly different about them it hijacks the usual social niceties. It does with me, anyway, unless of course it's offensive. Your day will not start off too well if you greet your contact with a 'My, how outstandingly ugly you are!' But in this case it was, I felt, within the rules to say, 'God, you're tall!' For he was Eiffelian, towering.

'Yes, I am,' Ben replied, as if no-one had ever pointed it out to him before.

Before I got into the where-do-you-get-your-trousers-from, we got into his Land Rover and sped off into the glorious hills of south Lanarkshire to meet the grouse at home, *en famille*. I have to say that, much as I respect their dress sense, their thriving culture and their apparent wholehearted passion for all things European, I really do have a problem with Scotland and heather. This devil needed to be exorcised, for try as I may to think otherwise, heather is to me the magnolia paint of the plant world – monotonous, predictable, over-familiar.

We finally stopped, and Ben switched off the engine. I marvelled at the complex, ancient hills and valleys, and the deep and distant silence.

'Let's go and take a look for these grouse, then.' And off Ben strode, my rather short legs working in comic overtime to his gigantic stride.

An owl flew overhead.

'That's a little owl. And a golden plover over there. Ah!'

Ben bent down, picked up some grouse droppings, and fingered them lovingly.

I was thinking of Sherlock Holmes. I always do when walking through heather. I think it's something to do with the hound of the Baskervilles. And there was something Holmesian about the situation. In fact, come to think of it, Ben looked remarkably like a stretched version of Sherlock Holmes. Ben (Holmes), leading the search, looking for *Lagopus lagopus*. It looked as if I was doomed to be Watson. But me, bumble? Pah!

This morning inspection had particular relevance for the grouse. I sensed they knew just what was being talked about.

'We've got to decide whether there are enough birds for the Twelfth,' announced Ben. 'I'm not actually too sure yet.'

Then, with a mad clucking, bustling and flapping, a family of grouse took to the air under our very noses, alarmed, no doubt, by reports of their imminent demise. You wanted to tell them to stay put and keep still. Just listen, and use Maoist guerrilla tactics, and you'll be all right. Flying powerfully low, the grouse family took off into the hills to warn the others. The time is coming. Prepare ye'selves. We're all doooomed!

Defending game shooting is not as easy as it once was. New tactics are called for, but since the British hold deep and passionate feelings about the welfare of animals, the runes do not read well. They will, for instance, man (and woman) picket lines as soon as the issue of transporting live animals appears in the press. They detest the idea of experimentation in the name of lipstick. They abhor dog beating, cat beating, swan abuse. They have banded together to save Spanish donkeys from certain death. Even retired greyhounds are cared for in their old age.

But, is there not just a tinge of hypocrisy in all this? How many of us can say hand on blocked aorta that we have never chewed on a meat pie? Or a sausage? Or a slice of bacon? All made from animals that have been raised specifically to be killed and eaten. They have never been allowed to run wild. They are not wild. They are fed on concentrated feeds we know little about. Our whole beef industry virtually collapsed when the system of feeding minced animal brain to herbivores was revealed as being the source of BSE. Dairy cows are kept indoors and milked to buggery. Even if the lot of pigs has improved somewhat in the UK, many are still being reared in conditions that would truly shock most of us. And as for the poor old chicken . . . This jungle fowl has been so overbred and abused that we have quite forgotten that the chicken was once a luxury, an occasional treat to be roasted for Sunday lunch. No longer. Globally, it is the sorriest story of all.

There is now a fairly pat, predictable answer to the issue of shooting and animal welfare. It is this: without rural sports the countryside would atrophy. Shoots would revert to scrub. Hotels would go bankrupt. Communities would become moribund. The countryside would lose its soul. It's a mild form of rural blackmail. But a significant tranche of the population disputes the defence that it is an essential part of the management of the countryside. To many it is simply indefensible, barbaric and immoral. Why, they may ask, should anyone in this day and age be allowed to shoot birds and deer for pleasure? And in the same breath, of course, comes opposition to hunting. This was Scotland, and despite dire warnings the banning of hunting has not caused all the doom and gloom that was forecast. Both hunting and shooting have become very public moral issues, so it may seem that the future looks pretty bleak. In the same way that hunting whales is now a complete no-no, and eating turtles would cause uproar, our morality evolves, and things change. We may well from now on be seeing packs of hounds merrily chasing aniseed trails and human beings all over the country, and I for one would have no problem with that.

Back in 1671, however, the Game Act gave the landed gentry what they took to be a God-given and exclusive right to shoot and hunt, a right they were reluctant to relinquish:

An Act for the better preservation of the Game, and for secureing Warrens not inclosed, and the severall Fishings of this Realme

And it is hereby enacted and declared That all and every person and persons, not having Lands and Tenements or some other estate of Inheritance in his owne or his Wifes right of the cleare yearely value of one hundred pounds per annum or for terme of life, or having Lease or Leases of ninety nine yeares or for any longer terme, of the cleare yearely value of one hundred and fifty pounds, other than the Sonne and Heire apparent of an Esquire, or other person of higher degree, and the Owners and Keepers of Forrests, Parks, Chases or Warrens, are hereby declared to be persons by the Lawes of this Realme, not allowed to have or keepe for themselves or any other person or persons any Guns, Bowes, Grey hounds, Setting-dogs, Ferretts, Cony-doggs, Lurchers, Hayes, Netts, Lowbells, Hare-pipes, Ginns, Snares or other Engines aforesaid, But shall be, and are hereby prohibited to have, keepe or use the same.

from *Statute of the Realm, 1660–1671,* CII, c22–23, 24–25, p.745; this section, 1671

Anyone with a rank of less than 'an Esquire' was therefore expressly forbidden not only to use a gun, but even to own one. Gamekeepers were permitted to enter houses at will to look for guns, traps or hunting dogs, and to pass the culprits on to the rural justices. This outstanding piece of biased legislation helped fuel a three-centuries-long conflict between the landowner and the poacher. In 1816, the Night Poaching Act was passed which allowed anyone caught catching rabbits to be transported and banished for seven years, and this was increased to an unimaginable fourteen years in 1828. Resentment was profound, and it became institutionalized.

The watchword for those owning the land became 'management', and in terms of grouse-shooting, by the late 1800s they were nurturing their resources so expertly that in August there was a veritable exodus from England of moustachioed men in tweed plus-fours and deerstalkers, their single- and double-bores oiled and at the ready. Crackling black and white footage shows the sheer numbers of birds these men shot out of the sky – in their thousands – and as I tramped across the moors over a century later I was frankly amazed at the number of grouse that appeared to be flying from the heather. Ben, however, was keen to point out that that didn't necessarily mean there were enough birds to justify a shoot.

'The thing about the grouse moor is that it's got to be managed properly,' he stressed. 'If you shoot *all* the birds obviously you won't last very long. So you need to keep them at just the right level.'

It's what's called 'wise use', and it calls for a fairly profound understanding of the habitat; of what the grouse feeds on, and what it needs to thrive; of its natural predators; and just as importantly of the enemies of heather. I hadn't realized until Ben stooped down to show me that there were different types of heather. The grouse prefers the shorter plants, and the young shoots at that, so if this isn't in good supply the grouse will grouse.

Ben pulled his own long face. 'There's not much young growth here at all. Now that is a worry. It's what the grouse like best. We've got a problem with this damned heather beetle up here. You can see the new shoots coming through here and there but I'm not too sure whether it's the same all over the estate.' Then, as if offering a cue in *The Archers*, he added, 'Oh look, there's Sandy. Let's go and talk to him about the shoot.'

Off he loped down the hill, striding over boggy ditches and peaty puddles, talking all the while. Meanwhile, writing things I knew I wouldn't be able to read later, I played the part. It was challenging. My admittedly short legs were being severely overworked. I fell into the ditches and generally stumbled in his wake while Ben, Mr Tall Grouse Shoot 2004, just swept on, oblivious, barely noticing the obstacles.

'So, this heather beetle, is it— aaarghh!' as I fell into the heather once more. The grouse must have been 'avin' a larf.

There is this problem, you see, in the form of a heather-munching beetle called by its friends and enemies *Lochmaea suturalius*, the heather beetle. The population is on the up.

When we caught up with Sandy, he looked as if he could yomp the moors for days without resting. He shook my hand ferociously. I noticed a few corpses tied to his quad bike – a weasel, a stoat and a mink, each with its pin-sharp teeth grimacing, each with a tiny trickle of blood rolling down its head. Sandy was obviously a fine shot. Ben began trying to get Sandy's permission to shoot on the twelfth. It was a curious dynamic, with none of the obsequiousness you might once have expected between a landowner and the gamekeeper. That is long gone. It's all managerial and focus-groupie now. This is a professional relationship, and it's Sandy Tomson who knows the moor more intimately.

Ben started to swing his arms, feigning a casual golf swing. 'Sandy, what do you reckon about the twelfth? I'd like to shoot if you think there are enough birds out there. We've just been walking the moors and I was surprised how many grouse there were actually.'

'Well, I'd prefer not tae shoot at all to be honest wi' ye.' This is broad south Lanarkshire by the way. Ben and I spoke London.

They continued this verbal quadrille for a while, then Sandy explained for my benefit some of the complexities of moorland management.

'What do I do? Well, I've got tae make sure there are some grouse out there to shoot first of all. And that means controlling the vermin, the raptors as Ben calls them, like these.' He held up his dead critters by the neck. 'But the biggest worry is the beetle. I've been here tharteen years noo and the winters get milder and milder, and it's just not killing off the beetle larvae like it used tae. We've tried to burn off the old heather, and that helps the young shoots grow, which is crucial for the grouse diet.' He paused while a grouse family clucked in agreement in the distance. 'Aye, and then there's a parasite that gets into the young grouse. It's not easy, ye know.'

Much of the problem seems to stem from climate change, which is something no gamekeeper, however expert, can do anything about. Research has shown that the number of ticks per grouse chick grew from an average of 2.6 (and believe me, point six of a tick is still nasty) to 12.7 by 2003. And it continues to rise. The ticks attack the blood supply of the young grouse chicks, often feeding on the eyes, which understandably affects the young bird's vision and its ability to feed or even see its mother. So they become weak and are easy prey to the grim-sounding beasts Ben calls raptors. Among them is the hen harrier, and this is where pest control becomes controversial, for there are many conservationists out there who are keen to see the population of this bird increase. It is rare. So who wins out of this one? The gamekeeper or the conservationist?

The economic reality is that grouse shooting brings a substantial amount of money to Scotland – about £17 million each year to be exact. Shots spend hundreds of pounds in the hotels and the B&Bs, and the money they spend on the shoot pays the gamekeeper his salary and gives the local economy a real boost. So if this were all simply to stop, the grouse moors really would revert to scrub, the hotels really would decline, and the economy really would suffer.

Not being one of nature's finest shots I cannot really write a glowing ode to shooting, but I did ask why these birds were a special draw.

'They are difficult to shoot,' Ben replied. 'They fly low. You've seen that already.'

Not far away, running up in a straight line across the moor, was a line of straw bales, with a pit dug just behind them. These are called butts – oddly, I thought – and are where the shot stands in wait for the grouse to fly straight at him. There is of course a strict, unspoken element of 'sport' in all this. In other words, you don't simply walk around the moor and blast at any grouse you come across. It all has to be done properly. As with any country sport, acceptance of these rules and regulations is crucial. So for a shoot to be done 'properly' you need beaters who walk up towards the shots, ensconced in their butts, flushing out the grouse, who then fly off to their doom.

Ben, being an entrepreneurial sort of bloke, has set up a business to sell the grouse from his shoot to whoever wants them (www.blackface.co.uk). These days, chefs in London are gagging for them. Regional produce is what the serious restaurateur is offering, and what many seriously want. The grouse has long been a spectacularly idiosyncratic British game bird, hardly known elsewhere, with a very particular and distinct taste.

Roast grouse

I am indebted to Martin Lam of Ransome's Dock for the minutiae of this recipe. It's one of the best places to eat roast grouse in London.

First, find your grouse, which will probably mean finding a good, reputable game dealer. Ask for a young bird, and one that hasn't been hung for more than a few days. Rancid rot is what you'll get otherwise. Allow one bird per person, and if you can, ask for it to be trussed, and for the wishbone to be removed. It makes it easier to remove the meat from the carcass when it is cooked.

The principal rule of cooking grouse is that the legs take longer to cook than the breast, so when they are done the whole bird will be ready. They are best eaten on the rare side. Also, remember to start with a bird that is at room temperature. Don't cook it straight from the fridge.

Make sure the cavity is clean and dry.

Massage some olive oil into the legs and rub some fat onto the breasts.

Season with salt and pepper.

Gently sear the thighs, legs and backbone in olive oil on top of the stove until brown. Don't cook the breast, which takes less time to cook.

Wrap some good-quality fatty bacon, or better still some pancetta, over the breast. The grouse has little fat so this helps keep the meat moist.

Place breast side up in a roasting dish over a slice of unbuttered toast (made from good bread, naturally) and into a moderately hot oven (gas mark 6, 200°C).

Cook for 25 minutes, then remove from oven and allow to rest for at least 5 minutes. To check if the grouse is cooked, try to pull the leg away from the body. It should come away easily. If it doesn't, put the bird back in the oven for another 5 minutes or so.

Serve on the toast, garnished with watercress. Classically, roast grouse is served with gravy, game chips and bread sauce. It also goes well with a buttery mash and red cabbage. You may find it easier to use a good pre-prepared home-made gravy since grouse don't give out too much juice of their own.

I wondered whether any of these professional chefs ever expressed the urban myth that the Glorious Twelfth is all waste and nonsense.

'Not at all,' Ben replied. 'Quite the opposite in fact. I find that they are all becoming far more interested in game, and in knowing where the food comes from. Grouse isn't all we sell, you know.' He pointed to the inevitable sheep. 'I'm selling quite a lot of them too. The only problem is finding the right name for them. They're black-faced sheep, so I sell them as heather-bred black-face lamb. I'd like to call them heather-fed, but that's not strictly true. Still, the chefs love them.'

These sheep are right at the heart of a revival of one of the most evocative of British dishes, mutton. Technically, this is meat from a lamb over one year old, but the best mutton comes from a wether lamb – a castrated male, that is. Each year, a few wethers are left on the hill and culled at two years to give a fabulously meaty, truly tasty piece of meat that calls for a different form of cooking to lamb. Long, slow, gentle stewing is what serves any mutton best, as any Orkney native you'd care to ask can tell you. The vagaries of culinary fashion have turned full circle. A few years back mutton was rarely sold, and rarely eaten. But look at any Victorian cookbook, Mrs Beeton or Eliza Acton for example, and the mutton section is long and varied.

The great Scots poet Robbie Burns wrote some of his finest songs and verses not far from the moor at Overfingland across which I had struggled, in a farmhouse in Ellisland on the banks of the River Nith. And that brought to mind Scotland's inevitable edible icon, the haggis, which has crossed the culinary border magnificently. Burns hasn't, and I'm sure he would be happy with that. But let's look at haggis first.

It started life as a way of preserving food, by using the precious sheep offal which if left untreated would have rotted in the time it took to tighten a sporran. If the essence of haggis is mutton and sheep fat, the bulk is provided by Scotland's auld favourite cereal, oats. Oats grow well in the shorter days up here in the north, and thrive where temperamental wheat and barley might not, so it has long been a fundamental part of the Scottish diet, still eaten in porridge, and baked into unleavened oatcakes. Its combination with chopped offal and mutton fat gave it an even wider role, and all this was cooked in the natural casing of a sheep's stomach. Or should be at least. As with black pudding, there are some who now use, shock horror, plastic.

Helping to preserve its pre-eminent role as Scotland's culinary icon is the Burns Night Supper. As 25 January approaches, dedicated groups around the country get into Burns mode and dream of steaming haggis and peaty fires. The tradition goes back a long way: the haggis is piped, fêted and washed down with copious drams of whisky. The very first Burns Supper was actually held in Greenock on 21 July 1801, the next in Dumfries in 1817, both on the wrong day. The idea is supposed to be to celebrate the birth of the great man, but for some bizarre reason the locals thought the date was 11 January. Wrong. Robbie Burns was definitely born on 25 January 1759 in Alloway, Ayrshire, the eldest son of William Burness and Agnes Broun. That's a fact. Anyway, despite these early errors, 25 January has since, correctly, been the night for auld acquaintance and sheep's stomach.

I stopped off at the farmhouse on the banks of the River Nith that captured the romantic heart of this prolific Scottish poet. It's easy to see what drew him here. Yes, there is a heritage sign, but then there's the Nith, peaty brown and full of fat trout, which slips and tinkles over the rocks so deliciously. Wild balsam flowers festoon the banks. Dragonflies dart about. The fast train to the south runs late in the distance, but all is serene in this loveliest of rural idylls.

Yes, it's all utterly enchanting – which was the problem with the place. Burns fell hook, line and sinker for Ellisland, but its soil was stony and poor, and it proved difficult to work. It had come to him by strange good fortune. In December 1786 Burns was in Edinburgh trying to arrange the publication of a second edition of his poems when he was introduced to a successful banker, entrepreneur and true polymath, Sir Patrick Miller. He was impressed by Burns' work, met him, and drank with him over a period of a few weeks in Edinburgh. Then he offered him the lease on some land by the Nith.

Now Miller had a passion for machines. He supported the construction of Scotland's first iron paddle steamer and introduced threshing machines and drills on to his land. His energy brought him to the attention of the King of Sweden, who was so pleased with his work that he presented Miller with a fine diamond-encrusted snuff box. Inside it lay the seeds of a plant that was as yet unknown elsewhere. The Swedes called it *rutabaga*, which roughly translated means 'red bag'. It was hardy, a sound, prolific cropper that wasn't too particular about soil fertility. The seeds were sown in Ellisland and the plant thrived. Its use quickly spread.

The English began to call the roots swedes, for obvious reasons, but in Scotland they were known as neeps, a shortened version of 'turn-neeps', to which vegetable they are closely related. Now, of course, it would almost be unthinkable to eat a haggis, especially on Burns Night, without bashed neeps, mashed with butter and just a pinch of nutmeg.

Haggis is a rarity, an obscure dish that has actually survived, nay thrived, in the world of culinary homogenization. But one has to wonder what on earth would have happened to this oat-stuffed sheep's stomach, Scotland's national dish, had the great poet never been born.

ORKNEY

Oatcakes, Clapshot and Bannocks

MEET THE ORCADIANS. THEY MOSTLY LIVE ON THE LARGEST ISLAND, which is simply called Mainland, and most of them in the capital Kirkwall, a bleak town, nothing like as endearing as it sounds. The most direct route to Orkney is to take the ferry from Scrabster on the Scottish mainland, a scintillating way to ride the oceans, and cruise past the massive brick-red stack they call the Old Man of Hoy. You begin to sense the mad rush of ornithology. There are birds everywhere. It is so busy it reminded me of a 1960s science-fiction picture of human cities with layers of monorails, everything just avoiding a catastrophic collision. I watched them, and tried to understand their birdbrains. Not once did I see a gull drop into the water and pick at a fish. They skimmed the water and followed us. Some birds, speaking a different language no doubt, slashed across the paths of the others. I assumed they were going somewhere meaningful. Gulls and guillemots. Delicate and spotlessly clean. How nice to see gulls back at sea again after their long sojourn in the rubbish dumps of the land.

If you take the ferry to Stromness, stay there instead of going on to Kirkwall. With its slate-grey high street and peat-scented night, it's a small town that lives with the ferry and feeds off the comings and goings. The seafront has endless quays that were once filled with the flapping of herring boats, and greasy, stinking fish gutters who followed them far down the eastern coast of Britain, as far as the fish would go. The herring have now gone. And the gutters with them. It's a strange thing how much of the country once moved with this mundane silver fish, and how much of a scar its departure has left on the land.

Of all the trips I had planned, this one had elicited the most calls and e-mails, all welcoming and encouraging. Come along, they said. There's so much to see up here. And it's true. Organic salmon was pioneered on Orkney. Cattle fatten magnificently on the grass. You can eat spoots (razor clams), dragged from the sandy beaches, and fine fat mussels. There are scallops, crab and lobster galore. Its food is thick, and elemental – soups, bannocks, and oats. Indeed, the oatcake is a distinctly Orcadian speciality, and they are taking over the world (it could be worse). Here are a few useful tips for those rootsy folk who have fields of waving oats outside the door.

Oatcakes

You will need the following implements:

- a spurtle, a.k.a. a porridge stick
- a bannock stick, a type of notched rolling pin
- a spathe, a heart-shaped iron mini pizza peel
- a banna-rack, or toaster

Put into a bowl about 4oz oatmeal, a pinch of baking soda, and salt. Melt 1 tsp of fat (goose fat is said to be the best, but it sounds a bit Gascon to me). Add the fat, and enough hot spring water to make a stiff dough. Turn out onto a floured board (a floured board for dough, oil for batter), form into a smooth ball, and slowly flatten with knuckles. Run with dry meal to prevent sticking. Bake whole as bannocks or in quarters as farls. Use a toasting stone if possible. Wink at your picture of Robert Bruce. Keep buried in the girnel, or meal chest.

Farming is intensive in Orkney, though less so than it could be to be sure. I had promised myself years ago that one day I would come to these islands where the grass was said to be as green as Ireland's, and the beef as fine. But it was neither cow nor pig that brought me here, but a sheep.

Before I set off in search of a good sizzling joint of roast mutton, I spent a while on Mainland, and became immersed in tales of the island's long-distant past, of Vikings, Picts, and Norse invaders. There are some extraordinary sights to be seen; Skara Brae and Maes Howe are but two.

One angry night in 1850, pounded by the waves and the wind from across the bay, stone roofs began to appear in the turf. The laird, William Watt, was informed, and he moved in, keen to remove anything of value from the site. He took the artefacts back up to Skaill House, but it wasn't until 1927 that a systematic study of what was known as Skara Brae began.

Five thousand years ago, the Orcadians were into stone houses in a big way. There were no endless dark forests full of wolves and evil spirits. The only wood available was drift-wood, flotsam from faraway neolithic America, carried over the ocean by the Gulf Stream. The climate was warmer then. Maybe life was even easy. Shellfish were readily available on the shore. Limpets, scallops and cockleshells abound in the middens that protected the ancient stone houses from the elements. Skara Brae seems to have been a place with little fear: there are no high towers, no sense of danger. The houses are intricately built, and closely connected. Fear was to come, though, and may well have been Skara Brae's downfall, for across the water the Norsemen were beginning to outgrow their land. Like hermit crabs, they sought new shells.

There is a startling uniformity to the houses on this neolithic sink estate. The raw material was to hand and easy to work. The local stone, Caithness flagstone, splits neatly into brick-thick slices. No axes are needed, just a keen eye for building. Each circular house, tightly fitting to the next, has a low-pitched door (you must stoop to enter) and a quern stone, which of course suggests grain and cultivation, fields and agriculture. It was wheat that they mostly grew then, the climate being that much warmer, which allowed it to ripen. This and what is called four-rowed or bere barley have been found among the ruins. And each house had its very own stone dresser, a central hearth, with a gently corbelled roof above, a fire below and even a stone water tank to keep shellfish fresh and alive. It all seemed positively inviting; neolithic life might really just have been sweet and arcadian in Orcady. Neuk beds, stiffly slab-lined, would have been softened by sheepskin and comfortable dried heather. Whalebones were to be found inside, and on the outside, layers of crushed detritus, middens of limpet shells and bones that suggest a comfortable life. Limpets are interesting. Seldom eaten, and often despised as food for the poorest of sea dwellers, they are excellent bait, and in each house these rubbery creatures were soaked in a clay-lined tank to soften them up for the mouths of the hungry cod and saithe that swam close by. Ancient Orcadians, like other neolithic Brits, also made grooved pottery, farmed cattle and sheep, and hunted the odd boar or deer (not indigenous creatures to Orkney) that wandered nearby. They rejoiced in the dead whales that were stranded on the beach. *Ebb maet* it is called in dialect – food from the shore. On the day I visited, I caught a peculiar scent in the air, more than the tang of tangle and the iodine blown from the sea, more than the sand and springy turf scent.

'Mmm. It smells of fresh flour, bran, or something like that. Is there a mill around here?' I asked, ever curious, in the bleak, windy Bay of Skaill.

'Ah, that must be the dead whale,' I was told.

Utterly untouched, of course. No-one would dream of eating dead whale now.

Now, it might have surprised you that limpets are interesting, but one fish with a multiple identity, the much-reviled saithe, coley or coalfish, is riveting. The Orcadians, like many Scandinavians, have a finely developed understanding of saithe which is so often dismissed by piscophiles on mainland Britain as being insipid and dull. But they are easy to catch, and each spring swim in immense shoals towards the shore. Indeed they were once so numerous that farmers would pull up nets bursting with saithe, and fill their carts with the stranded fish to fertilize their fields. Young saithe even had their very own name sillocks. A Norse reflection here, from the word for a finger length young herring – *sil*. An older fish, one or two years old, is called a ceuthe, or cuithe, from the old Norse *koö*, meaning a young fish. The words are still used to this day on Orkney.

Fishing for ceuthes (pronounced, by the way, with a French lilt as 'cooths') is a very evocative thing for Orcadians. It smacks of childhood summers, and memories. But their fishing was essential, for dried and salted cuithes provided protein in the winter, and were eaten, indeed still are, with clapshot – mashed potatoes and neeps, or swede. Orcadians also still like to eat blawn fish, fresh caught from their peedie (little) boats and hung to air overnight, or longer, which adds a tang to the taste; they are fine simply heated in boiled water and served with a bere bannock and butter. The eaves of the houses would once have been thick with fish drying in the wind, but the gulls and changing tastes have put paid to all that.

One of the few poets to write in dialect was a lady from Harray called C. M. Costie. She wrote this poem, 'At De Ceuthes', about two boys who go ceuthe fishing with their granddad:

I teuk me time, an' hid a smok'
Me pipe, sheu wisno new.
De peur t'ings baith wis bockan [being sick]
An Chon began to speu,
While Willie lay doon I' de bot
An' pleaded wae a sigh,
'Oh Grandad, if we can't get home,
Please will you let me die?'

Wae never teuk a ceuthe ava'
I turned de bot for heem,
Du niver saa sic' trachled t'ings
As baith o' dem dec streen.
Bit sometimes, min, hid pays a' right
Tae keep a silent tong,
For I got t'ree onse a twist, min,
For cheust niver lettan on!

from *The Collected Orkney Dialect Poems of C. M. Costie* (The Kirkwall Press, 1974)

Clapshot has to be the most Orcadian food of all. It makes the local population misty-eyed and even more reflective than usual. On the trail of Orcadian purity, I contacted one of the island's foremost clapshot devotees, Alan Bichan, half teacher half cook, and the author of the best book on Orkney cooking you'll find.

We arranged to meet for dinner.

'Is there anything you'd really like to eat while you're here?' he asked me over the phone.

'Well, how about clapshot and mince?' I replied.

Huge, extended guffaws.

'Well, that's easy enough, aye.'

So off I went for a *soirée de clapshot* in Kirkwall. And like all things to do with food, it's not *just* a mash of neeps and spuds. It's an earthy, poetic dish, quintessentially Orcadian. But let's look at etymology before gastronomy. The neeps first of all must be the root *Brassica napus* sp. *rapifera*, which, as I've already mentioned, you might know as the swede (as southerners do, or 'Sooth mothers' as we are called in Orkney), the neep, the turnip or even the rutabaga, depending on your own roots. Happy in cold climes, this thick, rotund root has a yellow to orange flesh up here, and is dry and eminently mashable, with its own very particular slightly cabbagey taste. The turnip that is known as such in the south would be called a white turnip in the north, but it is not as greatly loved as the swede. So how do we get to 'clapshot' from here? Well, nobody seems to be too sure. It might, I was told, come from an old Orkney word *klepp*, for a dollop of mash.

Whatever the truth, to make good clapshot you must obey the strict laws of clap. This is what Alan Bichan told me:

- Use a dry, floury potato.
- The best neeps are found after the first frosts.
- Frosted neeps should be peeled thinly.
- Choose a neep that is hard to the touch.
- When boiling, cut the spuds thickly and the neeps thinly so they are cooked at the same time, and so the clapshot isn't, God forbid, lumpy.
- Dry and drain the vegetables 'meticulously'.
- Add salt, butter and ground white pepper just before serving. The consistency should be smooth, and never lumpy, and the colour even.
- Serve with mince, or ceuthes.

Clapshot

450g swede
800g potatoes, peeled weight (floury type such as
Golden Wonder, Sharpes Express)
1 chopped onion
salt, pepper
butter

Cut the swede into small cubes so they can cook thoroughly while the spuds are boiling. Place all three vegetables in a pot and boil until tender. Strain, and dry on hob. Add salt, butter, pepper. Mash, and serve with mince, or haggis.

from *The Scots Kitchen* by F. Marian McNeill (Blackie, 1929)

Voilà. Here endeth the clapshot lesson.

The next day in Kirkwall was the monthly farmers' market, a very modest affair with a couple of English families selling meat, a fish stall with its own ceuthes and a lady from the WI with packets of fudge and woolly hats. None was doing a roaring trade, but the WI lady in her tinted specs was hiding a bere bannock (just the thing, remember, with blawn fish) by her cheesecake, a peedie sponge cake with absolutely no cheese in it at all.

'Ah, is that a bere bannock?' said I.

'Aye,' said she.

'And how do you make it?' said I.

'Well, I get the bere meal, but I don't think they make it here any more. I get it sent up from Caithness. You need the meal. I make it with about three-quarters bere, and the rest white flour.'

'Do you ever use buttermilk, or anything like that?'

'No, not I, but some folks do, mind. I just add a little

bicarbonate of soda, and some cream of tartar, and make dough, but you shouldnae work it at all. Just make it slightly sticky, and flour the girdle, and cook it for about three minutes each side. That's all.'

Easy.

'Do you eat it for tea?'

'Aye, for tea, with shellfish. Some folks even eat it with meat!' Said a little disapprovingly.

'Is there anywhere I can get some meal in town?'

'Aye, try the frozen food centre down the high street.'

I did. They did. They even had some fruit – a rare treat up here.

In fact, here and there you can still see a little bere being harvested, an ancient six-row variety of barley, *Hordeum sativum*. Hardy and quick-growing, bere can ripen within ninety days. It was often the last crop to be sown and sometimes the most productive of all. It was usually planted next to the homestead and the main source of manure, for it also made up a vital chunk of the rent under the crofting system. If you come to Orkney you will come across these bere bannocks, oversized scones that may seem a little heavy but are much loved by Orcadians. As the WI lady pointed out, they are simple to make and there is no need to knead. They do call for nimble fingers though. On my return, I set-to making bannocks with the enthusiasm of a zealot. The first lot were leaden. The second less so, but the third sublime, these having been cooked on a thick, blackened old iron frying pan, the nearest thing to a girdle in my house.

The complicated bureaucratic way we have with agriculture hasn't been kind to low-yielding crops such as bere, and there is now but one crofter who grows it, on the most northerly of all the Orkney islands, North Ronaldsay. So, now even bere meal is mostly brought in, along with just about everything else, on the weekly freight plane from Mainland. Don't get the idea that self-sufficiency rules up here.

Bere bannocks

50g bere meal
50g self-raising flour
1 level tsp baking soda
1 level tsp cream of tartar
pinch of salt
1 tsp cooking oil
approx. 60ml water

Sieve the meal and flour dry. Stir in oil and enough water to form a dough which leaves the bowl clean. On a floured surface, shape into 15cm rounds. Dust a girdle or thick iron pan with flour and bake for a few minutes on each side until risen.

from *An Orkney Feast* by Alan Bichan (Orcadian, 2000)

Orkney seemed cerebral, and calm despite the wild winds. The islands are almost treeless, and some are so low that incomers fear being stormwashed, that they will be drowned in a blow. And blow it does, frequently and fiercely. Some islands sit like marooned whales in the spume. On Hoy, the huge, severe cliffs take the breath away. Orkney is brimming with an ancient beauty.

I like the idea that we have within us something that relates to place, which may become hidden at times, lost, or grossly intermingled with the random effect of time and events. Yet Orcadians seem unsure of who they are. Some like the idea of being Pictish – the easy option, really, for we know so little about them. Yet in the ruddy Norman cathedral of St Magnus in Kirkwall, the seventeenth-century slabs that line the walls are quite Pictish in tone, doomy reminders of death and mortality, with skulls and devils carved into the soft rock.

Still, this is nothing compared to the astonishing tomb at Maes Howe discovered eleven years after Skara Brae. Built not far away at Birsay, on Mainland, the biggest island of Orkney, Maes Howe is a building made of massive slabs of stone, some weighing a mighty thirty tons and more. It was built with such skill and precision that it still seems almost impossibly clever. Maes Howe had fallen into disuse sometime before the Vikings came along and wrecked and pillaged this ancient building. Their graffiti remains etched into the stones, in weird runic *futhark*. And straight and to the point they are too. One inscription says 'Crusaders broke into [Maes Howe] – Hlif the Earl's cook (housekeeper) carved the runes'. Another made me smile: 'Ingebjorg the Fair widow – many a fair woman has had to lower herself to come in here whatever their airs and graces'. Like Skara Brae, Maes Howe dates from the neolithic period, but its very size implies that things had changed in the few hundred years that separated the construction of the two. It is thought to have taken well over a hundred thousand man-hours to build, to heave the giant slabs from across the island. Something of those people remains with the Orcadians.

Alongside the history, on board the ferry that brought me to the islands there was a mighty whiff of culture. Orkney has its poets, its soul, and it is proud of it. George Mackay Brown, from Stromness, wrote this on the opening of the town's first tavern in 1596:

From the kitchen, a fragrance and crispness of bread.
Beyond, clean bolsters and blankets spread.
A house of keeping it was for far-come folk,
With turf and driftwood to feed the welcoming flame,
Four days of silence. Nobody came.

from *George Mackay Brown: Selected Poems* (John Murray, 1990)

Another fine Orcadian poet, Edwin Muir, spent his early years on one of the most minuscule of the Orkney islands, Wyre. He eventually left, as many did, to seek a living elsewhere. But he was forever marked by this island childhood. Muirs still abound. As do Rendells. Robert Rendell was another Orkney poet. I stayed with his cousins.

Poets, wild landscapes, neolithic ruins, bannocks and clapshot. Words that make you smile, and an accent that is so soft, eloquent and poetic, it seemed that music had entered their very souls.

11

NORTH RONALDSAY

Mutton and Sooan

YES, I HAD PROMISED MYSELF YEARS AGO THAT ONE DAY I WOULD come to Orkney for its mutton. I pride myself in having a little of the gastronomic pioneer in me, and back in the early 1990s I had arranged a festival of British food in one of Sir Terence Conran's restaurants. The Chop House, it was called, a nice, evocative, well-established place that had, it seemed, the ideal location, slap bang on the River Thames in London. This was well before the upsurge in interest in all things regional, back in the dark days when French produce still tended to rule the culinary roost. Still, the Chop House was supposed to be British, earthy and carnivorous, redolent as its name was of the happy meat-eating joints that thrived in the seventeenth and eighteenth centuries, in the days when we Brits really were keen on our roast beef, our chops and steaks. There was even sawdust on the floor, and booths and wooden tables. The restaurant did well, and I suggested to the then plain T. Conran Esq. that it would be a good thing to bring to a wider public some of the disappearing foods that abound in the country.

Food writers and journalists, the great and the good were invited, and they came in their droves. At the restaurant entrance we wittily placed an enormous fat boar that snuffled and oinked its way throughout the meal, and greeted the guests with a knowing wink. It was one of the last remaining Essex boars, a breed that, then as now, was in danger of disappearing completely. Piles of apples, of varieties few had ever seen let alone tasted, decorated the reception. Britain's orchards were then, just as now, being grubbed up. I had also found some delectable native oysters, and sourced the finest cheese I could find, but the star of the whole thing was to be the weird and little-known seaweed-eating sheep from North Ronaldsay. Oh, what a marvellous pioneering thing I thought we were all doing.

However, it didn't quite work out as it should have done. The chef was stressed, and sank into a depression as things went from bad to worse. Serving a large amount of identical food at the same time to a discerning group of guests calls for special skills, and unfortunately he simply didn't have them. At the time I can honestly say I was completely oblivious to all this. I was actually thrilled to have got the produce there at all, as well as the boar and the guests. I made my little speech, told everyone what they were going to eat, and circulated. And circulated and circulated, until someone kindly pointed out that they had come to eat, not to see me circulate. Eventually the oysters arrived, and I breathed a little more easily. They were truly succulent, squirming still in their shells. A bit more circulating, still a bit more, and then the lamb began to appear.

Now, let me tell you a little about this 'lamb'. It was technically mutton – the meat from any sheep lucky enough to be over a year old, by which time it has changed its taste and texture and become far more robust – and had not, I was to learn later, really come from North Ronaldsay at all, but from an even smaller Orkney island, Linga Holm, which was being used by the Rare Breeds Survival Trust, a band of dedicated people whose main concern was to keep breeds from extinction. They were not, however, experts in getting the best to our tables. It turned out that they hadn't sorted out the uncastrated sheep from the castrated, or the males from the females, so some of our invited dignitaries were tucking into rancid ram meat, which is truly horrible. Moreover, mutton is only now beginning, just, to emerge from the culinary desert and to reassert itself; it was then a dirty word that smacked of gristle, fat, stews and poverty. Its grim reputation allowed mutton virtually to disappear. (The sheep haven't, though. They have simply been sold to more welcoming markets, both within and without the UK. Many ethnic communities have no fear of broken-teeth sheep, as they are called.)

Some of our diners were clearly appreciating the texture and gamey taste, others were struggling. The mighty Sir Terence himself was far from happy as his knife bounced off the meat. This was mutton cooked as lamb, and some of it tasted absolutely awful. If this was the best of British produce, we had a problem. But where would we be without these valiant pioneering attempts? It was the beginning of a forced journey of discovery and an early, perfectly avoidable blunder. The lesson for any food supplier is clear: do your homework and trust the experts.

The rest of the food was good, but it was a wonder I survived the day. Perhaps I did so because my heart was in the right place, for there was a serious point to be made. Just as many of us were becoming aware that there was still a struggling but vibrant subculture of regional food production in Britain, it was becoming increasingly difficult for the producers to survive the rigours and financial realities of a world where food was treated with almost pathological fear by bureaucrats. Brussels was creating ridiculous and anomalous regulations. The classic example was to forbid the ripening of cheese on wooden surfaces because of the alleged danger from bacteria; plastic must be used. The termination of a tried and tested process caused uproar. The result was that the plastic didn't allow the cheese to ripen in the presence of ancient colonies of helpful bacteria that developed the cheese's particular characteristics.

Go into any supermarket nowadays and you will find bacteria-killing chopping boards and bacteria wipes. The message is clear: bacteria are lethal! Now, to call this an over-simplification is a slight understatement. Yes, bacteria can kill, especially when poor hygiene causes cross-contamination. But don't bacteria also help us digest our food? To make yoghurt, bread, sauerkraut even, as well as cheese? The die, however, is cast. The average consumer assumes that bacteria are simply all bad, and dangerous to know; the consequences are even more mass-produced, tasteless food, and severe hardship for the food producers as they struggle to invest in white plastic surfaces, white coats and hats.

The story was, and is, full of irony. Take the North Ronaldsay sheep. They were being reared to preserve the gene bank, and were never really meant to be eaten at all, other than by the islanders themselves. But if they were to survive as a breed they simply had to enter into the wider food chain somehow. The whole Chop House event was an experiment, and one that didn't actually go to plan from the outset because government policy dictated that the sheep couldn't be slaughtered on the island but had to be taken across by boat to Mainland and dispatched there. Which added to their stress levels and toughened the meat.

It has to be said that bureaucratic institutions were treading a fine line by developing the theme that only officials were wise enough to know what we should eat, and they would tell us how to produce it, or the consequences might prove too much for us to bear. The BSE saga in the 1990s outed the British government as a band of shysters who were congenitally 'economical with the truth'. The problem arose because it was government policy to intensify farming, to continually cut costs and to pursue what was and is called a 'cheap food' policy. Thus our cattle were fed on meal derived from poorly rendered animal carcasses, to provide cheap protein. We all began to realize that the government, far from being the wise and beneficent arbiters of food manufacturing, were actually part of the problem. We learned not to trust their weasel words. We began to want, indeed need, to know how the food we were eating was being produced, so farmers' markets, brought across from North America, rather than the tried-and-tested European street market that we seem to enjoy only on holiday, began to flourish in the UK – the crucial difference being that only food that is produced locally is allowed, whereas in a French street market a stall may well have cheese from all over the country. It's more often taste that rules there, rather than principles of production.

Anyway, ever since those stirring days I had nursed an ambition to visit North Ronaldsay to see the sheep for myself, and to taste proper mutton *in situ*. Before I left Mainland, I asked Alan Bichan whether he had ever been to this diminutive Orkney island.

'Aye,' he replied. 'We all went there on holiday a few years back. Wild it was. Absolutely wild, but so beautiful. I take it you'll be going to see the sheep?'

I ayed back, and told Alan, a little sheepishly, about the bit of history between me and this wild, woolly Orcadian ungulate.

An eight-seater airplane, a mere ten subsidized pounds for a return ticket from Kirkwall, took me and another Willy, an incomer all the way from Stromness, to wild and wacky North Ronaldsay, population approximately sixty, famous for its cerebral inhabitants and, of course, its seaweed-eating, free-thinking sheep. This was no-frills flying at its finest: the pilot loaded the plane, he flew it, and he even checked our tickets. For all I knew he took it home at night and washed it at the weekend. There wasn't a frill to be seen, but thrills there were by the thousand.

Fifteen minutes in and the teardrop shape of North Ronaldsay began to appear below us. The plane scudded over the brilliantly pristine beaches, and water so turquoise you might have been flying into Bora Bora, but for the lack of a single tree. At one end stood an immense lighthouse, and a vicious, swirling sea. The island was peppered with dilapidated crofts, their slate roofs tumbling inwards, and a few newer houses, lived in and active with smoke issuing from the chimneys. Every homestead seemed to have a pile of wrecked cars outside. Running all the way around the island was a long dry stone wall – the Dyke, they call it – neatly dividing shore from land, which almost without exception was as green and pleasant as you would expect in Orkney.

You cannot fail to notice the sheep, cavorting and munching in turn, leaping from rock to rock, some sheltering against the wind, pressed tightly to the blasted wall, with their thick, gentle ochre fleeces flapping in the wind and their perpendicular, stick-thin legs tucked neatly underneath. But all of them, every sheep jack of them, were well and truly on the *outside* of the wall, the sea side that is, which seemed as odd as a fish in a desert. These sheep lived among the seals and seabirds, contentedly ruminating with their mouths stuffed full not of grass but bunches of slimy brown seaweed. There was barely a sheep to be seen on the landward side. But then perhaps not so odd, for they are becoming the island's unique draw, and its sole contribution to world gastronomy.

The plane buffeted its path through the breeze and drew to a stop on the clinker runway. We had arrived at North

Ronaldsay International, one of the world's dinkiest airports, to be greeted by a shed and a tractor, and a gaggle of islanders waiting for the huge rush of incomers – both of us. Not far away, a flock of sheep were plotting their escape. For the North Ronaldsay may be a wild, nervy breed, but, unusually, it is said to show distinct signs of intelligence.

Willy set off into the breeze. Waiting for me was the island's only taxi driver, its only car hire specialist, its water board engineer and road godfather, Tommy Muir, who with his wife, Christine, runs a bed and breakfast that is as warm and welcoming as a cup of tea, and whose resourcefulness and love of the craic constantly amazed me. Christine Muir once wrote a monthly column for the *Scotsman* about island life; the collection made for a beautiful book full of the harsh rhythms of the island. But even though that was only twenty or so years ago, that time seems distant now, long gone. She would say she is still an incomer after more than forty years on the island, but the Muirs know North Ronaldsay's every rocky pore. Both are islanders through and through who long ago mastered the subtle art of multitasking.

Which is precisely what crofting seemed to me to be, or to have been, about. For although its demise is not yet complete, crofting is not in good health. It is a continual struggle for survival, where the dark forces of politics and rent hikes were once matters of life and death. I wondered about using the term 'crofting' at all. Words used insensitively can so easily offend, but on the island, farming was happily called crofting. No-one seemed uneasy about it at all. Indeed, I was told more than once that they were not farmers, but crofters. A few days later, back on Mainland, I was told exactly the opposite: 'We don't like using the word. We say farmers down here.'

Until the nineteenth century, the island was divided into a complex weave of mini plots that had to support the crofting family. Rent, often to be paid in kind, was due to a selection of lairds and landlords, characters who ranged from the despicable Stewarts, bastard royals who built the palace in Kirkwall (whose ruins still gloomily glance towards the Cathedral of St Magnus), to the nineteenth-century lairds the Traills, a family whose name hangs in the air somewhat and whose descendants still own the laird's house on the island. It is called Holland, a name shared by several laird's houses, which ironically comes from the Norwegian *hoyland*, for high land.

Life on North Ronaldsay was long a matter of subsistence crofting. People fished, and farmed the land that was divided up into these tiny plots, a legacy of the Norse *udal* system where each of the offspring inherited some of the land owned by their parents. Its shortcomings were obvious. It encouraged many of the offspring to leave the island and seek work elsewhere for it was simply unsustainable for anyone to work the plots the smaller they became. And there was a perpetual pressure to seek better yields from the land.

The plots are now long gone. Neatly fenced fields cover the island instead. As I was driven down to the Muirs' house at Garso, built mainly from shipwrecked wood by the ever-resourceful islanders, we passed not one single sheep, just fields. Their house was conveniently right in the middle of the island, so I offloaded my bag, was greeted and tea'd up, and then I set off into the breeze to meet a man who could tell me all about life on the island, and the story of these bizarre sheep.

John Cutt is tall, and distinguished. He has that lovely, steely, soft accent of the islands, a firm handshake, and a slightly stern look about him. He has spent most of his life here and knows a thing or two about the 'bussy broes' – the bushy-browed sheep. He also had bushy brows.

It seems that once, all the sheep on Orkney were of the same stock, related to ancient Norse beasts. Hardy, almost goatlike, the animals survived where others simply expired.

'There's no danger of them mixing with other breeds up here,' John told me. 'Conventional breeds wouldn't last five minutes.'

In the seventeenth century, some of the lairds began to profit greatly from the sudden arrival of wealth from a completely unexpected source – seaweed, with which North Ronaldsay is supremely blessed. Some of the islanders worked the land on the cottar system – on ca', as it was called – where work replaced rent, and they became well versed in the business of seaweed dragging. Originally the seaweed was laid on the fields as fertilizer, but when the lairds learned of this new and apparently highly profitable market they were quick to divert labour wherever possible. Many of them were pretty impecunious as well. Piles of the stuff were carried up from the shore and burned in a particularly low-tech way to make a solid mass of kelp, which was then sold on to be used in glassmaking. Much of it went to Newcastle when the city was deprived of its habitual supply of Spanish *barilla* by Napoleonic blockades. The kelp boom faltered soon after that, though it revived once again in the twentieth century when seaweed was found to be an excellent source of iodine. The quest for increased returns from the land continued.

Meanwhile, in the middle of the nineteenth century, agricultural revolution hit Orkney, and the lairds of the islands began to think of ways to increase the returns from their tenants and the land. Until then the crofting system was almost the sole means of farming. Since it was neither a particularly productive nor profitable way to farm the land, agricultural progress was generally welcomed. In 1832, the island's factor, who acted as the laird's representative, decided to join the bandwagon and 'square off' the land, dividing it into larger fields more suitable for rearing cattle. Beef was then far more profitable than crofting.

These were particularly difficult times. Not only had the

kelp industry collapsed, but so had linen, and the nascent business of making straw bonnets, all of which were vital parts of the crofter's life. Elsewhere in Orkney, things were made even worse by the demise of the Hudson's Bay Company, which had drawn men from all over the islands, particularly Stromness, often unwillingly pressganged and taken away while the authorities were bribed to turn a blind eye. When ferry links began to be established, the lairds' thoughts turned to increasing cattle production, but all this called for more secure boundaries and larger farms – hence their enthusiasm for squaring off the land.

Quite how this was done depended on the nature of the laird. On the Scottish mainland the clearances were often brutal. Thousands died, and were simply evicted by the notorious Duke of Sutherland, but in Orkney things were different and the crofter was not automatically dispossessed of the land his family had worked for generations. Rents, however, did increase, and progress was characteristically double-edged.

On North Ronaldsay, the laird decided to allow the sheep to remain, provided that they were confined to the shore by a stone wall. It had long been known that the sheep were quite capable of eating the seaweed, but they had generally been allowed to wander over the fields to supplement their diet with good old-fashioned grass. So the islanders agreed to construct the Dyke, and to control the flock of sheep accordingly. This they did by establishing the Sheep Court, a group of eleven islanders, sheep owners all, who accepted responsibility not only for the sheep but also for the Dyke – a pretty onerous duty at times. The laird was happy for he received a set rent per sheep. Thus the North Ronaldsay sheep began a new life on permanent beach holiday.

The Sheep Court still exists, as John Cutt confirmed. 'We keep records, and meet every now and again, but the most important time is the punding. Oh aye. It's a difficult time.

Impossible t'ings they are. You see, they're not at all like normal sheep. Not at all. You go for one and it runs one way, and all the others run in completely different directions. Nervy t'ings they are.'

'How on earth do you know which are your sheep?' I asked.

'Excuse me,' he said, and got up to leave the room.

I wondered what I had said. A while later he returned, with a slightly worn red exercise book in his hand.

'This is how we know.'

On each page was written a family name, and a drawing of a sheep's ear. Every one was different, notched here and cut there. This was the islanders' way of distinguishing their sheep, ancient lug marks that were still used, though, as John added, 'We've all got to use tags these days. It's a European thing, I t'ink.'

The islanders look upon punding with mixed feelings, but it is planned with military precision. Twice a year all the sheep owners get together to round up the sheep into the punds. In the spring it's so that the lambs can be born on grass; in the summer, it's to clip them. First, they take a look at the tide tables to see when the tide is at its highest, for then at least the sheep will be confined to a relatively tight area and should be easier to catch. I mused on this. Sheep that show remarkable cunning and distinctly unsheeplike behaviour are rare.

If you do come to North Ronaldsay, you may just begin to wonder why you don't see an awful lot of the meat for sale. The main reason is that there's only one shop. It's run by the same couple who run the pub. I asked John where you could buy it.

'The frozen food centre in Kirkwall usually has some. Or Orkney Meat. I'm not sure. Willy Muir, Tommy's brother, would know, I t'ink. Ask him. But we never used to eat it all the year through. It's at its best in the winter when the tangle is blown onto the shore in the gales.' The frozen food centre was to prove an excellent, indeed almost the only place to buy local produce in Kirkwall. No namby-pamby delicatessens up here.

And how best to cook it?

'Well, we always used to cook it slow, like. Overnight, so it just falls off the bone.'

As I was leaving, he showed me his three ultra-privileged grass-fed sheep that he kept in his back field. Then I set off into the late-afternoon sun. It was a glorious, calm day, full of curlew calls, and oystercatchers flitting by busily. I walked past the island's desolate, ruined mill, and noticed that it had begun to softly rain. A broad rainbow flowed into the sky at the far end of the island. I stopped at the next house, thought about calling Tommy to metamorphose into a taxi driver and pick me up, then noticed the sign on the door. It was the pub. How perfect.

I pushed open the door, a little nervous to be sure, a little uncertain about how strangers fared up here. I stepped up to the bar and my old mucker Willy was there, talking in a dialect so strong I thanked God that everyone tends to be bilingual and to talk so that we strangers can get accustomed to their singsong words. The place was busy. I met the island's sole baby, gurgling happily, and the island's entire school population, all four of them. Their mum, learning that I too was soon to be a dad once more, handed me the baby, saying, 'You'll have probably forgotten what it's like. Have some practice!' Lilly, young blood on the island, gave me a very senior look, but didn't burst into tears and sat happily on my knee.

I had forgotten how solid and muscular little babies' cheeks can be from sucking on breasts and bottles, and just how sweet and edible they are. Deciding cannibalism wasn't probably a wise move, I asked Lilly's mum, 'Do you know anyone who might have a bit of mutton to taste?'

'Well, I'll tell you how to cook it. What we do is to stew

it for hours in the slow oven. Overnight it'll be fine. Just add a little water, and let it slowly slowly cook.' So there was at least agreement there. Everyone I asked said the same thing.

The landlady chipped in. 'You can try some of mine if you like. I cooked some last night.'

I wondered what I would get, but of course I agreed. Minutes later, sandwiched between a couple of slices of white bread, I ate my only mutton on North Ronaldsay. It was fine eating, full of a peculiar gameyness, but how good it would have been to be able to eat a fresh mutton stew or pie, here, *en place*, on the island. But, sadly, it was not to be.

Small mutton pies

12oz lean mutton
1 shallot
1 tsp minced parsley
½ tsp thyme
2 or 3 mushrooms
salt and pepper
1–2 tbsp stock or water
2 tsp Worcester sauce

HOT-WATER CRUST
1lb flour
4oz fresh beef dripping
½ tsp salt
½ pint water

Remove the skin, bone and gristle from the mutton and chop small. Peel and chop the mushrooms if used, and the shallot. Mix these with the parsley, thyme, salt and pepper, and set aside.

To make the crust, sieve the flour into a bowl, and add the salt. Put the dripping and water into a saucepan and bring to the boil; then pour immediately into the flour. Mix at first with a spoon or a knife, but when cool enough use the hands and mix into one lump. Turn onto a floured board and knead gently until free from cracks.

Put aside a third of the pastry to keep warm, and divide the rest into six pieces. With these, line six small ring tins, or mould them into small cases around a tumbler. Fill the cases with the mutton mixture, and just moisten with the stock or water. Cut rounds from the remainder of the pastry, moisten the edges, and cover the pies, pressing the edges firmly together. Trim with a pair of scissors, make a hole in the centre of each pie, and brush with a little milk or beaten egg. Bake for 35 minutes in a moderate oven.

Remove the pies from the tins, fill them up with hot gravy or stock flavoured with Worcester sauce or ketchup, and serve piping hot.

from *Recipes from Scotland* (Albyn Press, 1946), a fascinating book by F. Marian McNeill

There seems, however, to be some hope that tastes are changing so that one day we may actually be able to buy mutton, or at least to taste it. The London Hilton once had an Austrian chef who was particularly keen to promote British food, and used it to good effect. Skibo Castle – 'You know, that place where Madonna went,' I was told – used it too. But try buying it on the island and you will struggle. To be honest, many of the islanders seem to have OD'd on the stuff, but it always fitted in well with the annual cycle of scarcity and plenty, being at its best in December when other fresh food was hard to come by and when the beaches were awash with the sheep's favourite food, the sweet and delectable red-fronded seaweed *Laminaria digitata*.

The sky was beginning to darken, the sun was setting. It was magic to hear the birdsong, and to pass by the beach with its flighty sheep and fat lumbering seals about. Wild rhubarb grew along the ditches; 'It's from the old vegetable gardens,' I was told. I arrived back at the Muirs' to a fine fug and a slice of smoked haddock, and began to talk about life on the islands.

It has to be difficult. You expect it to be so. The school kids have to go to secondary school in Kirkwall, where they stay in hostels. That is how it has always been. It provided for a lively debate. Some thought it cruel – women mostly. Men thought it toughened them up. But that is just how things are. There exists, however, an overwhelming sense of concern about what the future will bring. The average age of the islanders is now over fifty, and new blood often comes to the islands for the wrong reasons.

North Ronaldsay really is as wild a place as I have seen, where storms and hurricanes rip up houses and lift off their great slate roofs, tossing debris through the air. But I was surprised by just how vulnerable everyone felt. At times, the great booming sea covers much of the island with spray so that crops need to be extremely robust to survive. Bere we have met already; another venerable and little-sown cereal is the black oat, *Avena strigosa*, again brilliantly hardy in the face of the constant battering, and highly nutritious. But it too is dismally low-yielding. These two crops conflict with the modern agricultural ethic of maximizing yields and controlled production so are almost inevitably on the way out. But maybe, just maybe, they will survive and flourish one day, when we know how to properly value traditional crops and breeds. And it's not just the old cry for maintaining bio-diversity up here, it's a cultural thing too.

Somewhere along the line, I had read of a curious type of pancake the Orcadians once ate called sooan scones, and I knew there was some connection with black oats, but no-one quite knew what. It had all slipped out of the culinary consciousness. Plain forgotten.

'I know,' Christine said. 'Why don't you ring up Radio Orkney? They have a programme on tonight where people exchange things. Perhaps somebody out there knows about sooans.'

Great idea, I thought, and rang them from my magnificently five-blobbed mobile.

'I am in the Orkneys for a few days and am trying to find out about some of the old food ways up here,' I said.

'Well, we'll see if we can help,' I was told by somebody with a distinctly English accent, 'but don't for God's sake call them the Orkneys. It's Orkney!'

A cultural whoops was thus avoided on air, and they called back later to talk live about the book and my strange request. The programme was as local as you can get: 'There's a request for a large duck on Rousay. If anyone has a large duck, please let us know. And someone on Shapinsay has a Labrador puppy that needs a home . . .' And on it went, until my bit came on air.

They asked me what I was doing, and what brought me to Orkney. I gave the résumé, then added, 'I'm looking for a recipe or any information on what I think are called sooan scones, or if someone can tell me what on earth "sids" are. I'm getting nowhere.'

Into the airwaves went the request, and the Muirs and I talked into the night.

A little later I received a call from Radio Orkney. 'You'll get a call from a Johnny Johnson,' they told me. 'He owns the mill at Birsay. They know all about sooans. Good luck!'

This was all incredibly neat and encircled, for this was the very mill within a Viking's lunge of Maes Howe that I had tried to visit a day or so earlier. And I knew I had to pass by on the way back to Stromness.

I hadn't entirely finished my few days on North Ronaldsay,

and began to feel at ease with the birds, and the obligatory nodding and greeting. The next day I was due to meet Tommy's brother Willy, who proved to be the most energetic and positive of all the islanders I met. His persona is as mixed as elsewhere, but he has the special responsibility for keeping the lighthouse blazing, and for organizing the Sheep Court. The energy that came from his carefully crafted words was clear. In the brittle company of a young Scottish woman who clearly felt uneasy listening to clipped London English up in these parts, and whose face would pucker like a dog's arse when I sat next to her on the plane back to the mainland a few days later, we climbed right to the top of Willy Muir's fiefdom, the North Ronaldsay lighthouse. Some 176 steps up, and 42 metres high, the islanders are proud of this enormous 150-year-old building, kept immaculately clean by Willy Muir himself, and his giant can of Windolene.

Until a few years back, the source of light was astonishingly simple – just a single paraffin light, as ornery and ordinary as you could imagine. Focused by the powerful and endlessly rotating mirrors, it worked a treat. A quick glance at the *Shipwreck Register* tells of its success. 'I beg to inform you', it read, 'of the loss of SS *Something*, lost in a storm on the . . . no casualties . . . no fatalities.' Although few have perished here over the past hundred years, seamen feared the thick sea fog most of all.

There are times when this lighthouse must seem a vulnerable place. Curlews have been known to crash straight through the outer glass, and hundreds of seabirds pile up in a storm, flying straight into the building attracted by the fierce light, doomed to a senseless death. Willy once counted 1,500 dead birds on the narrow ledge outside. The view from the top, though, is truly breathtaking. Built by Stephenson's, the master lighthouse builders, it replaced an older lighthouse (still standing) that could offer only a static flame, which so confused the skippers that they often mistook the lighthouse for harbour lights, and altered course right onto the rocks. So it was extinguished and replaced – wisely, I suspect.

Below the lighthouse there lie the old buildings that after years of patient negotiation have finally been taken over by the North Ronaldsay Trust, leading light Willy Muir Esq., and here there is hope for the future. The EU helped finance a loom that smells of thick wool and linseed oil; it churns and chugs in this most unlikely of settings, weaving socks and hats from soft-toned wool. There is hope also that the old lighthouse keeper's office will become a little museum, and the rooms a self-catering cottage with a thunderous view. At your front door will wander some of the two thousand or so sheep that live on the island.

Back with Willy's brother Tommy that night, I ate clapshot and more smoked haddock, followed by a fine rhubarb crumble, then went out into the breeze to smoke an illicit fag and listen to the sea rumble and the sheep sleep.

The next day I got my call from the mill. I left the island, and flew back to the airport at Kirkwall on the same old plane.

'Did you get to taste the mutton?' the pilot asked me.

'Well, sort of,' I replied, and set off to unravel the mystery of the sooan scones.

Radio Orkney had opened the mill's doors for me, and there waiting for me was Alan Bichan, who had kindly agreed to take me on a final extended ramble around Mainland, and then on to the mill to meet the third-generation miller Rae Phillips, who had been primed by Mr Johnson, the mill owner.

'You've come for the sooans?' Rae asked.

'Aye, I have.' Great. I was getting into this aye-ing thing. Not a lot of ochs, but *mucho* ayes.

'Well, I'll show you some black oats first.' And with that he dipped his calloused miller's hands into a sack full of the scrawniest-looking seed imaginable. Loose grains, dark and, yes, distinctly oaty, dangled from the stem.

Black oats, as we have seen, are, despite their rather feeble yield, highly nutritious and well suited to being continually battered by wind and rain. While the grain is used for fodder, or in the culinary repertoire of everyday crofting folk, it is the husk, the 'sids' as they are called, that are used to make sooans. And the chaff, which may not sound particularly enticing. So, while the grain was threshed at the mill, the husks were set aside, and the canny crofter would then place them in a narrow-ended wooden barrel called a sooan-bowie, cover them in warm water – good water, naturally – and leave them to ferment. For days, for weeks, until they gave off a mildly sour yeasty scent, the point at which the mixture was filtered through a sieve and the indigestible bits marooned. The liquid is the sooan, which was simply bottled up and stored in the cold, to be used as and when the whim arose.

As we left the mill, overawed by the misty bottles of sooan we had been given, we bumped into an old couple who were related to Alan's wife. People always seemed to know who each other was, signposted as cousins and second cousins. On North Ronaldsay you simply accept it as inevitable – you feel that everyone knows the colour of your pants and what you ate for breakfast – but on Mainland it struck me more. We fell into conversation, as one does, about sooan scones.

'Aye aye. We don't see them much any more. I remember eating sooan scones for tea, with jam. Quite lovely they were. Aye.'

A sooan scone has a distinct tang, and far from looking like a scone at all is more like a sourdough crêpe. I felt honoured to drag my sample back across the island, and all the way home to Oxford, and I spent a whole joyous afternoon trying the various recipes Rae had given us. There was one from Elsie Johnston of Dounby, another from Barry Norquoy of Birsay, and yet another from Birsay, by one Mrs Taylor. But the best, and the one I offer to you intrepid gastronauts, is this version from Alan Bichan. But first you need to get your sooans.

Sooan scones

Makes about two dozen

75g plain white floor, sifted
1 level tsp baking soda
225ml milk
25g caster sugar
pinch salt
200ml sooan

Put the flour and soda into a bowl and gradually whisk in the milk until smooth. Add the sugar, salt and sooan, and continue to whisk until uniform. Grease a medium-hot griddle or frying pan, and spread one tablespoon of the batter at a time to form thin pancakes. As soon as the bubbles burst, turn the pancake and cook briefly on the second side. Serve warm with butter, a dollop of home-made jam, and whipped cream.

LEICESTER

Chicken Tikka Massala

EVERY NATION HAS ITS LITTLE DREAM DISH, THE ONE HOMELY thing that gets the blood coursing through the veins and makes us misty-eyed and hungry at the very mention of its name. The British have, it seems, fallen hook, line and even sinker for chicken tikka massala, but any visitor to the subcontinent will be hard pressed to find it eaten there at all. And if this really is our national dish, why doesn't anyone know how to cook it? The story goes that it was first served to a stroppy Glaswegian who demanded gravy with his tandoori chicken. The chef set to and created a highly coloured sauce to silence the man, and succeeded magnificently. But, imagine a Frenchman being ignorant about his coq au vin. It seems we have achieved something highly idiosyncratic and fallen in love with a culinary sham — not entirely surprising for a country with such a long-standing tradition of culinary acculturation.

And a possibly toxic culinary sham at that. Some restaurants have been serving their chicken tikka massala laced with pharmacological levels of dyes. As well as eating dubious, intensively reared fowl, you may well be consuming alarming levels of tartrazine (E102) and sunset yellow (E110), and just a hint of delicious Ponceau 4R (E124), a cocktail that might well aggravate asthmatics, cause cancer or lead to vomiting, hives and kidney tumours, among other complaints.

Chicken tikka massala

Serves 4

600g skinless organic chicken breast cut into inch-long bits, seasoned

FOR THE MARINADE
500ml plain natural yoghurt
juice of two lemons
2-inch section of ginger, grated and peeled
pinch of black salt
3 cloves garlic, peeled and crushed
2 tsp tomato ketchup
1 tsp tomato purée
2 tsp garam masala
1 tsp ground cumin
1 tsp coriander powder
1 tsp red chilli powder
½ tsp ground paprika
5 tbsp mustard oil
salt and pepper to taste

FOR THE SAUCE
2 onions, chopped
3 cloves garlic, peeled and chopped
1 tsp cayenne pepper

½ tsp red chilli powder
300ml chicken stock
5 tbsp corn oil

Marinade the chicken pieces for at least four hours.

Remove and set aside, retaining the marinade. Preheat grill, stoke up your tandoori oven or, best of all, use a charcoal barbeque to grill the chicken.

Fry the onions for the sauce in the corn oil for five minutes, add the spices, and cook until onions and spices combine to a glorious non-toxic reddish colour.

Add the stock, and cook briskly for fifteen minutes.

Begin to grill the chicken pieces, either on kebab sticks or as they are.

Finish sauce by slowly adding the marinade to the stock and onions and boiling gently, stirring occasionally. This must be well cooked.

When the chicken pieces are ready, pour the sauce over them and serve with basmati rice.

Wondering what we had done to one of the finest cooking styles in the world, I planned a day in Leicester to hone my subcontinental food awareness. I asked the *Leicester Mercury*, a thriving organ in a city that appeared happily to laud its cultural diversity, whether they could put me in touch with a culinary mentor to help me sort out this peculiar love we have for chicken tikka. They followed up the request with a short piece in the paper, on condition that I agreed to an interview.

I did the usual spiel about the book, the journey around Britain and all that, but when asked why Leicester, and why Belgrave Road, my thoughts went along these lines. Firstly, I wanted to know about this enigma that was chicken tikka, and why we have all decided it is our national dish. Then there was the odd cultural mix that seems to be the essence of Anglo-Indian food. Britain has always been a multicultural society, not necessarily a welcoming one, and not always prepared to admit that it is; but our industrial success would have been far from assured without the powerful engine of cheap labour, which often came from abroad. And here in Leicester, the predominantly Gujarati community of Belgrave Road had found its pace, made its peace and flourished, and seems to have kept true to its culinary traditions. That excites me, and pleases me, but it's also easy to miss out on the cultural nuances without proper guidance. I needed help with my dhal. A lot of replies came from doctors and consultants who seemed to be remarkably *au fait* with the rise and fall of the restaurants of Belgrave Road, and talked enthusiastically of their own particular favourites. Drug companies are apparently very generous hosts.

In one of those moments of pure serendipity, as I was driving into Leicester I switched on BBC Radio 4 and listened to a restaurateur from Manchester pointing out that the very concept of Indian food needed to be treated with great care. Although going out for an Indian is now about as British as you can get, many of the country's Indian restaurants are actually run by Bangladeshis and Pakistanis who have helped to create an Anglo-Indian hybrid, offering food that would not necessarily be recognized in India. The food we call Indian is in effect a mix of British and Moglai, Madrasi and Bengali cooking.

The curry, our beloved brown chilli mush, is another dish with no clear origin at all. It has been nicked, in other words, absorbed and bastardized. Its roots are thought to be in the Tamil word *kari*, a term that describes a particular piquant runny sauce. Or it may have come from a Hindi word for a cooking pot, the *karhai*. Whatever the truth, curry has been around a long time: the first known recipe appeared in Hannah Glasse's *The Art of Cookery* back in 1747.

Driving in on yet another of those awful wet grey mornings, I was struck by the fact that Leicester's urban planners seem to have developed a gruesome weakness for roundabouts. They are everywhere. Maybe they were invented here, dollop upon dollop of meaningless concrete, built to test you and your steering wheel's strength of character. Leicester is a sprawling Midlands English city with a past that dabbled in hosiery, shoe manufacture and mining. All that is gone now. These days it has a struggling football team, makes huge amounts of potato crisps, and is in the heart of pork pie territory. It's fair to say that at first glance it is a fairly unremarkable city.

In a way, what had really drawn me to Leicester was a story from the 1970s that began many miles away in Central Africa, where one of the continent's more loathsome dictators, Idi Amin, later to be known as Idi Amin Dada, turned Uganda into a traumatized, abused and impoverished country. This unpredictable slob of a man with a penchant for human flesh decided to expel the entire Ugandan Asian community, many of whom were second-generation émigrés from the north-western Indian province of Gujarat. His reasons were entirely spurious: Amin felt he could gain political kudos promoting his own brand of nationalism by expelling the entire Indian community. The economy went into free-fall, and of those who left, many found their way to Leicester, where relatives had previously settled, or work was thought to be available. This showed up Britain in its paradoxical ways once more. While on the one hand accepting many through the hallowed gates, on the other the usual dark tales of immigrants swamping the population began to appear in the press. The *Leicester Mercury* excelled itself by placing an advert in the Ugandan papers saying that the city was full and there were no jobs available, which some say had the exact opposite effect and encouraged many to head straight for the area.

When the brouhaha died down and the Ugandan Asians were left to their diligence, many of them prospered to become some of the country's richest citizens. And their arrival gave a new identity to one particular road in Leicester, a far from pretty street with identical red-brick terraced houses running off at right angles, a road you should eventually find if you choose your roundabout wisely.

Belgrave Road was once deep in hosiery land; massive red-brick warehouse buildings still stand behind the terraced rows. Rich fodder for architects, I can well imagine them being converted into loft apartments one day, designer creations, with baths in the middle of the sitting room. These days it's trying to reinvent itself as Leicester's Golden Mile, but before you pop on your boots and hurry on down in the expectation of donkeys on the beach, it is gold in the form of finely worked jewellery that is at the heart of this particular epithet.

We know very little about the food of, say, Kerala, Orissa or Rajasthan. But here in Belgrave Road you can at least find a regional Indian food that is mostly unencumbered by any of this British fusion stuff, the tikkas and the vindaloos. It is more Gujarati than Indian, but it's not quite that clear-cut.

I had arranged to meet a young working mother, Sima Patel, for a morning's cruise around this Leicester 'burb. Sima is a second-generation British Asian whose parents had left not Uganda but Tanzania in the 1970s, and who knew Belgrave Road with what seemed to be an almost passionate intimacy.

'I love this road,' she told me, 'I absolutely love it!' And I had no doubt, no doubt at all, that she meant it. 'I eat here, I work here, and I've been living here since I was five, so I really can tell you what it's like.'

We had spoken on the phone, and she had suggested that we should meet up at Bobby's, a long-established restaurant right on the Belgrave Road, very much one of the old school. And right opposite Bobby's was the Sharmilee. I knew this place. I had eaten there years back and distinctly remembered that not only was my son violently sick on the premises, but that downstairs was a glittering emporium of sweets and sweetmeats. We were to visit this later.

But I wanted to try to avoid the classic, well-established restaurants. I sought something new, to see where authentic Gujarati cooking was going here in Leicester. So off we went to Sakoni's, a smart and busy buffet by day and a buzzy restaurant by night, cheap, comfortable and airy, and run by Punjabis but with a distinct culinary slant towards the predominantly Gujarati clientele. Its food is almost entirely vegetarian – sensible really, since 80 per cent of Gujaratis are too. We sat and talked for hours about life, food, and on being Sima Patel. She began to introduce me to the niceties of the bowl for dhal, the sauce for the bhel, the dhosas, and the pao bhaji. No chicken tikka darkened their doors.

What was really refreshing about Sakoni's was that there was a bit of culinary fusing going on right before my very eyes, for some of the buffet dishes had a distinctly Cantonese look about them, all cooked with an Indian twist, made acceptable in a way that echoed the creation of the chicken tikka massala. 'There's a lot of this sort of food appearing now,' Sima told me as I prepared to entertain my taste buds with the tang of tamarind and sweet sour of the Chinese. And that wasn't the only place where this was happening. Down the road we checked out a pizzeria that had famously created a pizza called the Eastern Delight. 'I know the person who started it,' Sima said. Belgrave Road, deeply urban on the one hand, still manages to have a villagey feel to it. Everyone seemed to know each other.

Sima began speaking Gujarati. I lost the drift somehow, but the pizza maker of Belgrave Road was stuck in a meeting. The Eastern Delight was a rip-roaring success, though. The pizza was loaded with onions, cauliflower, garlic, tomato, potato and peas, then rounded off with a hefty dose of chilli and spices.

We walked on to yet another restaurant, the Mirch Masala – we're still around Belgrave Road by the way – that not only served Indian vegetarian food, but Italian, Chinese and even Mexican, all tweaked and made acceptable, and selling very well.

Now all this might strike you as very normal, evidence of the cultural vibrancy of the UK, and I have to admit that was exactly what my thoughts were, until we went to meet the man who runs the Sharmilee, Mr Lalit Goswami, who began to tell his version of what was happening to Indian food.

Dapper, immensely polite and happy to talk, he promised he would sit down with us in a few minutes while we checked out the sweets, the *mithai*, below. Again we are in a minor linguistic bind here, for if you have never seen an Indian sweetshop, banish the thought of sherbet lemons and liquorice, of the scruffy chaos that is, or was, the classic English sweetshop, where the clients were usually impoverished kids. The Indian sweetshop is a different animal altogether. A better word is sweetmeat, in a way. *Mithai* are cooked and created from fresh ingredients, many using long reductions of milk, and decorated with nuts and gold and silver leaf. They are sweet. Almost overwhelmingly so. More fudgelike than anything, but softer and more subtle.

Sima noted that it wasn't always such a riot of colour. 'When I was young everything was yellow,' she said. 'The snacks were yellow. The cakes were yellow. Now look!'

And it was true that things had moved on since the early yellow phase. There were some sweets that looked like cut watermelon, some in tasteful magnolia, others in green, studded with pistachios and covered with a gossamer-thin waft of silver leaf. But yellow, the colour of saffron and turmeric, a colour with deep significance in Hindu culture, still predominated.

Banish also the idea that they were always a snack or a gastronomic postscript, for the Gujaratis will at times break the very principle I thought was almost inviolable: that sweet follows savoury. I had already noticed in Sakoni's the sweet rice pudding nestling in among the dhals in their buffet, and it is quite acceptable to start off with a little sweet something to keep, it is said, the company sweet. *Mithai* can be eaten as a snack food, or wrapped and given to friends and relations, brought by the guest, or given to the lover. Their sweetness helps on a functional level too: the oppressive heat of a subcontinental summer calls for much quick cooking, or a medium that is so sweet that bacteria would simply find it all too much. Humans don't.

In the Sharmilee, three cooks from Mumbai worked from five every morning in the kitchen down below, stirring vast pots of simmering milk – powdered milk is mostly used by the way – for the *barfis*, wielding huge tins of ghee, crushing cardamom seeds, and arranging all in a strictly formal pattern to be piled on the counters in the shop. Like a fool in a sweet-shop with a difference, almost overwhelmed by the spectacular piles and rows of *barfis*, *halvas* and the swirling, syrupy *jalebis*, I felt just a little unsure as to what on earth to buy, chickened out, and asked them to pack me a box or two, one as a gift, and the other just in case I should get stranded on the M1.

Lalit was ready now, so we climbed the stairs, and I could see once again the table where my son and I had sat all those years ago, and the uneasy false pillar. The Sharmilee opened in 1973, and was run by a family who also came from Dar es Salaam. They had run a successful hotel in Tanzania, which Sima could still vaguely remember. Everyone seemed to have heard of it.

'Oh, life was much easier, much slower in Africa,' Lalit recalled. 'When we came here, that all changed.'

Sima told her arriving-in-England story. For most, these centre on memories of the bitter cold. The long winters. For her, it was the shoes. And the feet. She could remember seeing thousands of strange feet in the airport. The image has stayed with her.

The Sharmilee is part of the hard core of long-established restaurants in Belgrave Road. Friends is another, as is Bobby's. All are completely vegetarian, but this is all quietly assumed, for that is simply what most Gujaratis are. Bobby's is different: it serves vegetarian food according to Jain custom. The Jains believe in an all-engrossing reincarnation, so that the merest insect may have a soul, and presumably could be a distant relation, which means that in order not to eat anything animate and living, roots and rhizomes are avoided. So no onions or garlic appear in Jain cooking, for example. They will instead use the incredibly pungent, almost overwhelming asafoetida, which also has the happy little name of *hing*. You can almost forgive it its vile smell with a sweet name like that! It comes from the reduced sap of a relation of the fennel plant. If you ever do feel the urge to buy it, be warned. It is one of those perplexing culinary foodstuffs like fish sauce and the Indonesian fruit durian, sweet and delicate to the habitués but utterly nauseating to the novice. I would suggest you buy but the minutest quantity in powder form before being evicted.

As we talked about the early years of the Sharmilee, Lalit told us how it all began.

'We served the local community. It was quite simple. We grew as they grew. Here we are, over thirty years later, still going strong.'

Sharmilee did well, and is now in happy middle age – no mean feat for a restaurant, believe me. People come from far and wide.

'We had a family of French here last week. They had come all the way up to eat here. They didn't really know what to eat, but they seemed to have left quite happy!'

'Are you still cooking the same dishes you were all those years ago, or have things changed at all?' I asked.

'Well, almost, but people are beginning to try different things now.' He got up, and brought me the menu. 'We get a lot of people who want to eat Chinese food. That's new. I think they like to eat it here because they aren't too sure about Chinese restaurants. The Chinese, they eat anything. So our customers try things here.'

They even have a section on the menu entitled 'A Selection of Chinese Dishes Indian Style', with offerings such as manchurium ('cauliflower with cabbage balls'), veg fried rice and veg haka noodles – all pretty tame stuff by some standards. I had assumed that all this had evolved from within, as Chinese cooking became so well known over here, but Lalit thought this wasn't the case at all.

'No, no. It comes from India. Things are really changing over there. People want to eat Chinese. Mexican. Italian. Everything. So long as it's vegetarian.'

As India has emerged from being an overly controlled, somewhat stifled economy, it has entered into a sort of mild culinary renaissance. And, British Gujaratis are now getting into the idea of widening their tastes a little. They like going out for a Chinese just as other Britons do, and to make it all comprehensible, flavours are adjusted, spices are added, and it can all be eaten in an easy, familiar environment. Which of course brings us full square right back to chicken tikka massala.

While rounding off the conversation with a strong cup of spiced milky tea, *chai masala*, brewed the way Gujaratis like it, Lalit, pillar of the local community and keen businessman that he was, pointed out something that had also seemed blindingly obvious to me.

'We're never really going to put Belgrave Road on the map unless someone promotes it,' he said. 'The council doesn't. I mean, there are no signs anywhere pointing to Belgrave Road.'

But there were a few roundabouts. So, councillors, burghers and aldermen, get out those brown signs. I saw one to a massive new hotel, the Four Horsemen of the Apocalypse Inn, and we haven't even touched on Leicester's Space Centre.

'Come back up on another day. Bring the family.' You could almost hear Lalit add, with his perfect smile and immaculate shirt, 'There's loads to do in Leicester!'

I had told Sima that I had felt deeply frustrated buying the raw materials for a Gujarati dinner, struck, I suppose, by just how little I knew. Even if this was a vibrant street in a dull city, a zone where the flock wallpaper had long gone, with its jewellers' shops, glittering saris and shops full of rice, *moolis* and herbs that I knew not, and that were distinctly alien to my cultural heritage at least, I asked whether she would escort me just a bit longer, feeling guilty now, for her daughter had just started school and she kept on fielding anxious phone calls while saying, 'No, no, it's all right. It's fine. Don't worry. We've got till four o'clock.' When her Renault will turn into a *mooli* and she will have to disappear. My guide and princess.

So off we walked, clock ticking, to what I guess is in a way the heart and soul of the Leicester Asian's home cooking. The shops that are half cash-and-carry and corner shop, brimming with bags of pulses, bunches of fresh *meti* (fenugreek) and strange medicaments with pictures of wise gurus on them. I bought one of these, but since the instructions appear to say 'leave on for six weeks' I haven't quite got round to squeezing the tube yet.

This is a brilliant way to stock up on those things your local supermarket never sells. Or if they do, it will be some bastardized, overpriced version. The shelves were full of dried fenugreek. Black sesame seeds. Ground millet. Tamarind pulp. And you can see too just how important is dhal – the pulses that are the protein base for almost all Gujarati vegetarians. 'That's good for dhal,' Sima told me, and we piled another thwacking sack of beans in the basket. Basmati rice cheaper than anywhere I have seen, including the most discounted of supermarkets. Cornmeal, lentils, beans – all eminently affordable.

'And take this too,' Sima said, thrusting a sack of millet flour my way. She told me how for six months after the birth of her daughter she had been fed and fortified by her mother with spinach, chapattis and this and that to bring her strength back up, and with my own baby only weeks away it all seemed to be another part of the peculiar dream that is late father-hood. The woman at the cash-desk gave me the strangest of strange looks when she got to the millet. Sima said something in Gujarati, and she smiled. This was quite an achievement, since she had just been attacked from all quarters for miscal-culating something deeply minor by a whole family of elegant, unsmiling girls – almost all the customers seemed to be women – and reacted not a jot when they broadly questioned her honesty before pouring out of the shop into their BMW.

'It takes all sorts!' Sima commented before leaping into her car.

I felt a huge surge of satisfaction in the knowledge that now I too could begin to hang around the Indian and Pakistani shops that can be found all over the country to serve their predominantly local customers. I became an Indian (Bangladeshi, and Pakistani) shop queen, and have without exception been treated with slightly bemused politeness. Once I packed what I thought were limes into the basket.

'You know these are lemons?' I was told. 'They're from my country, and we eat them like this.' Her country was Bangladesh, the shop in Cowley Road, which is my local multicultural drag. I was actually looking for something I hadn't seen since a trip to India years ago, and which had by now begun to remind me of that complex sour and spicy taste that to me is quite the most attractive of all the combinations. Black salt.

'No, we haven't got it, but try the Pakistani shop down the road.'

Which I did. And they did.

I felt just a little bit smug as I confidently flopped a bunch of *meti* into my basket, piled in more dhal, and bought a huge sack of basmati rice. Basmati is the best long-grain rice, generally preferred over patna for its taste and bouquet, and it can be widely found in the UK. Experts say the best basmati hails from the northern Indian town of Dehradhun, but I've never seen it being sold here.

Cooking Basmati rice

To help keep the grains separate, you might like to add a little lemon juice to the water, but in any case it's best to wash the rice first, and then soak it before cooking for ten minutes or so, retaining the water to use in cooking. The best way to cook rice is not to treat it like pasta and drown it in gallons of salty water, but to be a bit more scientific. This is how I do it, but read the instructions if you prefer.

Allow 95g uncooked rice per person.
Rinse in colander.
Add about 400ml salted water per person and bring to the boil.
After ten minutes, put in a hot oven, add a cinnamon stick and cover with foil. Leave for another ten minutes. It should then be a dish of perfect fluffy separate grains that will make you sing with joy.

Adapted from Yamuna Devi, *Lord Krishna's Cuisine: The Art of Indian Vegetarian Cooking* (Bhaktivedanta Book Trust, 1987)

Now, I might have done the matter of public eating, and public buying, in Belgrave Road, but I still wanted to satisfy that most difficult of urges, private eating. This has been a long-standing problem for me. I am profoundly nosy, and I absolutely love to eat in other people's houses – on the condition that they like to eat, that is. For, just as I love my food, I also like looking at mantelpieces and carpets, in the lavatory, at all the crummy old photos that conceal unknown joys, the grief, the passion of a private world only the family itself can really understand.

And so it was, with the rain still pouring from the sky, that I noticed it was the time that the hour doth rush. I had got absolutely nowhere trawling the shelves of the city's library, possibly the most unwelcoming and chaotic that I had seen, run by a band of flushed middle-aged ladies who were kept busy allocating computer terminals to all and sundry. They spent about 1 per cent of their time doing bookish things. I hurried out, and sought refuge in the rain. So Victorian was the whole experience that I felt a strong urge to eat a teaspoon of treacle, but I had to join the thousands of others leaving this sodden city, lemming-like, at the end of the working day.

Laden with my sweetmeats and pulses, not exactly hungry but still blessedly curious, I felt distinctly chuffed. I had been asked to dine with Mukesh Bhatt and his wife, whose son had kindly volunteered them after seeing the article in the *Mercury*. They lived many roundabouts away from Belgrave Road just near the enormous football stadium. I suppose landscaping stadia is not a practical point of architecture, but boy can they be brutal. Functional, I am sure, but I looked at it and thought, what about covering the roof in turf? You know, just like the Faroese do. Or dig it underground. But then I realized that frankly the surrounds weren't exactly pastoral and splendid. Just those damned roundabouts again.

I knocked precisely on time (this being a hardcore fetish of mine), and was asked in. It was going well. Through into the lounge. Or was it the sitting room? I offered them my box of *mithai*.

Mukesh was in his fifties, and his sons were part of that hybrid culture, their hearts not entirely in Gujarat, ambitious, bilingual in glottal stop and Gujarati, flipping easily from one culture to another. As we sat down to dinner, I noticed piles of huge pans stacked outside, the raw material for the weddings and feasts Mukesh cooks for his Gujarati friends. Of England he knew very little. Of Britain even less. When in London it was to visit relations. In Canada the same. His wife had recently returned to Kenya, for the first time since she had left over thirty years previously, again to see relations. For while Mukesh's roots were Gujarati with a touch of Uganda, his wife's were tinged with Kenya, more particularly with the palm-fronded beaches near Mombasa.

We immediately started talking of the past, the easy days of warmth, and then Britain and the solid memories of the grinding everyday life, the constant struggle in a country that even if it rewarded diligence and once celebrated the virtues of hard work could nevertheless be colourless and draining. In a sense, Britain still seemed to be an alien place to the Bhatts. His sons would come and teasingly suggest a little more broad-mindedness, and I would love to have shown them the sights of Oxford, but the Gujaratis have a great sense of community that has seen them through expulsions and prejudice which might seem like a tendency to turn inward. Mukesh is of that generation that has struggled and suffered but kept its culture remarkably coherent, through food and through the ceremonial. But in the meantime, all around them things have moved on.

We sat down to a bowl of dhal, and chapattis.

'My wife always makes them, you know,' Mukesh told me. 'Women make better chapattis. They have a more delicate touch than men.'

I found it almost impossible to keep my left hand away from the table – for this is the impure hand and should not be used to eat food – and to remember to scoop up food with my chapatti.

We talked of the feasts and the weddings, of those times when the family sat and ate together, and I began to get a feel that for his generation, the thousands who were summarily expelled from the land where they had been raised, the family is their solace, their hope, and their disappointment too. Mukesh spent the evenings sitting with his friends, chewing the fat. Meanwhile, of course, India itself seems to have opened its conceptual doors wide and taken to the thrill of pizzas and enchiladas. Maybe it will be as radical as the days when the Portuguese introduced the equally fiery thrill of the chilli, entirely New World in origin, a spice so well suited to the culinary repertoire that it is now almost unthinkable to eat Indian food without its vicious buzz.

So it felt quite the easiest thing to dip into the dhal once more, in this terraced Leicester house, to roll the chapattis – made by Mrs Bhatt, of course – around the table, to nibble on the delicious *puris* and the home-made samosas, and to reflect further on the twists and turns of who we are and what we eat.

13

MANCHESTER

Cantonese Home Cooking

'YOU LIKE HITLER?' ASKED MR SAN TANG.

A strange question, you may think. Not many do these days. I was munching on a bowl of the most exquisite Cantonese food I had ever eaten, deep in the heart of Manchester's Chinatown. Every day, on the first floor of a solid Mancunian building in a warren of rooms and corridors, a group of venerable Chinese ladies, along with the occasional husband, gets together for lunch. So, put down your mah-jong counters, meet the ladies of the Wai Yin Women's Society, and listen to their stories. I was their guest, and we settled down to a few hours of the most fascinating discussions that drifted from our thoughts on Hitler to the thoughts of Chairman Mao and back to life in a Chinese takeaway.

Having put my earnest enquiries about food, and the years gone by, I told my hosts with the snappy names of Wong, Pang and Tang the story of how a ten-year-old boy was once disciplined for selling Mao's little red book. Like many others,

I had become besotted with the enigmatic, powerful and brilliant revolutionary – no, not Tony Blair, but Chairman Mao Tse-tung himself, the man from Hunan. Officially, my initials are an M and an A, which has allowed me occasionally to abuse the system. When I was ten or so, I used to write off letters left, right and centre in the vague hope that I would receive endless freebies in the post. MA does after all mean Master of Arts, and many teachers have incredibly puerile handwriting. This, when combined with a sheet of school writing paper, often brought excellent results. I was at boarding school, and the lack of letters from the outside world could become very trying. A huge parcel was deep joy indeed, and gave you real prestige. I had already written off to Hovis and been sent piles of mini packs of wheat and barley, with thrilling pictures of combine harvesters. And in each booklet there was a magnifying glass. What fun we all had that summer starting bonfires in the July sun, incinerating insects on piles of dead leaves, scorching our names into the old wooden desks and, best of all, seeing how long we could burn ourselves until our skin seared. What an invigorating thing school was in those days.

Few images impressed me more than the pictures of millions upon millions of ardent Chinese gazing adoringly at Chairman Mao during the Cultural Revolution. What a style guru he was. The denims and the khaki were so of the moment, as was his natty quiff of swept-back hair. However plump Mao seemed he did at least have that devastating thing called charisma.

I wrote to the Chinese Embassy. I cannot precisely remember what I said, but several days later I received an immense package full of the Thoughts of Chairman Mao, neatly printed between brilliantly red plastic covers. I didn't have to wait long before they had all been distributed, but no cabals were formed; no acts of wild revolutionary fervour occurred in this particular Surrey school. We all just got on with life, fuelled by bowls of porridge, and stale bread. Thus was cultural revolution narrowly avoided in the peaceful parishes of Guildford.

Since my thing was our eating habits, I wanted to tackle the matter of the Chinese food we all know and love, the sweet and sour, the chow meins, and now, of course, that sublime, almost trendy upstart dim sum. But are we, as had most definitely seemed the case in Leicester, eating a complete bastard of a cuisine, a mad mix of this and that which few Chinese would ever actually eat at home? The Wai Yin Society seemed a brilliant entrée into reality. And indeed it proved to be.

The almost inconceivably enormous country of China encompasses Hans, Uighurs, Hunans, Szechuans and many more, all with their characteristic ways, their foods and languages, none of which truly unites them. Rice is almost unifying, and Mandarin Chinese may be playing a sort of neo-colonial role, but the glimpse we have historically been afforded of this unique culture comes from a very small part of the country, Hong Kong, at a time in its history when its people – certainly the ones I met – were young and idealistic. Hong Kong was claimed as a colony, on historical 'loan' to the British, and run by them along classic lines of divide and rule, of superiority and distinction. But, let us not fool ourselves into thinking that this was a benign and welcome occupation. It clearly was not, according to most of the people I spoke to at Wai Yin.

The vast majority of the Chinese community in Manchester are Cantonese speakers from Hong Kong, as indeed are most Chinese restaurateurs in Britain. Among them there was no long-held belief that Britain was the Golden Land, far from it. I sensed a very realistic appreciation of our shortcomings. They came here to work, and knew from contacts and relations who were already over here that the takeaways and Chinese restaurants provided a steady job and a dependable income but a hard life. You could succeed, if you were prepared to work long hours.

What appealed to me was the opportunity to taste Cantonese home cooking, to get away from the number 24s and 45s, and the bowls of egg fried rice. So when I walked into the Wai Yin dining room and breathed in the warm, starchy smell from a giant pot of boiling rice being cooked for *jo-fan* (breakfast), I cast any thoughts of toast from my mind. They were making congee, as classic and as restorative a dish as the Jewish mother's chicken soup, cooked with rice, water and soft spare ribs to give it a light carnal twang.

Congee

Serves 6

200g short-grained rice
200g glutinous rice
1½ litres of chicken stock with 2 tbsp soy sauce
1 small piece of fresh ginger rhizome, peeled and sliced
6 spare ribs

Rinse the rice thoroughly under running water. Place all the ingredients in a pot and bring to the boil. When boiling, reduce heat to low. Cook for 2 hours, partially covered, stirring frequently. The soup is done when it reaches a porridge-like consistency. Remove ginger slice if you have added it. You can add sliced spring onions, chopped chillis or pak choi, or small slivers of chicken.

I sat down and sipped my congee. Next to me, Mrs Wong admitted to a passion for Quaker Oats.

The Wai Yin Women's Society was started by an energetic lady called Silvia Shum, who had welcomed me with open arms. Silvia is a positive rocket of explosive energy, yin and yang combined. 'I am very proud of Wai Yin,' she had told me over the phone. 'We were the first ever to get a lottery grant, you know!' And she'd gone on to explain the trials and tribulations of getting onto the path of financial rectitude. 'One thing I always say,' she'd added, 'knowledge is very important to us. You know, we are happy to tell people about Wai Yin. The more people come then maybe the Chinese will be better understood, so come and spend a day, no problem. Come and eat with us too!' No further words were needed at that, and I booked myself in.

Silvia introduced me to Irene Pang, my guide and translator for the day and part of the team of sparky individuals who run Wai Yin, who had kindly agreed to help me mingle. Irene was young. She had come over during that last colonial flux when reluctantly the British accepted a degree of responsibility for the people over whom they had generously agreed to rule, and allowed the holders of Hong Kong passports to live and work in the UK. So she came to Manchester. 'I thought I would be more secure coming to England,' Irene told me.

Over the congee, we talked about breakfasts and about memories, of the old days in Hong Kong – the 1960s, that is, when the British were still in charge.

'May I ask you something?' one of the more passionate members of the group, Mr Tang, asked me. 'What do you think of the Commonwealth?'

'Well,' I said, 'if it's a place for equals, then fine, but otherwise it's irrelevant really.'

That wasn't quite good enough.

'No no. It's all wrong! Wrong! Why should any country rule over the others? Why? You tell me.'

I bowed to his feelings, and thought that even my revisionist understanding of the Commonwealth needed yet further revision.

I think all this started by my recounting a little something I had read in the paper. It had genuinely intrigued me. It was said that the one good thing Hitler did for Britain was to hasten the decline of our class system. Now, there are, I am sure, many of you who may well believe that it has far from disappeared. Or you could say that it is now simply based on money, and that Britain is a nouveau meritocracy. It made me reflect on China.

'How can it be', I asked, 'that a people who seem to be so fond of gambling and commerce could have undergone such an extended revolutionary past?'

The cat was well and truly out of the bag. We talked about Mao, and the turbulent days of the Cultural Revolution.

'But remember that we were a colony then,' Mr Tang said. 'We didn't always know what was going on over there on the mainland. Yes, we are all Chinese now, but then things were different.'

'So what would you say Mao did for China?'

I was expecting a swift nothing, but was then asked the do-you-like-Hitler question.

'Well, do you?'

'No!' I answered, suspecting I had fallen into some political trap, outsmarted as only we British know how.

'Well, as you say Hitler did some good for England, so we say Mao did some good for China.'

'How much good did he do?' I persisted.

'I would say seventy per cent good.'

Mr Wong came in at this point and reduced the pro-Mao quotient a little. 'No more than fifty, sixty per cent good,' he said. 'But there's too much corruption. You know it will take a thousand years to change that.'

I asked Mrs Wong about her story. She began her days as a rice farmer in the New Territories, wading through the paddy fields, planting and harvesting, all back-breaking work. And while she toiled, her husband followed the path of so many before him and left the steamy tropics, the mad, bustling, vertical city of Hong Kong, and came to England.

'We were told it would be hard. Very hard. But if you worked you could make good money.'

And where did Mr Wong end up? Grimsby. Yes, Grimsby. And the work *was* hard. As he waited on the English, he was astonished at how they seemed to love the sweet and sour pork, the chop sueys, dishes he would never have dreamed of eating at home. A few years later, his wife joined him.

I asked what was more difficult, rice farming or running a takeaway.

'Oh, rice farming,' Mrs Wong replied without a moment's hesitation.

So here was this couple who had spent almost their whole working life churning out chop sueys and watching the Brits struggle with chopsticks, and never quite finding a place to belong to. All of them told me that it was the language more than anything else that caused them such difficulty. The dining room was echoing to the sound of Cantonese.

Mr Tang, however, was more at ease in English. And his point of arrival was just as alluring – Gloucester, which may sound delightful but believe me, this is a city that also has its problems. He too came to work for a relation who had his own takeaway. He too was told that life would be hard. But work, and you can make it work. It was that simple really.

It came as no surprise that they smiled almost affectionately when they talked of the food they once cooked. Back home, rice farming was never a great earner, and they ate what they could. Neither the Wongs nor the Tangs could afford to eat out, and were fed instead on rice, *fan*, and whatever was to hand. Fish and pork mainly. The tradition was that the household kept a pig to fatten. The Cantonese make sensational pork sausages, hanging them out to dry for the festivities of the Chinese New Year. And as you would expect the rice farmers wasted not a single morsel, offering the head to the village deities. Ears, tongue and blood were all assiduously used, as were the trotters, which the Wongs could well remember being pickled in black vinegar and eaten with ginger.

Rice farmers didn't always start the day with a bowl of congee. They would be down in the fields early in the morning, and return at about ten. Then they would have their congee, for the heat in Hong Kong can be quite debilitating. Better by far to do as much work as possible during the cooler morning.

Cantonese cooking is considered by many to be China's finest. The use of the freshest, purest ingredients gives it an inevitable emphasis on the quality of the raw material, and this being said, it is hardly surprising that the Westernized version may make us suspect that Cantonese food has not travelled well. It is also said by some commentators that since the majority of the émigrés who came here from Hong Kong were not actually restaurateurs at all, they didn't have the requisite skills to recreate real Cantonese cooking.

The British have inherited some Cantonese habits. There is, for instance, the matter of drinking tea with your Chinese food. While Tsing Tao beer is preferred by some – a brand of beer, incidentally, created by Germans – we seem to like the idea of drinking green tea instead when out for a Chinese. It seems authentic. But it is apparently a purely Cantonese habit, slightly looked down upon elsewhere. And while we were passing through habits and the origins of dishes, I wondered about the sacred trio of our interpretation of Chinese food: chop suey, chow mein and sweet and sour pork.

'It was simply what the customers asked for,' Mr Wong confirmed.

There seems to be a bit of controversy over chop suey. The story goes that it was created in America by a culinary loose cannon at Trader Vics. But equally possible and far more alluring a version is that it actually evolved from a dish that was found in Toisan, in southern Canton, where many Californian émigrés came from, and is an anglicization of the Cantonese *tsap seui*, meaning 'miscellaneous scraps' — an ideal dish for the takeaway business. Chow mein is found in a Chinese and Chinese-American form; the latter uses fried noodles. As for sweet and sour pork, it is derived from a dish from northern China that was originally made with river fish.

The clock ticked on, the tea flowed, and we got nearer lunchtime. Giant pots bubbled, and the smell of onions and soy sauce wafted in the air. It must have been all this that turned our thoughts to food once more. Before long, lunch was being dished out. Plates began to arrive.

But first, a soup.

'We Chinese always like to start with soup,' Mr Tang explained, 'but thin soup. You English like thick soup. Funny, yes!'

This soup was something I had never once seen in a Chinese restaurant, light chicken stock and apple.

It's the food writer's old chestnut, but I asked what they would choose if they could eat anything at all.

'Moon han,' they told me.

Now this was not to be easily found, for 'moon han' means 'the food of the emperors'. They began to tell me about this curious, elaborate, forgotten food. Irene Pang slipped out of her role as translator and told me that she had once seen a moon han feast in Hong Kong.

'It was incredible. There were dishes everywhere. It was all so vast, but I never tasted the food. I just saw it on TV in Hong Kong! There's one dish they eat, bear's paw. They put the bear's feet on a hot plate, and it makes the blood flow down, and that is good. Then they cut off the paw and eat. And sometimes they ate monkey head too.'

'What, you mean it's true? People really do eat live monkey brains? I always thought that was just a story!' As apocryphal as the French eating ants covered in chocolate.

'Yes, for health. It's good for health. They place the

monkey under the table and cut off its head, and you take the brain out with your chopstick and eat.'

No-one had tried either dish. And it wasn't moon han day at Wai Yin. There is no real defence these days for such barbaric cruelty, but we have to accept that there is an elaborate network of tradition in Chinese culture that dictates that health and energy can come from eating the most obscure and often highly controversial foods. Chinese culture appears to be relatively uncomplicated by Western liberal thought, which means that, yes, they do still allow the illicit culling of tigers, and the consumption of dogs and snakes, and the awful extraction of bile from live bears. They also allow the whole-sale plundering of the world's diminishing shark population, and while the mainland energetically explodes and expands, the world awaits to feed this hungry monster. I have seen container-loads of dried shark fins awaiting shipment in the Red Sea to the gourmets of Hong Kong. I have seen people stuff illegally caught sea cucumbers into bags in the Galapagos, while enthusiastic environmentalists tried to let principle win over the allure of wealth. And before we all swoon over the evil and the sheer unsustainability of such practices, we should not forget those not-so-distant days when Imperial Britain allowed the wholesale massacre of tigers for sport, and the royals were happy to pose on their corpses. Neither should we forget the destruction of the North Sea cod. We should also perhaps remember the Chairman's dictum about self-criticism.

My day eating and chatting at Wai Yin made me muse a little on the word 'authentic'. I had been easily tempted by what was to me a rare opportunity to eat everyday Cantonese food – congee, bowls of pickled radishes, rice, and whole roast snapper studded with garlic, soy sauce and onions. The tastes were strong, not altogether unfamiliar, but somehow more satisfying than prawn crackers and a portion of number 25 served on a Friday night with a pint of lager. Once again I felt a touch perplexed, and slightly depressed that Britain's happy habit of fusing and toning down tastes and flavours means that eating out in a Chinese/Cantonese restaurant can raise as many questions as answers. What are we actually eating, a bastardized cuisine or something genuine? The same dichotomy between private and public eating exists to be sure; at least at Wai Yin I was allowed a taste of domestic Cantonese cookery, the evocative dishes such as congee that allow those essential cultural Proustian moments, causing minds to wander and the soul to reflect.

You can sense a precise, almost inevitable process of acculturation that occurs in the immigré foods we eat. A mass and cheap form of cooking becomes embedded, and has its distinctive edges honed. It no longer exists merely to keep the proprietorial community fed, but becomes a means of earning income. Then, as time goes on we all get bored, and seek something more 'authentic'. So the metropolitan centres begin to offer an element of regional variety – in the case of Chinese cooking, Pekinese; then a few Szechuan restaurants open up, and our experiences are extended. We will never be able to widen our culinary knowledge much beyond that, short of undertaking a lengthy trip to China, but we are now in the strange and rather ironic position in this country of finding it easier to glimpse a little more variety in Chinese food than in our own indigenous cuisine. It's even more perplexing that we have to use a French word to describe it.

As I left, my tongue tingling with chilli, and laden with dried mushrooms and radishes, a gift from the ladies of Wai Yin, I couldn't help but wonder yet again why we have lost our taste for the Hindle Wakes and the salamagundies of British cooking.

When I asked my hosts as a parting shot what British food they really liked, they all paused for thought.

'Ah, chips,' said one. 'I really like chips.'

'And roast beef too,' said another.

And I think they really meant it.

SOUTH

THE WEALD

Cauldron Cooking

IT WAS THE SIZE OF IT THAT SHOCKED ME. IT WAS MUCH TINIER than I had imagined. Three-legged, rather dinky, charred, seething even, but oh so radical. I felt an urgent need to pick it up and fondle it, but it was sitting at my feet on a bed of glowing, enflamed timber, and I thought it a little unwise. Here, before my eyes, was my very first fully functioning cauldron. I had dreamed of this moment. Adrenalin rushed everywhere.

Dawn Stevens was glowing with a ruddy milkmaid's charm, as was her willing helper. Although they politely denied that they were Tudor wenches, their dress screamed wench to me, and they seemed to share my enthusiasm for this very utilitarian metal cooking pot. I submit, m'lud, that the iconic cauldron is at the very heart of British cooking, and although people tend to prefer saucepans and cookers these days, it has shaped the way we eat.

Characterized by its three legs, and made of solid metal,

the cauldron could either sit directly on the fire or be suspended above it. Either way it was good practice to fill it up with as much food as possible, so while one part might have had a flitch of bacon pressed against the edge carefully wrapped in a floured cloth, another might have been filled with dried peas, beans, or even fresh vegetables, perhaps even a sausage or two. We know from archaeological excavations that the Anglo-Saxons used them. The Sutton Hoo ship contained three huge ceremonial cauldrons, one riven from a single sheet of bronze, but these were high-status cooking pots. Everyday households would have used thick iron cauldrons, which sloughed off microns of iron during cooking and possibly helped stave off anaemia.

I had driven down to West Sussex to visit the Weald and Downland Museum just north of Chichester. It was a place I knew well. At least I thought I knew it well. I grew up around these parts, and retain a lingering fondness for the flinty cottages and soft, springy turf of the South Downs, the fields full of moronic sheep and their endless neat little droppings. I had been drawn by an open invitation to meet the museum's cook, Dawn, and I came across her dressed for the part stirring a goodly Tudor vegetable broth.

The cauldron was particularly useful in the southern half of England, where trees were readily available to provide wood that was chopped, stored, then burned to provide fuel and heat. As soon as I walked through the kitchen door I began to put flesh on the theory of the primacy of this cooking pot. There was Dawn, bustling in her dowdy gown and bonnet, a rubicund vision of laughing rural passion. I hailed her in finest twenty-first-century English and noticed a pack of Wall's bacon on the slab. She was working in a reconstructed sixteenth-century kitchen of a house they called Winkhurst that had been gently hauled across the south of England from the adjacent county of Kent. In a brilliant retro makeover, it had once again become what it was originally meant to be. Winkhurst has sloughed off its multiple-layered persona, its years with new-fangled Agas and gymkhana rosettes, and once again become a fully functioning Tudor kitchen.

With the fire burning merrily at one end, you could easily see how much culinary multitasking was going on. The heat warmed the water and the bread oven; it roasted meat and boiled the soup in the cauldron. Hanging in the rafters were chunky hams and bacon imbibing all the smoke, to be left in this rot-free zone until needed. However, these days we are deemed to be so physically feeble, or the hams so dangerous, that the laws of the mighty health vigilantes dictate that museum visitors can taste neither ham nor bacon. That would be far too risky. Hence the Wall's Danish.

Perhaps this institutional fear is justified. We did after all popularize the carnivorous cow. The British have implemented laws with impressive zeal in the name of health and hygiene, but it is also true to say that British culture is particularly strong on its fear of foreignness in food, despite its strong multicultural roots. The French, for example, are weird because they eat frogs and snails. This seems to be yet another strand of the complex paradox that links the British to their eating habits. While the French and the Italians bemoan the demise of artisanal food producers in the face of ridiculous bureaucratic demands, the British attitude is less clear-cut, helped perhaps by the historical distance we have maintained from regular supplies of fresh food.

In this reconstructed Tudor kitchen there was no chimney at all, no quaint mantelpiece – a creation of many centuries later – no low ceilings, just a free-flowing space right up to the roof's rafters. Sussex was never big on chimneys during the sixteenth century – no whim of fashion this, for flint shatters when heated and cooled repetitively. This kitchen would once have seen great sides of flesh being basted and dredged over the spit set over the open fire. As time went on, novel ways were invented of turning spits. A clock spit used a giant, tightly wound clockwork spring, while a dog spit used a little breed of dog born to tread its life away rather like a Hanoverian hamster. The poor beast was trained by placing a burning ember at the foot of the wheel, which kept it in a fearful and fearfully non-PC perpetual motion. What an inventive lot we are.

As I took all this in, Dawn's lunch happily bubbled away on the trivet. She was feeding a bunch of earnest builders. I had unwittingly become attached to their group in the firm belief that we were to learn about Tudor cooking, but their interests seemed to lie elsewhere. They were actually studying the rise of the timber-framed building, so I sat listening to tales of wayney edges, lintels and grommets. I learned how trees were chopped by one-edge axes, and how wooden beams can be read by the eye of an expert. I clearly wasn't among them, but for the first hour I listened, fascinated by this rather intense lecture. The group had quickly sussed that I was a fish out of water when I asked, while looking at a magnificently gnarled beam, what sort of wood it was, only to be told with the politest touch of condescension that it was oak. All timber-framed houses were made of oak or elm, and this was clearly oak. Fool!

So I started fiddling around with the pots, lids and spoons, and the exquisite, roughly hewn wooden plates. How utterly bizarre it all seemed. Progress has consigned the Tudor look to the design cesspool. Yet the dream of rural simplicity lives on, and fuels endless volumes on the joys of the countryside. And yes, life was short then, but at least they had nice wooden spoons.

'Did you know', Dawn asked, 'that they didn't just put the soup in the cauldron, but they stuffed in as much as they possibly could? We've done it here sometimes. Put a bit of bacon in, boiled a chicken, and even shoved in a pudding or two.'

Which is the crux of the matter. Cauldron cooking

involved a judicious use of space, hence the British tendency to combine meat and sweet, in the form of a suet or steamed pudding, both of which evolved in the dumpy depths of the cauldron.

Puddings. The one thing upon which commentators seem to agree about British food is that we do a great pudding. And there is sometimes more than just sweetness to it. Of the savoury versions, the best known is steak and kidney pudding, one of those consistently popular classic British dishes, a judicious combination of meat and offal that has triumphantly survived. But it is the sweet variety for which Britain is most renowned – and we are not talking about delicate little things with a dusting of icing sugar. True British puddings are huge and hearty creations with names redolent of times gone by. Spotted dicks. Roly polys. Treacle puddings, cabinet puddings, and down here in the Weald the most delectable of all, Sussex Pond pudding, so called because as you cut through its steaming suet crust a rush of buttery, lemon-scented goo floods out. It's truly awesome, and truly belt-tightening.

This being the heart of Wealden Sussex, it seems fitting that we should fantasize a little on the luscious steamed suet puddings, the stodgy stars of British cooking, so dear to the hearts of all of us who have experienced their robust domesticity. But first, find your suet. This is the name we give the hard fat that surrounds the kidneys, and is now almost always bovine in origin, though at one time mutton suet was widely used. There is also now – I have to marvel at technology here – a vegetarian suet alternative that comes from the fat of vegetarian cows. Which are of course a rarity in the UK. Suet is combined with self-raising flour and cold butter and worked to make a suet crust pastry, the basic ingredient for all suet puddings. Add a little sugar, and it becomes a sweet crust, to be used in, say, Sussex Pond pudding; add some grated lemon rind and parsley and it's magically transformed into a savoury crust, suitable for steak and kidney pudding; it can be further tarted up by the addition of spices such as nutmeg or mace. Thus it became a staple of the evolved form of cauldron cooking that characterizes traditional British food.

The only problem is that it is now virtually impossible to buy fresh suet, which is much lighter and less cloying than the processed blocks most of us use. But puddings are still hefty dishes. Also, with the incomprehensible lack of designer inter-est in creating a manageable cauldron for use in the modern kitchen, we tend to ignore almost the whole repertoire of steamed puddings but for the occasional foray to a restaurant and, of course, at Christmas, when all true pagans may well eat a mince pie or two, and will almost certainly tuck into a Christmas or plum pudding, both of which use suet. If ever there was a sign of the importance of the blessed cauldron to British food, it is to be found in the hearty soul of the steamed suet pudding.

Sussex Pond pudding

This recipe comes from one of the finest books ever written on British food, now sadly out of print, *The Cook's Tour of Britain* (Collins Willow, 1984), written by the Women's Institute and Michael Smith, an early pioneer on the long path of the preservation of the delights of British cooking.

Serves 6–8

225g suet crust pastry
50g seedless raisins
50g currants
110g Demerara sugar
110g very cold unsalted butter
1 large unwaxed lemon

Make the pastry, adding 1 tsp of grated lemon rind to the dough. Generously butter a 1½-litre pudding basin. Line with pastry, reserving about a third for the lid. To make the filling, mix the dried fruit and sugar in a bowl. Prick the lemon all over with a bodkin (if not readily to hand, a skewer will do). Cut the refrigerator-hard cold butter into small cubes. Disperse half of this with half the fruit and sugar into the lined basin. Press the lemon in, then pack the remaining ingredients on top of it. The basin should be full. Wet the pastry edges, fit the lid and seal well. Cover with buttered foil, making a pleat across the top to allow the crust to rise. Steam for 2½ hours.

English puddings had a wide and excellent reputation. The French writer Frederic Misson, who spent some time in London, eulogized in 1719, 'blessed be he that invented the pudding. To come in pudding time is the most lucky moment in the world.' (His observations were unusually acute, although he did say that buggery was 'a thing came . . . from Italy'.) British puddings were of all things the most iconic, the most revered culinary creation, but the word originally implied stuffing or filling a container of some sort. Thus we have blood in a gut casing for black pudding. Into a basin for a plum pudding. The common ground is the need to be boiled and boiled and boiled again. And once upon a time this would have been done in – yes, you've guessed it – the emblematic three-legged pot we call the cauldron.

While Dawn chatted on, she stirred the steaming vegetable potage, thick with beans and potatoes, that was to be served for lunch. She had used two herbs that have fallen by the wayside as far as modern usage is concerned but were still lovingly grown in the kitchen gardens at the museum. One was lovage, a large and dominating plant for any kitchen garden that combines well with potatoes in soup if used sparingly, though its flavour can easily overwhelm. Secondly, there was a sprinkling of alexanders, *Smyrnium olusatrum*, a hardy plant that is similar to lovage, indeed is often called black lovage, but is less brutal. It was superseded by celery, which it vaguely resembles.

The soup was duly served by Tudor lackeys. Dawn then popped round to the Tudor fridge, showed me her shimmering brawn, and announced that the cheese course had to be prepared.

'Oh, wonderful! Home-made cheese!'

'Well, it's not actually ours.'

We both knew that while respecting the law is a wonderful thing, the deeply anal attitude the authorities have to risk and danger makes situations such as these utterly farcical. Especially on a day when I had driven 200-odd miles and risked life and limb on the motorways. But we couldn't ban cars, now could we?

I passed on the cheese. But I was allowed a taste of Dawn's sweet and spicy prune suckets (candied prunes), on which note the meal ended. The builders and carpenters wandered off, looking distinctly downtrodden, and I set off to look at the rest of the museum.

Not far away from Dawn's Tudor domain stood the more elaborate Bayleaf Farmstead, another Kentish building, but one this time with its own flock of geese, and a garden. There is a marvellous band of well-informed volunteers that works at the museum, so all the houses have their own timelord in command. I fell into conversation with a wise and ancient man called, I think, Godfrey Sniff. (I really hope I read his nametag right.) His fifteenth-century domain had an open fire blazing slap bang in the middle of the bumpy floor, with the central hall reaching right up to the rafters. But at both ends there was an upper level, a first floor indeed, two mini mezzanines that were design features of the times. The family would sleep at one end, the servants at the other. This was, Godfrey thought, probably a bailiff's house, a man of some substance who worked for the landowner rather than knocking on doors repossessing televisions.

The glassless windows could be shut tight with neatly fitting wooden boards. They even had a truckle bed, a crazily clever creation on wheels that stacked under the double bed to be used when required. Looking at its mattress of tightly woven straw and the woollen blanket, I was amazed that Godfrey didn't sneak under the bedclothes every day and fall fast asleep. But being a man made of sterner stuff, he showed me the curfew that was placed over the fire each night. It looked remarkably like an upturned Spanish cooking pot. 'Curfew' is an etymologically fascinating word, coming from the French *couvre feu*, meaning to cover the fire.

But what got me thinking was the size of the room that you entered. It was still called a hall, but not yet in the modern sense, i.e. a tacky ground-floor corridor. This large, open, central space was essentially the heart of the house, full of a wonderful array of three-legged chairs and trestle tables. It is extraordinary how beautiful these rough and elemental houses can be when you see them cleared of their modern riff-raff.

'What do you do with *plectranthus*?' asked a plaintive voice. The answer was quick and erudite.

I was in the garden office of West Dean House, just next door to the Open Air Museum, where the Edward James Foundation is fiercely committed to encouraging arty things such as restoring clocks and tapestries. Back in the 1990s, the trust appointed two highly ambitious and enthusiastic gardeners, Jim Buckland and Sarah Wain, to renovate and resuscitate what was then a rundown and decayed mess. It was an awesome task. But the walled garden is once again an ocean of fertility. Espalier apples cling geometrically to the edges, and the glasshouses are all sparklingly clean. Thick-stemmed figs and apricots, and beautiful blushing peaches thrive in the earthy warmth of summer. But it hasn't been simple. There has been much learning and experimentation since most of the garden records were lost, but the rewards are there for all to see.

'Before the war there were twenty-two gardeners working here,' Sarah told me as she escorted me around the gardens. 'That's just not possible any more, so we have had to cut corners and improvise.' She spoke about her own private hero, the 'God-sent Dutchman' who she noticed was looking at the vines in minute detail. 'He was amazing. He had worked with vines all his life and showed us what we were doing wrong. That sort of thing happens quite a lot. We are learning all the time. And even if we use as many of the local varieties as we can find, we will never be able to recreate the garden completely. And to be honest, we don't really want to. West Dean has a different role to play these days.'

This has become an ogling garden, a living fossil in a way, but it has nevertheless found an important role in the local community. There's an annual chilli day, a tomato day, and the almost obligatory apple day. The locals assemble, marvel and nibble at the Thai food stalls on chilli day, and stock up for their *salsa festa* at home. Come Apple Day, there is a far stronger element of traditional jollity. You can bob apples, carve pumpkins, and temporarily forget about the awful hegemony of the tasteless gas-stored apple. But as is so often the case in Britain, it's the past that is of real interest. Why is it that such gardens were ever built? What purpose did they serve?

The golden days of the estate came at the end of the nineteenth century, when Edward James's father William, profiting from the success of his railroad empire, ploughed in huge amounts of money to create a magnificent walled garden, enormous glasshouses and a fine kitchen garden. This was more than a decorative whim, however. West Dean was a fairly typical pre-war Edwardian country house, with a well-connected and ambitious family who entertained and circulated, and who would no doubt have commuted up and down from London in order to work and socialize. There was this peculiar British phenomenon called the London Season, which was to have a lasting effect on both the social structure of the country and, perhaps surprisingly, on the food we ate.

During the eighteenth century, country gents were usually happy to mould the landscape as much as they could in search of that ideal of a rural idyll. But come the 1800s there was a subtle change in the role of the gardener, from someone who implemented the grand designs of the master to a professional who sought a bit of independence. It was his duty to provide the household, and the weekend guests, with the most prestigious and beautiful fruit and veg. Estates gained much kudos from growing the first asparagus, or the finest grapes, and this expanded with the rise in the complexity of the glasshouse.

The most extraordinary effort was expended on growing the pineapple. It required prodigious amounts of energy and expertise, for the hothouse was never allowed to be less than 60°F so that the plants could survive the English climate. The initial growing season was during the winter, for the one aim of a successful pineapple grower was to be able to send his fruit to London in June, just as the summer season was beginning. But by the end of the First World War this way of life fell into terminal decline. Estates all over the country sank into a sorry and fast decay. The pineapple lost its social cachet after it was planted in the Azores and did so well that it began to be more widely available. By the end of the nineteenth century the nascent canning industry in Hawaii was plotting a global conquest that was eventually so effective that it is extremely hard to imagine just what a stir the pineapple once caused. So think of that the next time you plonk a pineapple ring on your gammon steak. West Dean House allows us to glimpse a way of life now long and for ever gone.

The London scene involved a constant round of entertaining and socializing. Guests would come and stay, shoot, and mingle. Gardeners would be hard pressed to supply the kitchen with its needs for the year. Sturdy pots forced sea kale in the spring, and rhubarb after that. There was a continual and repetitive cycle of fruit and vegetables that were picked and plucked by the host of gardeners. Much thought went into the varieties that were grown. Each part of the country had yet to homogenize its apple varieties, so odd pockets of ancient trees flourished all over the land.

It became a fundamental part of entertaining among the elite to be able to offer the best food in as unfussy a way as possible. This contrasted explicitly with the popular conception of French food, which was its very antithesis. French food was transformed food. Haute cuisine created dishes of great complexity. It was an expression of the mastery of man over the raw material, and reflected a tendency of the French aristocracy to be somewhat dismissive of the *noblesse campagnarde*. The British took a different route. After years of toying and teasing with the idea of imitating the French, it finally returned to a more earthy style of cooking, where the excellence was in the raw material rather than the skill of the chef. It is still one of the perceived characteristics of British food. This was also encouraged by a change in the way food was presented. With the arrival of what was called *service à la russe*, the display of fruit became an integral part of the dinner. Courses were served one after the other, rather than being laid directly on the table for the guests to serve themselves, which in essence was what happened with *service à la française*, which preceded it.

All this slotted in perfectly with a desire for plainly roasted meats, and with the British habit of offering vegetables to be eaten with the meat course, again different from the French, where they were eaten afterwards as *entremets*. It was the expression that for the British a meal is only really a meal when it is some form of our beloved meat and two veg. We really *are* a conservative lot.

15

HOOK NORTON

Ale

IF THE PERCEPTION OF THE BRITISH AND THEIR FOOD IS INTIMATELY involved with plates of sizzling meat and boiled vegetables, then we also have to try to nibble away at their equally passionate fondness for drink. Particularly beer. So I decided to don my woolly sweater and enter the mindset of an everyday pub drinker. Slightly lost on the edges of the Cotswolds in a time-warped valley at Hook Norton is one of the country's last remaining independent breweries, where I spent a day immersing myself in the everyday story of country brewing folk.

Stewart Maine exudes an infectious nervous energy. His Scottish veins are bursting with passion, for brewing, for beer, for malt, for barley even. But it's not really that woolly-jumper, bar-propping enthusiasm that beer can sometimes engender, but a deeper, almost manic passion, a respect for perfection, and a joy I think that at last, at the end of a long and distinguished career, he might just have found his own private nirvana. So off I respectfully trotted alongside him while he transmitted this enthusiasm with proper evangelical zeal, dutifully acknowledging everyone's 'Good morning, Stewart'.

Inside the brewery, you really are engulfed by otherworldliness. Almost the first thing you see is the muscular iron steam engine that has pumped and powered the brewery since it was built in 1895. It is quite extraordinary. This twenty-five-horsepower cast-iron machine still provides the energy for the business of brewing. It is the heart if not the soul of the brewery, a beautiful Victorian masterpiece that throbs, hisses and agitates the air.

Record-keeping at the brewery has been meticulous. Every single brew that has ever been made can be looked at, analysed, and repeated if necessary. Handwritten records are to be found neatly scribbled in the rows of stout, musty notebooks that line the shelves of the master brewer's offices, full of secret recipes, of the blends of malts, and gloriously named hops – Fuggles English and Champion, to name but two. These records satisfy more than just a curious interest: they are actively used to recreate beers and ales that worked long ago, and in some cases even to create 'new' brews, to add to a constantly changing list of seasonal beers.

'It's like a dream come true, working here,' Stewart told me, a glint in his Caledonian eyes. Being a complete beer dunce, I listened to the story unfolding. How the brewery grew, and survived. There were awkward moments.

It really starts with malt, or more properly malted barley. I had always thought of malt as a sticky brown gooey liquid. The reality is somewhat different. Rather than goo, I was shown sack upon sack of delightful tumbling golden grains of malted barley – infinitely more appealing it has to be said. Malt comes in sacks, not tubs, and is dried, semi-toasted grain – barley in this case, as it is for most beers, although the Belgians have apparently always been rather adept at malting wheat. They are rather good at waffles too. We all have our talents.

Under the very eaves of the brewery, to the constant whooshing of liquids and the unhurried thumping of the steam engine way below, Stewart initiated me into the wonderful world of malt.

'Here, try this one.'

I nibbled on the grain, trying not to break my fragile teeth, and struggled to find a word that encompassed both its sweetness and its nutty mysteries.

'It's quite sweet and nutty, you'll find,' he said.

'Wow, you're right. It's amazing. Sort of sweet and nutty.'

'Now try this one.'

And I did. It tasted distinctly of chocolate.

'What does that suggest to you?'

'Chocolate?'

'Yes, that's right.'

I had passed. Stewart turned the label of the jar that held the grains; thankfully, it was labelled CHOCOLATE.

There are many varieties of malt, and it's all in the mix. This is a crucial variable that gives the brew its character. New and old types can be combined in almost infinite ways, and a master brewer can vary the recipe according to the beer he is making. Chocolatey malt gives a darker brew, lighter malt a pale brew – hence pale ale.

First stop for the malt is the grist mill, another ancient piece of equipment at Hook Norton, yet more solid Victorian engineering. This mill has been in continual use since 1899, and has crushed millions upon millions of grains of barley in its time. The malt is then soaked in what brewers call liquor. We call it water. Whether brewers go home and fill the bath with hot liquor remains a secret. They are a secretive lot. But water is a vital ingredient, its purity being essential for a really classy brew, and here at Hook Norton the brewery has been handily and quite deliberately built on an old spring.

This mush of malt and water is then left to soak in a masher before being passed into what are called mash tuns where it is left for a couple of hours. As you would expect, the tuns are massive and ancient too. Well, one mash tun is. There is another which is just massive, a modern upstart that is pragmatically accepted as an improvement. They are well aware at the brewery that progress isn't entirely a dirty word, and have been adept at keeping what is best of the old ways without turning their backs on the new. In the tuns, the magic really begins. With the grains crushed and properly soaked, the water activates the enzymes in the malt, which turn the starch into sugar. Which is the basis for fermentation, and the arrival of the marvellous, stupefying, mysterious substance we know as alcohol.

But we're not quite there yet, for this odd mix, sweet to the taste, has as sweet a name: wort, a delightful, little-used, rosy-cheeked word, one of many that dart in and out of the story. The wort is left to suppurate for a couple of hours, busily releasing its sugar, and is then run off into the vast coppers below, where hops are added, again in distinct and specific combinations, to give the beer its characteristic bitterness. But let's reflect a little on the wort, and its easy sweetness, for this was the basis of the drink that resonates of the days of earthy floors and taverns, of ale indeed, for this is exactly what ale once was: hopless beer, a drink we all would have known, one that even children once drank with unashamed regularity from the Middle Ages right up until the seventeenth century. Water then was often notoriously impure, and this ale was mostly a light-headed brew.

The wort is heated, more fiercely now as the hops are added, to release their essential oils, then cooled, once more thanks to the energy from the steam engine that powers the pumps that drive the liquid up to the cooling towers at the top of the brewery. Then it's on to the final stage, fermentation. Yet more secretiveness here, for this is when the yeast is added. Every brewer guards his yeast jealously, for it is a complex thing. And it isn't just paranoia at work here, for in order to make a consistent brew the yeast must be nurtured and kept alive. It seeps into the very walls. Indeed, Stewart was quite adamant that this was actually one of his biggest headaches.

'What keeps you awake at night, Stewart?' I asked.

'Well, nothing really, to be honest. Except the yeast. If it fails it's an absolute disaster, and it can happen.'

Poor thing. Yeasty nightmares, of bubbling vats and screaming brewsters. Sounds horrible.

He invited me to inhale a little of the fermenting brew. The froth was spilling over the edges and bubbling gently like a Jekyllian potion, but there was a vicious chemical kick to it; the gas produced during the process is quite natural. We poked it with a thing that had a special name – we would call it a stick, or a poker – and bubbles rose to the surface. I nearly passed out.

The beer, for we can call it that by this stage, is left for at least seven days to brew. It may sound simple, but it calls for much skill in its perfection. Hook Norton produce what are called cask beers.

'Um, Stewart? Forgive me. I know this might seem odd to you, but can you tell me what exactly is the difference between cask and keg beers?'

I had to ask this. We had been joined by the young MD by now, James Clarke, a descendant of the brewery's founding father, Edward Clarke. He had come to sit in on the discussion, a paean to the joys of cask beer.

'A keg is used to create a more standardized product. It really is much easier to handle. Basically, when the beer is brewed, it is passed into a keg and cooled. Fermentation stops. The beer just stays as it is. It was very popular in the sixties. Remember the Watney's Pale Ale sort of beer? Well, that was a classic keg beer. Good, but rather boring. No depth to it at all.' Mild scoffing?

Indeed I did remember the Watney's brew, a popular beer from a brewing giant in whose shadow Hook Norton was but a gallant minnow. My dad used to buy the stuff. He'd appear with a great fat can, pierce its lid with a sharp triangular bottle opener, and attach some mini tap to its top. We, as teenagers, were allowed the odd glass when we wanted. Especially if we cut the lawn. I couldn't honestly say I liked it. In fact I thought it was quite nasty. I had always loathed that gagging smell of giant breweries we passed by, I can't quite remember where, on our travels.

The Hook Norton story was very heartening in a way. A family tries hard to survive in the face of nasty old brutal capitalism, devotes itself to quality, and actually succeeds. We all puffed and preened a little at the happy reality. But it has to depend on more than just happenstance. The drink, the beer itself, the end product of all this froth and fermentation, has to be good. It was time to taste.

So, off we went to their own mini pub in the old malt-house, to be greeted by the resident barman who plays the part with real skill. Blazer. Bonhomie. *Really* funny jokes. And a dedication to the loveliness of the beer. During a gradual revelation, and a convenient one at that, I began to see the light. I actually began to quite like this drink, bitter. I no longer felt the need to retch and gag. This mellow, almost floral brew – their Best bitter it was, a prize-winning beer – flowed down my gullet with ease. I listened to their commentary.

'It's doing well, isn't it?'

'Yup. Coming along really nicely. I noticed it yesterday. Really pleasant drinking.'

There was none of that 'hint of blackberries' and 'essence of road surface' nonsense you get at wine tastings, simply a genuine appreciation of the experience, the sensation of drinking something of which they were justly proud. The brew had successfully reached its adolescence, and was just 'doing well'. I liked that. All I needed now was a pub, and a depressing landlord. And that was within easy reach. I set off back home, to my village pub to try out my newfound love of bitter.

The tradition of drinking beer in a poorly lit, smoky pub goes way back into the swirling medieval mists. Pubs have gently evolved from a now defunct prototype called the alehouse, a modest, simply furnished place that would go down a storm these days with its wooden benches and sawdust floor. The brew was made on site, but had never seen a hop so had none of that intestinal bitterness we seem to love in our finest bitters. It was called ale. Closely related, as I said, to the wort we tasted at Hook Norton. Ale, not beer, is our ancestral brew. It was a lightly fermented drink produced as part of a householder's weekly domestic duties. In other words, it was mostly women who brewed. In medieval Britain ale provided everyday nourishment for one and all – 'the warmest lining of a naked man's coat' wrote the Elizabethan poet John Taylor.

Since ale was a more fragile and easily spoiled drink, the alewife, or brewster, needed to tell the world when fresh brew was available, and this she did by pulling a small bush or even a bunch of barley up the end of a wooden pole for all to see. Which was called an alestake. Now alehouses, and their descendants inns, taverns and much later pubs, also needed a way of distinguishing themselves, and began to use a more elaborate version of the alestake, one that blew high in the wind, again for all to see. Some of the alehouses began to take on a name to distinguish themselves from one another. Back in my village in Oxfordshire, there's the Plough – there is still agricultural land around here after all. And the Thatched Tavern, which does at least have a thatched roof. But it calls itself a tavern. Not an inn, nor a public house, but a tavern. (Records show that the term 'pub', from 'public house', is actually a nineteenth-century innovation.) Further on there's the Eight Bells, simple again really, for it is within easy earshot of the local church and its eight-bell peal.

But if we venture, God forbid, into the adjacent villages, the names become more enigmatic. There is, for example, the Bear and Ragged Staff, in Cumnor. There is someone very close to me who thinks it was called thus because the people who worked there were particularly scruffy. Not true, alas. This pub lies on land that was once owned by the Earl of Warwick whose original ancestor – we're talking Arthurian legend here by the way – was said to have been so powerful that he wrestled a bear to the ground, an everyday Arthurian occupation. And the staff? Well, a few generations later, another Earl of Warwick, Morvidius, showed courage and great skill by slaying a giant with a wooden rod, his staff. They were a pugnacious lot in days of yore. This pub is said to have its very own ghost. One of the barmaids told me of a room upstairs, a cold and strange place where the dog never enters, but whimpers and scurries on downstairs. The gents is on the ground floor.

While trawling through endless tracts about pub signs, I read – spinetingling this – about the woeful story of Amy Robsart and the village pond that never froze. On the day I spent engrossed in the awful story, with the ghastly screams of the unfortunate Amy practically ringing in my ears, it was deeply and bitterly cold. Oxford was sublime, its gothic towers dusted in snow. On the way home, in the midst of a blizzard, I drove past the village pond that never froze. It was frozen solid. And it turned out that it wasn't actually the pub that was haunted at all but nearby Cumnor Place, where in 1560 Robert Dudley the Earl of Leicester's lawful wedded wife 'fell', or was pushed as legend would have it, down the stairs to free him for a possible marriage to Good Queen Elizabeth. In the end it was not to be. Nevertheless, the staircase where Amy fell was said to have been so haunted that the house fell into disrepair, collapsing under the weight of its spooky past, and despite a well-recorded exorcism during which nine priests were said to have committed the evil spirit into the village pond, the ghost seems to have moved on to the local pub. Wise too. The food there is the best around.

Tavern names even became family names, evidence that the habit of hanging around drinking has for long been one of the nation's most treasured occupations. In London in particular, anyone called Edward who hung around a tavern called the Cock would in all likelihood have been known as Edward atte Cock, which became Attcock.

But brewing ale was not destined to remain a merely domestic affair. Although the homely old brewer began to move with the speed of a medieval capitalist to towns and villages, she was to be outmanoeuvred. Hers was an amateurish business largely untroubled by any need for great expense, other than a mash tun and a supply of water. Most of the ale was drunk on the premises. True, the poor tended to arrive with a bucket to be filled with ale, but the natural tendency was to linger, to drink, to gossip and chat. Sounds familiar? The alehouse was indeed a rough and ready embryonic version of the pub. But the problem was that the ale wasn't always that good, which proved to be its downfall, as the Elizabethan poet Andrew Boorde so graphically tells us:

> Ich I am a Cornish man, and ale I can brew
> It will make one to cacke also to spew
> It is thick and smokey and also it is thin
> It is like wash of pigs had wrestled therein.

Back in 1347, when one of our more belligerent warrior kings, Edward III, was battling to keep the French enclave of Calais as an English fiefdom, the business of supplying the marooned garrison town with home-brewed ale became simply too challenging. So the authorities turned to Flemish beer brewers instead. There was at that time a relatively sophisticated brewing industry in northern Europe, but this brew was different. They used hops, and made what we now call beer. The hop was not entirely unknown in Britain. The Romans, ever imaginative, called it *Lupus salictarius*, believing that a hop plant would cause havoc among a crop of willows, like a wolf among sheep. But it was only in the early sixteenth century, when immigrants from northern Europe, Flemings and Alemaines (Germans) mostly, settled in London and began brewing their way, that our long love affair with beer started. Some of them moved up to East Anglia where barley was in good supply, and thrived. Originally the new drink wasn't much liked – we always were conservative in our approach to food and drink – but it soon became apparent that beer had far better keeping qualities than ale, and was a far more profitable brew. In 1574, Reynolde Scott published his design for a 'perfitte plateforme of a hoppe garden to encourage the English to grow hoppes successfully', and the voracious plant began to be more widely cultivated. The willows pulled through.

Now, it may strike you as a touch ironic that the very soul of our drinking culture wasn't actually British in origin at all. But, rest assured that it wasn't long before it slipped into the collective unconscious, and beer became subsumed into our very own cultural baggage.

With the arrival of beer, the alehouse began to morph into the tavern, and the alewife's days were numbered. Learned books were written telling of the art and mystery of brewing, and the alewife eventually became redundant. Not entirely forgotten, however, for she also became the butt of endless jokes, the object of ancestral mirth. Untrustworthy, dirty and pitiable. This unflattering ditty was penned in the sixteenth century and describes the then renowned alewife Elinour Rumming of Leatherhead:

Droopy and drowsy
Scurvy and lousy
Her face all bowsy
Comely crinkled
Wondrously wrinkled
Like a roast pigs ear
Bristled with hair.

Taverns retained a bawdier, looser approach to drinking that the alehouse had created. They were for drinking and wenching, particularly when the serving staff played the game of titillating the customer. Much of this may sound familiar. There was eating too. The choice was stark, but it tended to be cheaper than the local inn, a classier place altogether. At times, poorer customers might even bring their own food to be cooked on the premises – some roadkill perhaps, or something that had fallen off the back of a stagecoach.

In 1577, government figures calculated that there were approximately 17,000 drinking establishments in the thirty counties of England alone. Small houses and a lousy domestic life have always pushed men out of the home, and they fell into taverns quite happily. Apprentices and journeymen who were learning a trade and getting paid very little for it, and single men who liked to drink and liked to get drunk, learned that drink could be had on spec, and that the landlord often knew where work could be found. The taverns that did well often had whores as well as buxom serving wenches to whet the hormonal young appetites, and drew on the vast ravenous population that loved the excitement of the cities, London in particular.

Inns tended to be strategically placed on highways and the main routes between cities, in university towns and in all big commercial centres. They were often used as staging posts, and were a vital part of the intricate business of travel around a fast-growing country that from Elizabethan times was rapidly urbanizing. Inns had stables, rooms and a range of drinks from ale to brandy, and by the Hanoverian period began to be significantly smarter still, with ticking clocks, carpets and uniformed waiters. They flourished during the Restoration when a protean network of roads and highways developed countrywide. Inns could provide both stables and some stability for the traveller, often highly vulnerable away from home to the unknown and, in truly Rumsfeldian ways, the unknown unknowns. Many of those thick-walled British town hotels with a clear entrance to the side for the stabling of horses were almost certainly once inns. And, as a halfway point between town and country, and between professionals and their clients in all senses of the word, the inn became one of the preferred locations for striking deals and doing business.

Inevitably, there was the problem of drunkenness to deal with. Public drunkenness, that is, that offended the religious and the upright, the lawmakers and the pure at heart. Not that any government was fool enough to try and stamp out drinking altogether. The tax revenues were far too significant for that. In 1625 in *Healthe's Sicknesse*, William Prynne reflected a growing concern with the work, as he thought, of the Devil, the Prince of the Air: 'Of all the gross and crying sins which have of late . . . overspread our nation . . . there are few more common, few more dangerous, hurtful and pernicious than the unnatural, unthrifty, odious and swinish sin of drunkenness.'

Despite Parliament passing four Acts relating to drink, things didn't improve in the seventeenth century. The Dutch were blamed. The Devil was blamed. Papists and Catholics too. With a touch of irony, one of the lasting results of the Puritan revolution was that churches no longer allowed games and festivals to be held in their grounds, which helped taverns flourish, and fostered throughout the country the rise of bar games such as shove-halfpenny, guile bones, noddy boards and bowls.

The Church did, however, hold sway with its profoundest

belief, that the Sabbath was to be a day of reflection and worship, a day wholly unsuited to drink and pleasure. Thus, a typical urban Sunday in eighteenth-century London was full of people wandering around with little to do; there's a marvellous description, 'London's Low Life', penned by Ned Ward in 1748, of the cold-hearted city one typical Sunday, with scenes of squalor and depredation on a drinkless Sabbath. It was also, in an era when liberty was shockingly fragile, the one day of the week when it was not permitted to arrest people for debt. Before 1725, anyone could be arrested for debts of a few pennies. In the late eighteenth century, apprentices could be sent to the prison at Bridewell simply for not appearing for work. Tallymen and debt collectors hung around the pubs feeding off local contacts, lying in wait for the indebted victim. And in prison, what would there be but a tavern, and a chance to drown your sorrows once more in beer, and to amass even more debt? In a bizarre reversal of the norm, there was even one pub, the White Lyon in Southwark, which had a prison inside it.

The modern-day pub has evolved from all this. So if you wonder why so many of us like to go out on a Friday or Saturday night and get completely out of our heads, it really is nothing new, nothing radical. In fact it is, I believe, a solid reflection of our Anglo-Saxon roots, as I would find out in the Norfolk village of West Stow. Unravelling beer-drinking's origins doesn't necessarily tell us why, but at least we can see the wherefore. Binge-drinking – please note, purveyors of populist politics – has long been around.

16

GREENWICH

Whitebait, Eel, and Pie and Mash

ONE DAY I DECIDED TO VISIT AN OLD THAMESSIDE TAVERN, TO EAT a fish that never existed. *Clupea alba* was its name, and it drew from scientists much umming and ahhing. It is also known as something infinitely more palatable – whitebait, even though it is silver rather than white, and was not used as bait for very long. It simply became too valuable.

In Britain, whitebait are tiny fish that are traditionally fried, served with a squeeze of lemon and a pinch of Cayenne pepper, and eaten whole, eyes, brains and all. It is a rare dish in that the English are not remotely squeamish about eating them, and have relished this riverine delicacy for hundreds of years. Cooking them was easy. Fished directly from the Thames, they were brought to the kitchens of the riverside inns and taverns, soaked, washed, and then coated with fine white flour and fried in lard in huge copper cauldrons. A multitude of taverns and inns along the Thames riverbank offered sizzling platefuls to one and all. The fish were freshly caught and cooked under the very noses of the travelling gourmets who flocked to Greenwich to make a real day of it and eat a whitebait dinner. One Thomas Pennant rather haughtily described the scene in 1776: 'During the month of July there appear in the Thames, near Blackwall and Greenwich, innumerable multitudes of small fish, which are known to the Londoners by the name of White Bait. They are esteemed very delicious when fried with fine flour, and occasion, during the season, a vast resort of the lower order of epicures to the taverns contiguous to the places they are taken at.'

How we would all worship at the temple of whitebait these days. An entirely local and seasonal fishery that enticed Londoners – yes, even lower-order epicures – into sitting down and eating freshly caught fish. They were cooked with infinite care, for there was, it seems, some pretty fierce competition between the riverside taverns, each of which tried to outdo the other to serve the very best. Some Londoners preferred the Artichoke Inn at Blackwall, others Mr Lovegrove's in West India Docks. In Greenwich there was the Trafalgar, the Ship, and the Crown and Sceptre, all vying for business. People took steamers downstream from Westminster and dressed up for the occasion.

The problem was this. By the end of the eighteenth century, whitebait were becoming rather too popular. Inevitably with such high demand, fishermen were tempted to profit from what was a pretty easy and lucrative fishery. All that was needed was a boat, some oars and a small net, habitually a fine-mesh trap with its mouth kept open by small wooden beams. By the early nineteenth century there were over sixty fishermen working from Greenwich alone, but the other Thames fisheries were suffering. Sprats and flatfish became scarcer, and the situation was not helped when in 1812 the government decided to hold its celebratory end-of-Parliament dinner on the river and served crisp fried whitebait in immaculate white linen napkins. Thus began a long association of a non-existent fish with politicians.

Inevitably, whitebait dinners became even more popular and fishermen continued to grumble. The water bailiff and a deputation of Thames fishermen petitioned the Lord Mayor to impose tighter controls. The smelt fishery had been wiped out, they complained, and shad and flounder were hard to come by. The whitebait fishery needed to be closed. But the whitebait fishermen had a brilliant riposte. These were not juvenile fish at all, they argued, but fully grown fish of an entirely separate and distinct species, as yet to be named. William Yarrell, an expert on the Thames and the author of a history of British fishes, agreed with them and suggested that the fish, which everyone could see was remarkably similar to the herring, *Clupea harengus*, should be given the scientific name *Clupea alba*, or white clupeid.

For a while the whitebait fishermen carried on as usual, on the assumption that they could never be accused of fishing juvenile fish, for this was a separate diminutive species. When zoologist Achille Valenciennes and anatomist Georges Cuvier published their groundbreaking *Histoire Naturelle des Poissons* in 1849, it was clear that they too had been duped by the *Clupea alba* story. Indeed, they decided that the genus was so special it should have its very own name. So *Clupea alba* briefly became *Rogenia alba*, and whitebait was still to all intents and purposes just a small fish.

However, other fishermen were quick to point out that there was an obvious flaw in the argument. For within virtually every catch could be discerned a number of clearly distinct species that varied according to the season. It was clear that the single-species story was, to put it mildly, dubious. Eventually, science turned full circle and accepted that whitebait were in reality the fry of a number of species, primarily sprats with the odd herring, shad and roach thrown in, and by the beginning of the twentieth century this had been accepted generally. *Clupea alba*, or *Rogenia alba* for all you zoologists out there, was no more.

There aren't too many places where you can still eat fresh whitebait in London. There aren't too many whitebait left either. The only significant whitebait fishery left in the UK is downriver in Essex; most of the whitebait we eat is caught in Holland, and frozen. The British season is short and tightly controlled, and can supply but a minuscule amount of the demand. But if you steam down to Greenwich there is one solid Regency pub called the Trafalgar where you can eat whitebait on the banks of the Thames. I walked in one summer's day, accompanied by someone whose pedantry would have terrified any politician. My nine-year-old son, Sid.

Earlier that morning, after luxuriating in a giant coach from Oxford, we had crossed London and taken a driverless train from Canary Wharf to Greenwich. I looked below as we clattered over Billingsgate fish market. It was all very *Mission Impossible*. I gawped. There was the place I used to park. Oh, look, and there's the kiosk where I was arrested. The same old seagulls careering around with squashed herring dripping from their beaks. It made me go all nostalgic and gushy again. I used to drive there every day, I told Sid; that was where you'd go to buy the fish. And that was where you'd have a bacon sandwich. My life centred around a van stuffed full of fish, around chefs and fishmongers, around selling and buying the best fish available. I lived and breathed fish. I stank of it too, right to my very core, but never really noticed it. To this day I still love the smell of fish. I'd hang around fish markets all my life if only I could make it pay. The bright eyes, the surprised faces, the brilliant colours and that scintillating, vulgar, 'avin-a-larf sort of humour.

I remember the day the fish market first moved to Docklands. It was in the 1980s, and the final day of old Billingsgate, back in the heart of the city of London at Lower Thames Street, was typically tragicomic. Everyone was convinced that as soon as the electricity was turned off the ice in the deep-frozen arches below would melt and the foundations would crumble.

Billingsgate would be no more. Over in Docklands there was more than a sense of waste and desolation. It was totally moribund. But, in the spirit of modernization, everyone agreed that the fish market should join the bandwagon of progress, and get itself a car park.

There were immediately dark mutterings. The new market was just as restricted as the old. The corridors were not even wide enough to use a forklift, and had been deliberately designed, all us fish buyers thought, so that the porters and bummarees could keep their jobs. Which was fine by us. They were an eccentric bunch of villains and poets who seemed to live odd, sleepless, double lives. Many boxed. Others drove taxis. Some presumably went home and slept.

My thoughts turned to Sir Henry Mayhew. He would have been amazed at the scene. No more costermongers. Children in school. Not even any dancing bears. Mayhew loved to cruise the streets of Victorian London, accosting street sellers and market workers with endless questions. When his *London Labour and the Poor* was published in the late nineteenth century, it prompted the philanthropists and the inquisitive to thoughts of reform and education, to bring the streets under control.

London was a city that lived on the streets. Families crammed into tiny garret rooms tended to spend as little time in them as possible, and plied whatever trade came to hand. In Mayhew's day there were thousands of costermongers mooching around; these days no-one has the faintest idea what a costermonger was. Costermongering is no longer a wise career choice.

This is what they did: they sold food on the streets. Sounds simple really, but life was the inevitable constant struggle. This was Victorian England after all. The Police Act of 1850 specifically forbade them to stand still and make a sale, so they were constantly on the move, announcing their wares with hearty, loud yelling. It is hardly surprising that many of

Mayhew's informants were distinctly uneasy when being inter-
viewed. One female costermonger, he noted, found it very
difficult to know where to put her hands. Costers had their
own language, an early form of cockney rhyming slang.
Clodhoppers were coppers, or policemen. Mince pies, eyes.
Some spoke words backwards, so sey was yes, and top o'reeb
a pot of beer. All designed to outwit their deadliest enemies,
the police.

Each borough had its coster king, and however hard life
became they would all look after one another as much as
possible, by 'passing the basin' as it was called and making a
collection to keep a particular coster family in food. It was said
that no costermonger died alone. The word is thought to come
from an even more ancient street seller from medieval days
who sold costard apples before graduating to selling virtually
anything that was edible. They would buy up what were called
the stickings, scrag ends of meat, to make into meat pies, and
apparently weren't averse to using the odd dog or cat.

Costers were part of the great waves of Londoners who
used Billingsgate market – the old market in Lower Thames
Street, that is. Records show that a fish market had been
trading on the river for nearly a thousand years, so memories
were at full stretch on the last day of business. Costermongers
were allowed to buy fish only after seven a.m., once the city
fishmongers had taken the best and made their way back to set
up shop and start a good day's mongering. But they had a very
particular role to play. They bought all the stuff that no-one
was going to be able to sell. Something had to be done with
all that surplus. What they did was to buy and fry, and sell it
on the streets, which is almost certainly the origin of fish and
chips.

If costermongers went the way of all flesh, their
descendants came in droves. But, on that final day of old
Billingsgate, the future looked bleak for the Dickensian host of
dossers who hung around the green market outside and laced

their tea with whisky and brandy. They emerged from the mists each morning to help the market porters push their towering trolleys, stacked with fish and jellied eels, lobsters and mighty salmon, far up the hill. The cry of 'Up the 'ill, up the 'ill!' brought wiry, bristly men running to help push trolleys up towards the Monument, or along the river to Young Tommy's stand – a man of great age by the way – where my fish van was parked. And for their trouble they were given a bit of money, or a drink.

Every morning, Lower Thames Street would be half closed as the fish market breathed and shone in the dark London night. A blast of manic energy would hit you slap bang in the old mince pies as you walked in to see the stands alive with bright-eyed fish, some piled into wooden boxes, others in cardboard that would split and disgorge its contents in minutes. Then along came polystyrene and all was well for a while. They just collapsed.

When I traded in the market, a few of the porters were still called bummarees. Not many of us had any idea why. Nor did they in Mayhew's day: 'I asked several parties as to the origin of the word "bummaree", and how long it had been in use. "Why, bless your soul, sir," said one Billingsgate labourer, "there always was bummarees, and there always will be; just as Jack there is a 'rough', and I'm a blessed 'bobber'." One man assured me it was a French name; another that it was Dutch. A fishmonger, to whom I was indebted for inform-ation, told me he thought that the bummaree was originally a bum-boat man, who purchased of the wind-bound smacks at Gravesend or the Nore, and sent the fish up rapidly to the market by land.' These days it is thought the word comes from the French *bonne marée*, or good fish, which in anglicized form could just work.

The bummarees were the ones who bought and sold from the merchants and would then sell these aquatic odds and sods to the costermongers. With a slap of the palm, a deal would be struck and the costermonger would take the fish back to be battered and fried and sold on the streets of London. By the time the old market moved bummarees were still around, but few and far between. But the merchants still needed to shift their fragile stock as soon as they could, so the market began to welcome immigrant families, West Indians, Chinese, Bangladeshis and Sri Lankans, who struck a quick cash deal when all the main buyers had long gone. It is they who have replaced the costermongers.

London's Dockland had basically died a long and rather agonizing death, so moving the fish market there was thought to be an excellent idea at the time. The docks had simply become too small and impractical for trade, and container ships were too big to manoeuvre into the narrow wharves and ancient quays. Something needed to be done to the aquatic wastes of a dead city. The river had lost its meaning. Polluted and filthy, the old docks were filling up with shopping trolleys and dead dogs.

Sid asked why it was called Canary Wharf. 'Is it because there were lots of canaries flying around?'

I started a no-son-it's-because-London-was-once-a-thriving-port-which-traded-with-all-corners-of-the-globe speech. 'It's all offices now,' I concluded.

'It can't all be offices,' he said. 'I can see some restaurants over there.'

'It is, just look.'

'What do they do all day long then?'

'I don't know. Work, I suppose.'

But whatever the exact number of offices, there was at least life down there. There were restaurants, and they were heaving. The driverless trains were heaving. Canary Wharf lives on.

We got out at Greenwich and set off for a day of discovery and delight. It was time for another fatherly talk. Listen, son, there are one or two things you should experience in life, but before you do, listen to me. I had long felt that he was ready for a culinary *rite de passage* of real significance, his first plate of pie, mash and liquor. Maybe he was still too innocent for a jellied eel. We walked into Goddard's Pie Shop and did the deed.

'Pie, mash and liquor for him, please. And I'll have the jellied eels.'

Goddard's is a long-established pie and mash shop, a marvellous London institution that evolved from the days of costermongering and selling pies on the streets. Originally pies were highly complex creations that were baked in a pastry case that wasn't always eaten. Over time they became more down-market, and were filled with the bits and pieces of meat left over from the great chunks of roast meat served in cookshops. Thus the meat pie was born.

Pie shops are profoundly Dickensian, and Goddard's is no exception. They have a very specific look to them. Pies are stacked in the windows, both meat and fruit, baked on the premises and served quickly and cheerily from the counter at the back, the latter drowned in tumults of custard. You sit at a long marble table and take your plate with you. No waiters. No elaboration. They have their regulars. There are the sad characters with pinched, drawn faces, the smarter suited regulars, and here in Greenwich the experimenters. We were among them. Next to us sat a French couple, clearly enjoying it all, lapping up the strange, anomalous pie shop.

Here at last, I felt, was a significant nugget of our culinary past that hadn't died the death. The pie is a very moveable feast. In Kent you might have found a conger eel or oyster pie. In Leicester a homely apple pie, or a fine raised pork pie. In Somerset there were mutton pies, and in the north of England, in the Lake District, the precious freshwater char was used. Steak and ale, and beef of course, fallout from the delectable sizzling joints of the finest British beef, were also put to good use. Dirt cheap, copious and sublime was the food at Goddard's, and, well, if even a French couple had made their way here then the pie shop has a chance of pulling through the culinary Darwinian process that has deprived us of so much. Yet liquor, a thickened sauce of flour, stock and parsley (exact ingredients secret), was once a natural accompaniment to eel, and there is surely significance in the fact that what originally adorned an eel pie is now sploshed onto a meat pie. The eel, semi-monstrous to the average British eye, has travelled to the land of the inedible. That old squeamishness again.

Eel, pie and mash shops are so Londonish it almost makes you want to say, 'Cor love a duck, me old cockney sparr'er.' The eel might have lost out to the meat pie, but it wasn't always so. Before the Thames was gifted with locks and pollution, eels swam up and down river playing out the extraordinary drama of this most bizarre of life cycles. They are what are called catadramous fish – fish, that is, that live most of their lives in fresh water but reproduce thousands of miles away in the sea. And not just in any old sea water, but for some incomprehensible reason in one of the most obscure of all the seas on the planet: the Sargasso.

Come the spring, the eel fare began. This was what river people called the annual migration of elvers upstream, the fish that had made it back to the river, oozing forward in unimaginably colossal numbers. In 1832 a scientist worked out that there were about one and a half million eels passing a fixed point per day at the height of the eel fare. Accounts record wave upon wave of these minuscule, almost transparent fish dealing with the newly constructed lock at Teddington in the only way they knew how – by sheer weight of eels. The first cohorts covered the wooden lock gates with their bodies in the vain attempt to swim upstream, and even if they never made it their desiccated corpses helped the later arrivals at this mass self-sacrifice. Even though they died to save the others, there is as yet no religion created in their name.

But it was the downstream migration of adult eels that provided the richest bounty. Wicker buck nets were set in their path in the late autumn, but the locks and pollution quickly put paid to the Thames eel fishery, and by the mid-nineteenth century alternative sources had to be found. For eels had already entered into the culinary consciousness of the English, and were there to stay. The answer was provided by the Dutch, who began to send over eel *schuyts* that were fitted with wells to keep these Dutch eels alive in transit. They moored off Billingsgate, and were allowed to sell to market traders, relying only on the watermen to deliver the eels to the customer, and vice versa.

Some costers specialized in hot eel, sold covered with a thick, floury parsley sauce – the origins of 'liquor' – and it wasn't long before this estimable London speciality was taken off the streets into the first eel and pie shops. It seems that the first was opened at Highbury Sluice, and another at Twickenham Ayte, which soon became known, as it still is, as Eel Pie Island. By 1860 there were over twenty eel pie houses in the London area. Meanwhile, the original pie shop at Highbury decided to smarten up its act, for it had a reputation for being rather insalubrious. Dog fights and rat killing were banned, and it changed its name to the Highbury Sluice House Tavern, famous not only for its eel pies but for its gardens and concerts, and its 'people's platform', where you could dance genteelly in the evening air.

Pie shops sprang up all over the outskirts of London, particularly in the costering cockney heartland to the east. The business is peculiar in that it has long been dominated by a few families, the Cookes, the Manzes and the Kellys, who have kept the eel and pie shops little changed over the years. They are still almost all run as family businesses.

The street piemen began to have a hard time. A tradition of tossing (not off) the pieman was begun possibly to boost flagging sales. The idea was this: you tossed a penny, and if you won the call the pie was yours for free; if you didn't, you lost the penny. But thankfully there were no piemen to toss as Sid and I left Goddard's.

'That pie was *lush*, Dad!' said Sid.

'So you'd go there again, would you?'

'Well, yeah, if I can have some custard and crumble next time.'

We walked down to the river, ogled at the *Cutty Sark*, took in the Maritime Museum, and walked up the hill to wrestle with the problems of longitude. Of all the tricky matters that I have tried paternally to explain clearly, this one really took the biscuit.

'Why', Sid asked me, 'does time begin at Greenwich?'

It was a hugely complex question, and I was struggling. I thought the best way was to look at it through the remarkable case of the Powder of Sympathy. Somewhere tucked into the displays and the gorgeous complexity of John Harrison's chronometers is this little model of a man stabbing a dog. It seems a little weird to say the least, but it was apparently a firmly held belief that if you applied the powder to a weapon and stabbed a dog at exactly midday in Greenwich, then took the dog with you on your travels, it would yelp at exactly the same time as the initial stabbing if someone rubbed a little of the powder at noon in Greenwich. Pain by sympathy, in other words. You could then easily work out just by looking at the position of the sun above you where on earth you were. Despite the work of many a learned physician, the idea somehow failed to prove effective.

By the time we had grappled with all this, the day had slipped by, and we walked back down to the river, to the Trafalgar, and our very own sizzling plateful of the fish that didn't exist.

SPITALFIELDS

Offal

I LOOKED THROUGH THE WINDOW OF ST JOHN — SLIGHTLY BLEAK
and white-walled, but buzzing — to see if there was a space I
could squeeze into. I was greeted professionally, smiled at, and
gently guided to a table from which I could see the bustle of
the kitchen, and the piles of loaves, flour-dusted, freshly baked
and voluptuous, sitting quietly on a counter, exuding that scent
of divine breadyness.

St John has a special place in the hearts of urban
gastronomes. It has slashed a magnificent trail through our
notorious reluctance to eat offal. The bits, that is, that literally
fall off the carcass, one's attitude to which has more to do with
psychology than taste. In a society that has historically held the
consumption of meat and two veg to be the ultimate in
achievement, offal was often thought of as simply too awful to
eat, food for the poor, not the sort of thing to be seen to dine
upon unless in the direst of straits. But with truly poetic
justice, all this is changing. Eating cheek is now chic. Fergus

Henderson, the culinary brains behind the restaurant, has been fêted by food connoisseurs in the UK and the US, largely encouraged by the bonhomie and enthusiasm of Anthony Bourdain – who, you will remember, was the man who jettisoned the glamour and told us all about the seedy life of the restaurant world, the drugs and the sleaze that is.

And sleaze there was aplenty, believe me. Perhaps there is less now than when I was plying my trade as a fish seller, but I suspect it still lurks. Once, not long ago, the brown envelope was king. You would have found it hard to supply many of the hotels in London without a generous wodge of dosh stuffed into a manila filla and delivered lovingly every Saturday. Everyone knew what was going on. Even the backdoor man at the House of Commons was 'bunged' – allegedly, that is. They were all at it. The fish supplier, the veg man and the butcher. Quite a handy extra income for the needy chef.

And drugs were everywhere. I was arrested once on suspicion of hiding cocaine inside a tuna fish, and I spent the night in the cells. (I hadn't, by the way.) Chefs can get hugely pumped up during service and need an hour or two to wind down. Victims are not hard to find. There was, for instance, the sad case of Gordon Ramsay's sous chef who died during a post-shift binge. It was a tragic waste of raw talent.

Where you rarely found such dodgy behaviour – illegal dodgy, that is – was among the band of passionate self-taught chefs who ran their own businesses, where margins were so tight that extra costs were almost suicidal, and a bung meant almost inevitably that you simply paid more for your food. Fergus Henderson is a gentleman among this band of chefs, and has survived partly due to his love of offal. It is often cheaper to buy than meat, you see, and is a canny business wheeze as well as a clear indication of style. It fits with St John's minimalist decor. Offal is rough and unrefined, and to the surprise of many, St John sails blissfully on its own course to eternity and fame.

There are now two St Johns: one, the original, just to the north of Smithfield, London's hugely ancient meat market; the other, the one into which I had just stepped, juts out opposite Spitalfields, a curious and almost indecently fascinating part of the city that seemed to me as perfect a location as you could think of for an offal fan. Welcome, then, to St John Bread and Wine.

Its reputation for roasting squirrel and serving pigs' tails has in a way gone before it, for the restaurant is actually an awful lot more than that. As I perused the menu I felt a streak of Ebenezer Scrooge growing within me, and being a passionate allotment holder I did baulk a little at paying £3.50 for a plate of fresh peas in the pod, although to the deprived a plate of fresh, succulent peas really is a gastronomic high. I would have gladly paid to eat some wild rabbit, something I strongly approve of. You cannot imagine the depths my misery reaches when I cycle down to the allotment and see that those brainless furry little things have without reason or apology slaughtered my lovingly nurtured *cimo di rape*, or my glorious purple beans. It's enough to push you over the edge.

But I was drawn by the brawn. A foul concoction in the wrong hands, but a wonderful dish in the right, light hands. Brawn uses the bits and pieces that are naturally rich in gelatin, often a pig's head, and is an ancient dish. At St John it was served in the classic British manner with pickled red cabbage – or, as they spelled it, red cabbadge. This fine vegetable goes well with all things offaly, and was traditionally eaten in the north with many of their finest dishes – tripe for one, a dish I still have never once seen on a restaurant menu anywhere in Britain (even in Lancashire).

Offal is often greeted with disgust. While in France, Italy and Spain its transformation is almost an art form, we are still hampered by the solid meat-and-two-veg syndrome. M2VS, I think I will christen it. Secondly, offal smacks of poverty in Britain, so part of the problem may well lie in the social importance of being seen to be able to afford a choice cut of roast meat for Sunday dinner. It was the desired goal of a successful family. In one account, I read of an Edwardian family in south London sitting down to lunch and clicking their knives and forks loudly on empty plates so that the neighbours wouldn't suspect their dire straits. Kidneys were acceptable food only in the form of a steak and kidney pie or pudding. Sausages and pies might be able to play the M2VS role in the week, but never ever on a Sunday. Our natural dislike for offal once again expresses the distance we have established between food and how it relates to living things, to both plants and animals. But food fashions move on, and it is this, if anything, that will resuscitate our love of offal. Nothing else will.

While I was marvelling at all the studied simplicity, the waitress came up and said in a delightful Gallic brogue, 'We 'ave some veree nice sea bass today cooked whole for sirty-eight pounds if you want.'

I did not want. I stuck to the brawn, and gently swooned when some perfect crusty bread arrived, achingly fresh, the very thing that still eluded me in my kitchen. (I habitually blame my oven, though just in case I was the weak link I was planning a trip to Dorset to sort out the problem once and for all.) The brawn was magnificent. A gelatinous, light slice of good tasty pork, or as it is called by the ever-romantic Americans, headcheese. It is not an easy dish to cook at home. You need a pig's head first of all, which you are unlikely to find at your local butcher's, let alone any supermarket, where the British buy most of their food. Marinating the head for seven days and boiling it for three to four hours would suggest that here is yet another classic British dish that is quintessential slow food, thoroughly unsuited to modern eating culture. I wondered how many of the punters really knew what brawn was, and how many would have baulked at it if they did.

Later on that day I met up with Henderson, and talked to him about his love for offal. Are things really changing? I asked. Is our love for offal blossoming? Will we all be nibbling on marrow and aorta sandwiches before long? Henderson was revealing. 'We're still cooking the dishes we have always cooked,' he said. 'Nothing's really changed. But I like eating offal. It's the food I used to be given when I was young.'

One of his real claims to fame (and you'll notice it is not of an offaly nature) is that he proudly serves squirrel when the time is right, which is early spring.

'It makes perfect sense,' he told me. 'Here is an animal that is a pest, and is widely available. They are good to eat, so why all the fuss? Every year I get a call from one of my suppliers who sends a few squirrels down. We cook them and then put them on the menu, if they are fat enough. What I didn't realize was just how controversial it would be. It was picked up by the *Today* programme and I agreed to go on air and talk about it. The next day I started receiving some fairly worrying calls. So I called the police. They sent someone down, and he asked a few questions. Then he said, "Mr Henderson, is there any reason you can think of why you are being threatened, anything you can tell me about?"

' "Well, I have been cooking squirrels."

' "Squirrels, sir, did you say? Ah."

'He gave me the strangest look, and that was that. Never heard from him again.'

Spitalfields has a very particular feel to it. The old market still lumbers on, but it is now a hodgepodge, a jumble of lentil stalls and tapas bars, of brilliant bright cushions and long wooden benches, where you can munch your baked potato with organic pride. Surrounded by a constantly looming vertical presence as banks and insurance companies slowly close in, the building needs a purpose, a focus before it has its life gently snuffed out.

On the south side, there are still some outposts from the Georgian days: a marvellous food shop, A. Gold, and a place called the S and M Café. Great name, guys, and despite it being a chain, with all the horrible connotations of roll-outs and profits, it is one of those rare places that shamelessly celebrate one of our most wonderful culinary creations: sausage and mash.

But while the connection between the original St John and Smithfield is pretty obvious, locating site number two, St John Bread and Wine, in Spitalfields has a less clear logic to it. Fergus Henderson, affable man that he is, revealed that the reason was actually rather mundane. 'We came here because the bakery side of the business was getting too big,' he said. 'And this place seemed just right. It's an old bank actually.'

Among the streets around Spitalfields are some of London's most beguiling examples of Georgian architecture, rows of tall, elegant houses that sprang up during the eighteenth century when Spitalfields was enjoying its golden age. Its soul, how-ever, is rooted elsewhere, in the lurid machinations of domestic French politics. In October 1685, Louis XIV revoked the Edict of Nantes that had given French Protestants a degree of freedom to worship, albeit subject to tight constraints. All this rapidly changed when the treaty was revoked, and Protestants were ferociously persecuted once again. This caused a period of mass emigration to countries that were deemed to be more tolerant. Over a period of ten years, more than 200,000 people fled. Some went to America, others to the Netherlands and some to the colony at the Cape of Good Hope, but a vast number – estimates vary, but the figure seems to be around 40,000 to 50,000 – came to England. Of them, almost all were eventually to find their way to London.

It's a little odd, but nobody seems to be too clear as to why the French Protestants, or more accurately French-speaking Protestants as there were many Walloons from the southern part of the Spanish Netherlands among them, were actually called Huguenots at all. The explanation most often proffered is that the word is derived from the Swiss-German

Eidgenoss, a term used to denote a confederation by Jean Calvin.

The great amorphous city of London has often gorged itself on the diligence of immigrant communities. It still does. When the first Huguenots arrived they found a city that already had a small French Protestant community, right in the heart of the city in Threadneedle Street. This community, and the church that served them, had been actively encouraged by one of Calvin's most trusted colleagues to organize itself along the official Calvinist line. The Huguenots settled around the Savoy church in the Borough of Westminster, and worshipped using a direct translation into French of the English Prayer Book. The two communities soon diverged. In the west, the Savoy Huguenots became wig-makers, goldsmiths and restaurateurs. The English retained their mighty ambivalence towards the French, and Huguenots were simply deemed to be 'French' rather than French Protestants. The Huguenots were stuck with all this and many chose to hunker down and quickly became assimilated. Further out to the west of London, in Wandsworth, another Huguenot community settled, became felt- and hat-makers, and thrived and died. A small Huguenot cemetery can still be seen just off the South Circular Road.

But by far the most interesting were those who chose to settle just outside the city walls, away from the immediate, confining influence of the city guilds, most notably around Spitalfields (there was already a small Walloon community that had been established in London since the reign of Elizabeth I, and they had settled around Bishop's Gate, just next to the old market of Spittle), where they began to specialize in silk weaving. When a skill is in the mind and the hands it is eminently portable, and the Huguenots, particularly the Walloons, thrived. The markets in Britain and America were booming. The Huguenots were said to make the finest of all silks, and their inventiveness created new materials, fabulous taffetas, finely worked velvets. Spitalfields flourished.

Glorious, imposing houses were constructed, with fine Georgian exteriors and garrets high up in the rafters where the weavers worked their magic. The Huguenots' love of design and decoration extended to their gardens, which were said to be among the most beautiful in London. The streets were full of the warbling of caged canaries, and the twang of French filled the cafés and taverns of the area. Weavers worked long hours, clacking and shuffling in the high eaves of the houses into the late hours. During the golden age in the eighteenth century it must have been an enticing part of the city, wealthy and busy.

Not a lot of weaving and spinning goes on in Britain these days, let alone in Spitalfields, but there is one house you can visit that simply guides your senses on a weird and wonderful trip. It's called 18 Folgate Street, on the city end of the road, within easy reach of Bishopsgate. Turn the corner and you will see the flickering of a flame, and high above you a red bobbin, once the sign of a weaver. You need to prepare yourself for this: book ahead and read a little; check out the website www.dennissevershouse.co.uk; but I seriously suggest you don't get too far into asking who Mr Severs was. Leave it till later.

I was lucky, and was allowed in outside regular tour schedule hours, which meant that I could actually talk. Usually, talking is forbidden. It's a house rule, not to be broken, on pain of a scowl and the power of peer pressure I assume. My companions were two very erudite old ladies who completely ignored me when I told them I had no idea what the name of an obscure piece of porcelain was. For I, like you I suspect, had assumed the place to be an authentic survival, but began to wonder when I found myself in a room which was an almost exact reproduction of an old Hogarth print, accurate right down to the very last splinter of broken glass.

The house is exquisite, wildly atmospheric and one of the most marvellous things I have ever seen in London. I urge you all to get along there post haste. It was once a Huguenot house, a weaver's house no less, with its tall windows and high ceilings, but the whole thing was appropriated by one man with an ardent spirit, an American by the name of Mr Dennis Severs. Fittingly, I think, he is no longer with us, though very much among us at 18 Folgate Street. And do not worry too much about the notices that tell you to be quiet, or the notes that ask if you have got it yet, for you will, eventually, I am sure.

I asked Mike, the house's custodian, what they were trying to do, for I was genuinely unsure.

'Hmm. What are we trying to do? Well, we are trying to get people to use their senses. On Monday nights the whole house is lit by candles and we insist on absolute silence. It works. You just have to imagine each doorway as a picture frame; enter and look around. It's what we could call an art installation.'

It is reconstructed, yes, but with extraordinary passion. I loved the way I began to feel almost overwhelmed. To look at the candied pineapple in one room, and the oranges stuffed with cloves, both signs of wealth to be sure, and then to witness the abject poverty of the final days of the declining silk trade, killed off, as you can probably guess, by the Victorians' beloved laissez-faire which opened the silk markets wider and wider so that the cheapest man won.

Later on that day, I walked over London Bridge, closed my eyes and inhaled. Deeply. I sensed those intoxicating carcinogens as the taxis and buses lumbered by, and a vague fishiness from the Thames that flowed beneath me. I reflected again on the eels and whitebait that used to swim by. Once you might have sensed something a little more enticing, the gentle wafting smell of oxtail soup blowing in from Bermondsey to the south. Huguenot tanners are said to have brought a love of oxtail with them, from boiling the tails of the beasts whose hides they cured to make leather. I thought how fitting it was that St John in Spitalfields was one of the only places in London where you can still find a thick bowl of oxtail soup to eat.

18

OXFORD

Coffee and Quince

ON A DAY FULL OF THE USUAL TRAGEDY AND DESTRUCTION, I SAT down for my daily fix of *macchiato* and thumbed a broadsheet. It was all horribly grim and familiar. A randy female tortoise had mistaken a blazing light bulb for a hot male, mounted it and burned its owner's house down somewhere in England. Poor thing. It was probably an al-Qaeda operative.

My thoughts turned to the coffee, and the curious fact that I was sitting at the site of Britain's very first coffee shop, which had triumphantly opened its door to the public over 350 years earlier. It was not, sadly, called Ye Olde Starrie Buckie, and they probably knew not what a *macchiato* was in those days. The Grand Café on Oxford's high street, or the High to Gownies and the Oxford cognoscenti, is a much better bet for a morning shot of caffeine than any of the coffee chains that litter this and almost every other city in the land. Here you get palm trees and high ceilings, and the added bonus of sipping this enigmatic brew in a building that has a very particular connection with coffee.

Most of the time the Grand Café is full of students trying to pretend they are having a jolly and civilized time to their visiting parents who know only too well that they are not. Loud horsey girls sip Bucks Fizz, and the boys seem unsure of whether to be a stallion or curmudgeon. Yes, things have changed little over the years.

Oxford is my home, my base, my urban paramour, but it really pisses me off. I want to wander around the colleges, but I can't. I want to destroy its hideous car parks, its junkie-filled conveniences, but I can't. I hate its crazily impractical way of clogging up the traffic, but this is Oxford, with its streams of dermatologically challenged students. It is a smug and beautiful city. If you have a strong desire to tear up pavements, come on down. There's a strange tradition here. Every few months the main shopping drag, the Cornmarket, is resurfaced. Every single time something goes wrong.

So what's good about the place? The sublime architecture, for one. The celestial Bodleian Library and its vast collection of books, for another. The occasional flurries of courtesy, which if you have lived in London can be a refreshing change. And then there's the Pitt Rivers Museum, full of musty old artefacts of dubious origin. The river, the punts, and the quiet dappled corners you can come across both down and up the Thames – the Isis, as it is called here. And there are the arcane rituals you brush up against every now and again. May Day at Magdalen tower when people rise early, or go to bed late, and sing from the heights. The Botanic Gardens and the fritillary fields in spring, and the best PYO I have ever come across down Binsey Lane, a far better stop than the nearby pub, which despite its glorious riverside position I found surly and unwelcoming, and barely capable of feeding a dog let alone a human being. Every spring, when the PYO's asparagus sign appears at the end of the road, it is time to unrustle, to metamorphose, to prepare your senses for the chance of eating something unique. Fresh green English asparagus, even better here than at Evesham just to the north, where asparagus growing is a local speciality.

Much of Oxford fills up with visiting foreign students as the year moves on. The French cruise around flirting with one another and saying things like '*C'est vachement chouette ici*' (or in English, 'it's cow-ly owl here'). Intellectual tourists hover around the Bodleian and are even allowed to look at the tall, sombre books in the Duke Humphrey library, so long as they've got nametags on (the wanderers, that is).

Frank Cooper's old marmalade factory has morphed into a club, and cheap offices, but the city still has a covered market to make up for all its architectural horrors. At Christmas you might even spy the odd ostrich carcass hanging outside to amuse the vegetarians. It has a particularly fine cheese shop, and a vegetable stall that positively buzzes most of the time. The fish stall right opposite just hums. And there are sausages in profusion. You can even find the long-forgotten Oxford sausage, which is supposed to be a blend of veal and pork, just the thing to eat with slices of lardy cake and pasties – also freely available, though having little to do with Oxford. On the first Thursday of the month, Oxford even has its own farmers' market. Eager people truck their way towards the city with crates of fruit juice, plastic-packed bacon and some earthy, glisteningly fresh vegetables.

One sunny autumn day, with cumulonimbi scudding overhead, I decided to take a topless bus tour around the city. I was feeling a bit embarrassed by my nimbyism, and had spent far too long peering intimately into the life of other towns and cities. I kept on asking the guide obscure questions, some of which he actually answered.

'Psst,' he said at one point, 'promise not to tell' – as if – 'but as there isn't anyone else on the bus, do you want to hear a bit of gossip?'

Excellent, I thought. Music to my ears.

With a nod and a wink, he revealed, 'A mate of mine used

to go to the same college as that famous daughter of . . . well, let's say a famous American who couldn't keep his trousers on. Well, neither could she. She used to like to party while her boyfriend wasn't around.'

Gossip pervades the streets of Oxford; perhaps this is why I love it so. Walk in any direction and there will be a couple of students saying things like 'I got really hammered last night. It was great. Can't remember a thing about it.' Nights of drink. 'Yeah, but I just don't know how to tell him, yeah? I mean it was only once, and now he thinks I'm his. I mean. Get a life, yeah?' Nights of love. And, since it is Oxford, we also expect a bit of intellectual class. I have walked past students chatting about Descartes, donkeys and druids. Not simultaneously though. Clean-looking, ruddy-faced Englishmen speaking fluent Chinese. People log on to Korean websites, absorbed by that jumble of ideograms. And if you want to know a little more about Oxford's history, you only have to join a tour group and listen to the stories. Tourists just love to hear about riots over a flask of cider.

St Scholastica's Day in 1355 was an exceptionally bad St Scholastica's Day. A minor altercation over the quality of a flagon of cider ended in a pitched battle. Before long sixty-three students lay dead, and the authorities called on the military to restore order. Town and gown were never well matched, and they still loathe each other. Even now you can see it. Town is grey, and poor. People's faces are pinched and pale. Gown is secretive, and speaks in weird tongues and gestures.

But if alcohol fuels the evenings, and the long weekends, it was the *macchiato* that made me wander mentally far away, to the hot, dry plains of Araby, to Yemen. (Eh? Has he finally gone mad?)

I remembered flying there on a bizarre trip to find a decent fish supplier near the Red Sea. Rumour on the global fish grapevine had it that fish were cheap out there. I drove for hours through this maddest of countries, dodging the cars and getting poetically transported around the souk in Sana'a. Once, we stopped to escape the blistering dry heat at a roadside restaurant with a towering view. On the slopes below were rows of coffee bushes. Below them a man in a pure white ankle-length djellaba worked a field with a depressed half-baked ox. This is the land we once called Arabia Felix, and a few hundred miles to the north lay Saudi Arabia, now far from being felix at all. Baskets of bread and the sizzling sound of lamb roasting on the oven greeted our entrance. All was serene.

'What's that you're eating, Naji?' I asked my guide when we were served with a spicy dish of eggs and tomatoes. 'What do you call that?' I was expecting something lyrical.

'Yes, it is very good,' Naji replied. 'We call it omelette. You have in England?'

Just as the British can get edgy at tea time if there is no chance of a cup of tea, so Naji got edgy – well, positively vitriolic – in the late afternoon, in the daily search for his beloved qat. It's a pretty strange habit. But then he thought we were pretty strange coming all this way to look for fish: Naji had been given the job of taking us down to the Red Sea port of Hoddeidah. And back again, thank God.

Imagine chewing on a privet bush and leaving it, hamster-like, in your cheeks for a few hours and you will get a sense of this crazy habit. The whole country drives with manic tension at qat time. Policemen get jittery. Qat is a stimulant, and to buy the best you need to be in Ethiopia, on the other side of the Red Sea, hardly handy for the Yemenis. But, magically, Naji always seemed to know where to get some good gear, though he was reluctant, probably with very good reason, to let me come along on his afternoon search for the local qat market. Eventually he relented, and I, for my sins, was allowed to chew and chew and chew on this most disgusting stimulant. I found it quite difficult to masticate for five seconds let alone the two or three hours expected of you. I spat it all out, and Naji laughed.

Yemen is the spiritual home of another stimulant, one with which we are infinitely more familiar – coffee. It was here that the Sufis are said to have learned that it too, like *qat*, kept them awake for their divine reveries. This was the drink they called *qahwa*. In fifteenth-century Arabic the word didn't solely mean coffee, but was thought to have included *qat* as well. In fact the coffee bean was called *bunn*, but *qahwa* eventually became the linguistic root of our word coffee.

Coffee drinking proved to be as problematic for Islam as it was for Christianity. Was coffee an intoxicant, and therefore forbidden under *sharia* law? Or was it permissible under the Qur'ān? The fifteenth-century Yemeni Sufi Muhammed al-Dhabani was the first to write about the strength of the drink, and he sparked off a long doctrinal debate.

Coffee had been drunk in Ethiopia for some time. It slipped across the Red Sea, as did *qat*. Gradually its use widened, and was actively encouraged by the Yemenis, keen to profit from the powerful drink. Soon it was found in Cairo, and then Istanbul, but almost always in the context of social drinking. It made you voluble, and kept you from sleep. Coffee houses sprang up, and stories filtered back to Europe of a strange soot-black drink that kept Turks loquacious into the small hours.

It came to Europe much later. Venice had long treasured its powerful hold over trade with Istanbul and took to the drink with gusto. *Qahwa* became *caffè*. Genoans and Venetians sent their agents to seek out yet more sacks of the beans that made this peculiar, bitter, captivating drink, and by the beginning of the seventeenth century travellers were beginning to bring their own sacks of beans to keep them wired and attentive well into the long winters.

During the time of Oliver Cromwell, when the traditional tipple had for long been ale, and beer, which if not exactly frowned upon was nevertheless tarred with the brush of the great British curse of drunkenness, coffee was at first looked upon with interest. Cromwell was nothing if not a pragmatist at heart, and under the Protectorate in the 1650s trade with the dynamic Tuscan port of Livorno, or Leghorn to us in English, thrived. This vibrant city was the only one in Italy where Jews were allowed to mix and move freely, and was the likely departure point for one particular man simply and somewhat unsympathetically known to history as Jacob the Jew.

It was he who in 1651 opened the very first coffee house in England, a country that also took to the brew *con brio*. And where did he choose to open his coffee house? Why, Oxford of course, an excellent location with its wealthy students and avid intellectuals addicted to verbal tussles. A wise choice? Maybe. But it wasn't long before Jacob went bust, and he disappeared into the historical ether never to be heard of again.

But the idea took hold. Other coffee houses opened in the city, and then in London, where coffee-house culture really took off. By the time the Hanoverians had come to save us from Catholicism, the coffee houses were well established. They had a certain style. Coffee pots were handed out from the counter. Servants took pipes around the tables, and there was much chatting and discussion of the world's problems. In some of them, a small box sat on the counter for the coffee drinker to drop in the odd coin or two. TO INSURE PROMPTNESS was inscribed on the front – the origin of the word 'tip'. The coffee house was the place to go to catch up on the news, the place to go after a hard day's drinking. Lloyd's of London grew out of Lloyd's coffee house, so business was at least a possibility in such establishments. Sobriety and the constant exchange of news and information were colossally important in this pre-electronic age.

Moreover, while alcohol was bad for the very soul, many believed that coffee was actually good for you. It was good for the eyes, they said, if you held your head over a steaming cup. Despite this, the coffee houses didn't manage to survive. Taxes were deliberately imposed on the crop, and tea drinking was actively encouraged in the early nineteenth century, despite dark mutterings from some quarters that it was a weak and insipid drink, dangerous to the health and moral fibre of the nation. Even now we still consume a relatively modest amount of coffee – a paltry two kilos per head on average a year, compared to Europe's most avid coffee drinkers, the Scandinavians, who each consume a staggering eleven kilos per annum. Maybe it's those long dark nights.

But we are catching up. Have we been bitten by the bug once more? It certainly seems so, for just about every city in the land has its own selection of identical coffee bars that vie for our newfound love of the *cappuccino* and the skinny *latte*. It has become a lifestyle thing. But what we have fallen in love with has nothing to do with the coffee house and very little to do with European coffee culture. It is a direct clone of the North American coffee bar. It is somewhat spooky to note that two of the more radical new developments in British food and drink, farmers' markets and coffee bars, have both winged their way across the Atlantic. Still, I for one rejoice that it is now an awful lot easier to find a decent cup of coffee than it was twenty or even ten years ago.

Not necessarily in the home, though. The British are all taught how to make a decent cup of tea – boiling water, one for the pot, and all that – but who really knows how to make a decent cup of coffee? And how do we navigate through the piles of blends and arabicas that fill the supermarket shelves?

Every food and every drink has its own passionate expert, and I needed some coffee input here, for frankly I was not at all sure that we were getting it right, and even less sure that the coffee we are drinking is really at its best. The business is supplied by huge conglomerates that do their utmost to supply a standard blend that will keep us happy at all hours, but why is it that sometimes coffee seems so harsh and unpalatable, so bitter and unpleasant?

No-one I found in Oxford seemed to have any idea. The baristas could certainly conjure up a fine skinny *latte*, but few knew anything about the coffee they were using, and even less about how it was produced. You could try our head office, I was told more than once. We're not really told about that, sorry! 'We're always having tastings,' another replied, 'but the espresso blend we use in the *macchiato* is a closely guarded secret, I'm afraid.'

I called a restaurateur friend of mine who suggested I contact Jeremy Torz, who took his coffee very seriously. I met him a few weeks later in as unlikely a place as you can imagine, within earshot of one of London's more troubled and consistently useless football teams, West Ham (sorry, I'm an Arsenal supporter). Jeremy was once an optician – a singularly irrelevant beginning for a coffee expert, I thought. While cruising around northern California he was struck by the excellence of the coffee, and by the coffee-bar culture that was beginning – we are in the early 1990s here by the way – to seep down the west coast from Seattle. And like a true pioneering entrepreneur, he just knew that this was to be his great mission, to bring to the poor, coffee-deprived Brits the 'real' thing, the best, the finest brew that could be found. So he and his business partner Steve Macatonia set off to acquire the knowledge, to cram into months what could have taken years, and came back to the UK full of zeal and vigour.

Things grew slowly at first, but took off when they managed to get the vital contract to supply one of Britain's better coffee bars, then part of the Seattle Coffee Company. They found a willing and eager partner who had got just about everything right apart from the coffee, so they set about imparting their knowledge. To good effect. When the company was taken over a few years later by the mega corporate *bête noire* Starbucks, they pocketed a little dosh, moved on and embarked on another world tour to brush up on their coffee. The final part of their success story has been the creation of the Union Coffee Roasters, boldly belogo'd, well respected and knowledgeable. Their coffee can now be bought by one and all either online or through some of the country's supermarkets.

If there's one thing that gets my juices flowing it's a bit of passion, and it was gushing from their very doors. But to be really successful in the coffee business, you need more. You need to understand the very essence of the bean, the growing, the cultivation; everything must be known and analysed, noted and improved. And then there is the skill, which comes, according to Union, in the roasting. 'The moment of inter-pretation' Jeremy called it. The name of the company has been chosen very deliberately. 'Union' may imply angry workers and unreasonable behaviour to some, but the intention is to impart a true sense of unity, of a company that takes serious pride in its business.

'Number one is the quality of the coffee,' Jeremy told me, 'but we still want to do the right thing by our producers.'

They are in a business that has been at the forefront of the Fair Trade movement, so it would be almost financially reck-less not to take this into account. But I am almost ashamed to say that I get distinct feelings of cynicism when it comes to fair trade. All trade seems to be fair. Just as in the fish business where everyone swears on Neptune's knob that they are devoted to the cause of sustainability, so in the coffee world everyone pays fair wages, and plays the fair trade game. Idem bananas. Union also have their fair trade agenda, but at least it comes across as part of a genuine and passionate commit-ment rather than pure business. When I probed Jeremy for a bit of Maoist self-criticism on the possibility that coffee pro-ducers are suffering from a mild case of bandwagonism, he told me that Union take a fair trade-plus attitude, which in his words meant that they believe the whole coffee business from grower to drinker should be a process of a constant exchange of knowledge, between the producer and the trader, and the trader and the end user, all working along clearly defined rules that ensure that wages are paid and that there is no exploitation along the way.

Look, for example, at the story of the Abahuzamugambi cooperative in Rwanda. This land experienced a barbarity that is simply beyond comprehension. Hundreds of thousands of people were butchered during the frenzied years of mass genocide, and the world largely tut-tutted and did little more. Rwanda has no oil after all. But this is where fair trade begins to become real. The Maraba district of Rwanda was producing coffee beans that had long been lost in the global commodity markets, but some devoted coffee experts thought that something could be made of the mellow and subtle brew from the Bourbon tree, an increasingly rare form of arabica. Union agreed to help the story become real, and placed the Rwandan beans in one of the country's biggest chain of supermarkets, to great acclaim. So, here we are with a real story, and an apparent success, that reminds us of how things have evolved from the days when the coffee business was simply too remote for anyone to care about how the coffee was actually grown. Even if you are tempted by the path of the cynic, there is a very real contribution the thinking consumer can make. And that cannot be bad at all.

While we tasted cups of delectable Ethiopian yergachef, and the Bourbon Maraba from Rwanda, I asked why it was that even within a city like Oxford nobody seemed to be able to get my *macchiato* just right. There was such a variety between the coffees I could drink. Some were acrid, foul-tasting; others just acrid, barely passable. And they were definitely consistently so, for with the whole business being so totally the property of the corporate world, blends are created and rigorously reproduced in each and every outlet.

Jeremy took matters in hand and talked me through the problems.

'A lot of the espressos we drink, and in Italy too, are made with a blend of robusta coffee,' he explained, 'which is less refined than arabica, and can give an acrid brew. It's cheaper too, so when there is pressure for greater profitability, robusta helps the bottom line. You should try a pure arabica blend or a single estate to get a really good brew. And even then it can be ruined by a poor roast. We think that the secret is in the roast, which is why we pay so much attention to the whole business. It's the artisanal side of our business, if you like.'

With a seriously professional air, Jeremy moved across to the line of coffee machines and ground a little of his purest Guatemalan Arabica from the Finca Santa Aña la Huerta for me to try. With a hiss, and a lordly dribble, a thick, luscious shot of coffee filled the bottom of the cup. One of the signs of a good espresso is the *crema*, that brown emulsion of coffee and steam that sits on top of a good brew. Its transience is also important. Drink it quick, Jeremy told me. Every espresso has a sweet spot that fades after thirty seconds or so.

I have to say, his *macchiato* was simply the best I had ever tasted. Attention to detail pays, you see.

A few days later, I drifted into the kitchen back home, fixed by my now much improved morning *macchiato*, and decided it was time to indulge in one of my own culinary passions. Which was why, an hour or so later, I was standing over a seething copper pan full of quinces that were bubbling volcanically, splattering and burning my arm.

I love the quince. Some of us get off on the smell of toast. Others buxom figs, or wanton mussels. There are probably fans of dead chicken carcasses for all I know. But for me it's the quince, *Cydonia oblonga*, with its flash of the Kasbah, and gentle, spicy autumnal wafting. It is the Isadora Duncan of the fruit world, fast and smiling, but underachieving. Perhaps it's

the virginal fluff that covers the fruit, or the porcelain hardness of the flesh. Or just that heady scent, that mild hint of
compost, and the deep purple fruitiness.

I have always loved quince jelly, but had taken the Tiptree
route until one year, when living in the wilderness of
Northamptonshire, a neighbour came calling.

'I don't know if you can do anything with these,' she said,
thrusting a plastic bag nosewards. 'I never get round to using
them at all, and I remembered you said you liked them, so
here they are.'

'They' were a bagful of some rather scrawny, cankered
quinces, but wafting almost too headily through the bag. I had
talked quince with her a few months earlier, and had told her
how glorious, how rich and luscious home-made quince jelly
could be. When she told me she had a little quince tree, and
that something did it bear, I laid my claim. But I had long forgotten all about it. There were even a few medlars in the bag,
and they were even more mysterious to her. She pronounced
them 'med-lahs'. They were once called 'openars', for they do
indeed strongly resemble a human arse. In France they have
been given the more bestial name *cul de chien*, or dog's arse.
Despite all this, medlars make excellent jelly. The only thing
you need to remember is that the fruit need bletting,
otherwise they are inedible, too astringent. To do that you can
either leave them outside or store them in a cold shed. The
fruit begin to ferment and only then become interesting.
Medlar jelly has a pleasing pink colour to it, but the raw fruit
are more of an acquired taste. The only way to make kids like
them is to draw attention to their interesting anatomical
design. They'll love that.

The quince has, it seems, fallen out of favour, but God only
knows why. It is versatile, has a long history, and most
varieties eventually crop reliably. OK, it is difficult to eat raw
– it will make your mouth pucker uncontrollably – and it
doesn't grow too well in the north, but the quince has much

going for it. Back in 1629, the plantsman John Parkinson wrote that 'there is no fruit growing in this land that is of so many excellent uses as this, serving as well to make many dishes of meate for the table, as for banquets, and much more for physical virtues . . .'

We know that the quince has been around in England since at least the Middle Ages. References to the 'chaire de quyince' are made in John Russell's *Boke of Nurture*, written in the middle of the fifteenth century. It was baked or boiled in dumplings, and made into pies, often added to enrich an apple pie to give it extra depth. But it was as a sweetmeat that the quince was most widely used, which of course raises the question, what on earth has happened to British sweetmeats?

Sweetmeats come from the time of troubadours and banquets, a time when sugar was so expensive that it was sold in small doses at the apothecary, a precious substance way beyond the reach of all but the wealthiest or the most extravagant. The English word 'sugar' comes from the Arabic *zahara*, for this plant was first known and grown around the Mediterranean basin, although recent research has shown that it might first have been cultivated on the island of New Guinea, and diffused westwards via India.

The European sugar trade was originally closely controlled by the Italian trading empires of Venice and Genoa, and was sold refined to various stages of purity. The very best was known as *mucchera*, double-refined, white and pure, sold to sultans and the richest of the rich. Then there was *bambillonia*, from Babylon as its name suggests, less refined but still extraordinarily expensive, and on down the scale to *cafetino*, *musciatto* and *dommaschino*. The trade was mostly based on the middle grades sold in thick loaves weighing up to four kilos each that would find their way into noble houses, apothecaries and shops, where sugar hammers would be used to chip small fragments off to be sold, sucked and eaten.

Not all the sugar that was used in Britain was bought from

Italian merchants, however. The Portuguese had succeeded in transplanting sugar cane into their own colonies, São Tomé, Madeira and Brazil, where vast plantations began to be developed, processed and harvested using a workforce that comprised the dwindling remains of the indigenous population and, in the case of Brazil, imported slaves from Africa. An eighteenth-century description of sugar describes it as 'a reed crushed by rollers turned by negroes'. The sugar trade was a dirty business.

During the eighteenth century, the British, always keen observers of the world of trade and exploitation, began to develop supplies from their colonies in the West Indies and Guyana. Particularly the island of Barbados, so that by the end of the century sugar was in such constant supply that it was becoming far more affordable, even for some of the poorer members of society. This meant that the market for all things sweet expanded rapidly, and the kitchens of the cities, and of the rich in particular, began to produce variations on the ancient themes of sweets and sweetmeats. A flurry of books appeared. Confectioners became skilled members of court kitchens.

Among the most enduring sweetmeats were fruit pastes, highly reduced fruit pulp, boiled down to the thickest of pastes, with sugar added, to create a concentrated, long-lasting sweet that would have been served as 'banqueting stuffe'. In other words, exactly what I was recreating in my kitchen that day. It's interesting to note that banquets were once occasions on which to eat uniquely sweet foods, where sweetmeats and kickshaws – a word derived from the French *quelquechose*, a 'little something' in other words – were served in all their complexity. There would have been 'subtleties' made of sugar stiffened with gum dragon and worked into miraculous forms, and jellies and creams. The guests would retire to an elaborately decorated table, dressed with all these exoticisms, and rejoice in the sumptuousness of the feast.

So, here I was with my very own pot of quince bubbling away, watching it slowly transform into this most ancient of things. But fruit paste? Is that really all we can call it in English? It seems so mundane. Why do we no longer use the delicious-sounding quidini, or quidonny, used in the seventeenth century by Sir Hugh Plat, whose *Delights for Ladies*, published in 1609, was among the first to record recipes for all those essential everyday things, including 'the most kindely way to preserve plums, cherries, gooseberries &c, how to dry Rose-leaves, or any other single flower without wrinkling, to boil Sparrows or Larks, [and] how to hang your Candles in the ayre without candlestick'? We also once called quince paste 'condimacke'. The Tudor herbalist and gardener Gerard refers to it in his *Herball* as 'cotiniate'. Both words can still be found in modern French (*cotignac*) and Italian (*cotognata*). *Cotignac*, the great speciality of Orléans, is still made; it is distinguished by a characteristic imprint, often of the greatest of local heroes, Jeanne d'Arc, made by a special wooden stamp. In Spain, quince paste is called *membrillo*, the name that most people used when they tried my version. Odd, that. A Spanish equivalent is now imported and happily eaten with *manchego* cheese, but the English version is virtually extinct. They are one and the same. Sadly, the elaborate art of making English – though not Indian – sweetmeats is virtually dead in Britain, doubly surprising considering the British palate's overwhelming love of sweetness.

However, the fine art of sweetmaking has its roots in the sweetmeats of days long gone, when sugar was still, almost laughably, associated with promoting health, when highly perfumed cachous were taken to sweeten the breath and aniseed was thought to ward off colds and fevers. Comfits were also used, more highly and distinctively flavoured sugary creations derived from the French word *confit*. The comfit is the ancestral forefather of such endangered sweets as the gobstopper, covered with layers and layers of highly refined and coloured sugar. Flavours were often unimaginably strong. Confectioners used ambergris, ground pearls, musk and the strongest of peppermint oils.

Another particular favourite was the sucket. These were essentially candied citrus peel, and were part of the popular European repertoire that moved from Italy through to France and then to Britain, bringing with it words that became quickly anglicized. Thus, the Italian *zuccata* became *succade* in French and sucket in English. The sucket was much closer to the fruit paste, but was almost entirely dependent on a raw material, citrus, that had to be imported. Vain attempts were made to use something a little more readily to hand. In Colchester, candied sea holly roots, or eringos, became very popular, but they too have since disappeared.

To round off the quince story, we can turn to the breakfast table and that great British favourite, marmalade. This has a clear association with citrus fruit in the British mindset, particularly with the bitter Seville orange. Yet the Portuguese word for the quince is *marmelo*, and *marmelada* was yet another word used for sweetened quince paste – a further source to confuse matters. Boxes of *marmelada* were in all likelihood shipped across to Britain along with barrels of the port wine we were so fond of. Richard Hakluyt, the Elizabethan explorer, wrote of giving 'gifts of marmalades in small boxes'. The quince was nearly always found in its cooked form; its high pectin levels meant that it set readily and could be easily combined with other fruits to create real variety, so it wasn't long before the *marmelada* began to be made with the peel of citrus fruits, which were already eaten as suckets.

Quite when these thick, finger-held slices became a variation of jam is vague, but, true or not, the belief is that it was the Scots who were the originators of breakfast marmalade. Recipes started using greater amounts of water, with the emphasis on the peel, so that eventually we all completely forgot that marmalade ever had anything to do with the quince. It was a fruit that was peculiarly ill suited anyway to any wild expansion of demand. It takes many years to crop and is generally one of the more unpredictable of fruit-bearing trees. Much easier to concentrate on the citrus fruit that were readily available by the boatload, and consign the role of the beautiful, enigmatic quince to the culinary dustbin.

Gervase Markham's marmalade

To make red marmalade of quinces take a pound of quinces and cut in half, and take out the cores, and pare them. Then take a pound of sugar and a quart of faire water and put all in a pan, and let them boil with a soft fire, and sometimes turn them and keep them covered with a pewter dish, so that the air may come a little at it; the longer they are in boiling the better colour they will have; and when they be soft take a knife and cut them crosse upon the top; it will make the sirrop goe through that may be all of a like colour; then let a little of your sirrop to coole and when it beginneth to be thicke then break your quinces with a slice, or a spoone, small as you can in the pan, and then strew a little fine sugar in your boxes bottome and so put it up.

from *The English Huswife* by Gervase Markham (1615)

Britain once had thousands of types of apple, but very few varieties of quince. I planted two of them. Quince tree number one was a Portugal. Difficult, allegedly, and it quickly got a touch of leaf spot. The Portugal is a descendant of the great seventeenth-century plantsman John Tradescant's original tree, which he called the Portingall. John Parkinson, a contemporary of Tradescant's, wrote that the Portingall was so 'sweet being fresh gathered that it may be eaten like unto an apple without causing offence'. The other was a Balkan upstart, Vremja, which grew well – accustomed, it seems, to adversity – and was the only tree ever to bear fruit under my regime. Sometimes I wonder if my Portugal ever did fruit.

Thus, with talk of my Vremja tree, this curious culinary journey comes back to the seething mass of quince bubbling away in my trusty copper pan. Time flies when you are making quince paste, quince cheese, or whatever you choose to call it. There is much to reflect upon as the pulp slowly takes on that deep maroon colour, and you imbibe that marvellous scent – powerful, inimitable, quincy. After an hour or two of stirring (and musing), the mass should be thick enough to hold a wooden spoon upright, so that when you draw the spoon across the base of the pan it leaves a clear mark. The paste is then ready to be scooped out and laid across baking trays, to a few centimetres' thickness, to dry. Line them with grease-proof paper to stop it sticking. Then just leave them for a day or two, to solidify – in an airing cupboard if you have one.

When you feel strong enough to finish all this off, when you have stopped having repetitive quince dreams, cut the paste into neat, bite-sized squares or lozenges, and that's it. They'll keep until Christmas, at which time I cover some of them in a layer of melted dark chocolate, which provides a delicious contrast to the fruit inside. I cut and shape, the kids cut greaseproof paper to line a few elegant little chocolate boxes, and that's my Christmas offering for friends and family. I like the idea of giving sweetmeats to people for Christmas – precisely what John Parkinson encouraged 'ladies and gentle-men' to do, to 'bestow on their friends, to entertain them'. The quince, he thought, offered a way to help 'close the stomach, the perfect way to end a meal'.

19

LOWESTOFT

Red Herrings

ARRIVING IN GREAT YARMOUTH ONE AWFUL NIGHT, WITH SLEET
and hail bouncing merrily off the car, I began the traditional
hunt for an affordable bed. The first hotel was welcoming, but
laughably expensive. Things looked up at the second stop, and
as the snow was piling up inside I asked the very nice-looking
lady if she had a room available. She was definitely a lady
because she had dyed black hair piled up on her bonce, wore
thick lipstick, and sported a museum of wrinkles.

'Well, I can't really show you the room, I'm afraid. I've
got someone here.' She nodded towards a completely silent
man in the corner, stroking his glass of beer.

'Oh well, don't worry then. But can you tell me, is the
room nice and warm?'

She looked quite shocked, as if I had asked her to remove
an intimate part of her clothing.

'Well, it will be when I turn the heating on.'

I thought it might be a good idea to move on, so I drove

around the corner to the real hot spot of Great Yarmouth, the Pleasure Beach, for there, I dreamed, must surely be endless rooms just waiting to be filled. Especially as it wasn't exactly Pleasure Beach weather.

And what a sight awaited me. The glorious electric twinkling was outrageous. Leisure land. Pleasure land. Blowzy and beautiful. I parked in one road for no particular reason, got out of the car and stepped into the welcoming arms of a real old-fashioned B&B, dirt cheap, clean and as warm as a proverbial slice of toast. I was asked for no name, no credit card. No blood samples. No urine samples. And how nice that was. In the corner sat an old man enjoying his retirement, with a pile of stubbed-out cigarettes beside him, and the football on the telly. He never stirred but gave me a smile, and if it wasn't for that I would have sworn he was Jack, the drunken old priest in *Father Ted*. (Feck off, did I hear?) There was even a Full English Breakfast included in the £15 per night. And clean sheets. And a telly all of my own. Even a toilet.

To get in the mood for breakfast, I crossed the road in the blizzard to eat and fell into even more warmth and comfort, and weird curly chips called twisters that I had never heard of. This was another place that had to be named to remind you to be happy – Joyland. So in I skipped joyously. There was a bit of a theme here – the American Diner. But the hamburger was quite unexpectedly excellent, the twisters twisted, and the coleslaw was home-made. What was going on here? You sort of expect grim food, surly service and grubby seats in British seaside towns, but none of it was to be found here. The floor was spotless and the service was fab. The chefs even wore those checked trousers that express real professional intent and a terrible dress sense simultaneously. Perhaps there *is* resurgence out there. Perhaps the dirty weekend has given seaside resorts life once more. Then again, perhaps not.

I too had a theme. It was sleek, silver and smelly. The herring, a fish that has had possibly the greatest role of all to play in our past, and the fish upon which the riches of Yarmouth, before it was Great, and its eternal rival Lowestoft to the south, have been built.

In the morning, the snow had gone and the sun shone brightly, but the beach appeared to be in disgrace, or had been removed entirely, for there was a long rabbit-proof fence that ran alongside what was allegedly sand, blocking it all off from view. I drove the few miles to Lowestoft and started looking for a rusty old hulk called the *Eva May*. It was the last herring drifter to have been in commission, a boat that was apparently in desperate need of help. Financial, that is. I felt close and sympathetic before I even got there.

Something seemed to be happening in Lowestoft that day. Something big. Something so big that traffic was at an absolute standstill. But somehow I jiggled around the back streets, did desperately illegal things, and found this poor old wreck way upstream being looked after by Harold Steptoe's dad and a gentleman called Dave. They lived in a caravan and appeared to smoke quite a lot, and to drink a little too, but they were the fitting guardians of the wreck and very courteously showed me around. Dave was from Derbyshire so he knew a thing or two about the sea and herring fishing, as did his mate, who, come to think of it, was also called Dave. Anyway, Dave Steptoe really did know loads but had a tendency to mumble, and a strong accent the like of which I had never heard in my life, a soft, almost Somersetian lilt which was all very fascinating. Only I couldn't understand a lot of what he was saying.

The gist of it went like this. The *Eva May* was on the verge of sinking and needed money as fast as the water rushed into the bilges, and where else to look but the blessed National Lottery, the Patron Saint of All Lost Causes. We are apparently being encouraged to save the *Eva May* because it was a lousy design whose bows were built so high that they tore the nets when they were being hauled in. I wasn't really very convinced by this dismal, rusty, leaky old drifter, but we did at least begin to talk about how Lowestoft once was.

Dave 1: 'Oh no, there's no fishin' down 'ere any more. All the boats have gone. There's Birdseye, down there, they are the biggest employer these days. Nothing much else here to be honest. Loads of unemployment.' This last said with relish.

Dave S: 'Mmm, mmm. I can remember when you could walk across the drifters, right across the harbour. It was mmm, mmm. Mmm. The problem is, you see, the herrin' have all gone. Fished to buggery I would say.'

The *Eva May* was one of several hundred drifters that would leave the port and follow the herring up the coast, shoot their nets, and bring the fish back to port. Just as had been done for hundreds if not thousands of years. Herring are pelagic fish that swim in vast shoals (when allowed to), at times quite close to shore. So it didn't take too much effort to sail out and throw a net into their path.

Within a herring's flip of the Birdseye factory, tucked in between a car showroom and a bathtap wholesaler, is a build ing that suggests something a little different. It produces neither frozen fish nor tap handles, but smells of fish, of smoke and tar. This is J. T. Coles, one of the few remaining herring curers in Lowestoft, and one of only three I had heard of that still produce our once infamous red herrings.

Red herring are whole fish, cured in salt and then smoked for as long as three weeks, with their guts still in place. Being treated thus makes them acquire a reddish hue, and they become desiccated, hard to the touch, and fiercely strong-tasting. They were a peculiarly local creation, traditionally the speciality of these two great herring towns and old foes, Great Yarmouth and Lowestoft.

Yarmouth is said to have been founded on the sandy strand by a Saxon known to us as Cerdick in the year 495. He called the settlement Garmuth. Quite when the Garmuthians first noticed the herring is impossible to say, but we know that by the thirteenth century a herring fair had begun to be held on the beach front. And it almost immediately caused problems. The Yarmouth herring fair lasted for a biblical forty days and forty nights and would begin on the Feast of St Michael. Records show that the first fair was held in 1267, but it seems that it was organized by the powerful Cinque Ports authorities who sailed up from the south coast of what is now Sussex and Kent. They knew about Yarmouth and the herring shoals, so they arrived, dried their nets on the beach, laid claim to part of this piscine heritage, then went off herring fishing. They were an astute lot, it seems, and were soon staging elaborate feasts and banquets to assert their dominance. After the towns-people accepted that the fair was becoming too dangerous – in one year over twenty-five local boats were sunk in a vicious bloody dispute – the boys from the Cinque Ports became the herring fair policemen as well. Domination was complete.

So, here I was on the edge of a gloomy industrial estate in the once mighty fishing town of Lowestoft, excited by the idea of finding someone who spends his whole day producing things I thought had simply disappeared. This makes me feel great. I want to ring people up and say, 'You'll never guess what, I've just met someone who still makes red herrings!' But there really isn't anyone I know who would be at all interested. It's not just the rewarding sense of discovery, but that tangible link with the past, and the opportunity to ask why on earth is anyone still bothering to make red herring?

The man to quiz on matters herring was Mr Colin Burgess, who is and always will be Mr Red Herring to me. He has the gravitas of a herring, the look of a herring, and almost certainly the smell of a herring. He isn't red, however, though he is a man to avoid playing Scrabble with for he uses a barrelful of the most extraordinary words in the English language. He talks of speets and pales, rhivers, crans, luves and marns. Verbal fossils. But this is hardly surprising. The East Anglian herring fishery is, like the whole business of producing red herrings, not only very ancient but sadly on its very last legs. It is an exhausted fishery. And not many people seem to want to eat red herring any more. This highly smoked fish that was once shipped around the Mediterranean, to Livorno, to Rhodes, and sent to the West Indies, and more recently to Africa as cheap protein, has never really entered into our food culture. We are more likely to know it as a phrase than as something edible.

I could see from the outset that there was a problem here. For a start, the herring are now all bought in from Norway, the best source for the fish. Norwegian fish are graded and analysed with Scandinavian thoroughness.

'Why do you have to get them from Norway?' I asked Colin. 'Why can't you just use the local fish?'

'Well, it's quite simple really,' he replied. 'The problem is that there aren't any left down here any more. All gone. And when I buy Norwegian fish I can specify just how fat they should be.' Norwegian herring fit the bill nicely. Fat to the right degree – 15 per cent is best – they are a Volvo with fins.

I began to wonder why it was that the herring had long gone from our coasts.

'It's not that they have *all* gone,' Colin said. 'There are still some fish out there, but they're just too small. If you look at this' – he picked up a mighty Norwegian – 'you can see it's a good size, and we can't kipper fish that are the size of a goldfish, now can we?'

Quite.

Herring are and always have been fickle fish. The shoals come and go with notorious unpredictability, but the reason why the Norwegians, and the Icelanders, still have such good supplies is simple: they look after their stocks with a degree of efficiency that the rest of us Europeans have never even begun to approach. It might sound boring, but good fisheries management is the key.

Colin then proceeded to demonize seals. (They don't all do this in East Anglia. Further up the coast, in north Norfolk, you can take a boat trip to see these raucous creatures that fishermen, in fact anyone who has anything to do with fish, want to see assassinated.) 'It's hardly surprising there's no fish left', he said, 'when you see how many seals there are out there. There's bloomin' hundreds of them. Just think. Every seal eats about a stone of fish a day. That's a lot of fish that just goes down their gullets.'

We began a tour of the factory.

'We don't just make red herring here, you know,' Colin informed me. 'There wouldn't be much point in that. The fish we sell most is the kipper.' And in the distance one of his happy herring workers was working through a pile of herring, getting them ready for kippering.

In fact, there's a complex repertory of herrings being produced at J. T. Coles. Even if they don't actually produce a huge amount of red herring these days, they do turn out a mean kipper. The home market ticks on, and filleted by hand, with the bone always on the left as tradition requires, the kipper — Norwegian, though, not English, or even Scottish — makes up the backbone of their business. A kippered fish originally meant a spawning salmon, caught when its fat reserves had run low, and therefore not all that good to eat fresh. The word comes from the Dutch *kippen*, which does actually mean 'to spawn'. And then there's the bloater, called thus, it is said, after the Swedish *blota*, used to describe their lightly smoked and infinitely delicate version of the smoked herring. Among the cognoscenti they are possibly the best of all types of cured herring now available. Together with the divine, hot, smoked buckling.

There are times when the herring are suitable for one but not another type of cure. Historically, thousands of people were required to sort out the fatty fish from the slim, and the 'full', in-roe fish from the spent. So, the greater the variety of products, the more likely it was that the curer could function with almost any type of fish. As soon as the drift nets were pulled on board the selection could begin. But without ice the herring could spoil easily, so they were covered with a layer of salt instead. Now, a shoal of herrings could be a mighty thing, and when the steam age began in earnest at the end of the nineteenth century enormous quantities were brought ashore to be cured, smoked and barrelled as the curers saw fit.

The fish were 'roared' into a series of vast concrete pickling vats that once lay along the shore at Lowestoft, covered with even more mounds of salt, then left to suppurate for a few weeks. Each of the tanks held seventy to eighty cran, and with twenty-eight stone to a cran, that is an awful lot of herring. The fishing season started in the summer, in order to catch the fish on their way to a jolly good spawning. The poor things were then molested by line upon line of fishing boats, drifters and trawlers, and hauled aboard. Their fishy lust came to nothing. Much of the work was carried out in the wide open on the beach, and Lowestoft must have been an extraordinary sight, raucous and bawdy.

The first catch of the season was often pretty paltry. They were graded out as seconds, and used for pickling. It wasn't until later on in the year, when the herring had had time to put on a little weight, that the really creamy fat fish started to arrive. They would be selected to become the sweet bloaters that made Great Yarmouth in particular famous. Pales were popular in Italy, herring that were put under salt and then smoked. Then there were the hardcure at the other end of the herring spectrum, fish cured to a wooden hardness with a high salt content which might have been hung for anything up to twelve weeks. They were exported as far away as possible.

'We used to send them to Kinshasa,' Colin told me. 'They took about two thousand stone a month. That's a lot of fish you know!'

Whatever the cure, whatever the product, this was always a very labour-intensive business. When the fish were taken out of the pits and washed, they were hauled up into the company's yard and threaded onto long wooden staves called speets. It must have been mind-numbingly tedious work.

'How do you spell that, Colin?'

'Speets, S-P-E-E-T-S. That's it.'

'Who did this then?'

'Well, the reevers, the Scottish women who came down each year with the herring. A wild lot they were. They'd fill up these wicker marns and carry them out to be packed in barrels or smoked. Depended on how the fish were really. When they were on the speets, it was up to somebody to stack them in the luves.'

'These words you are using, can you tell me what they all mean? It's quite sad really hearing that a whole industry that's said to be dying on its feet uses these weird words, and there aren't many people apart from you who have any idea what they mean.'

So we sat down and began to create the world's first English–Herring dictionary.

'Now, before we go on, what other words should I know about?'

'Well, there's the names of the fish for a start. We called them matties, fulls, spent and mattiefulls, and each one had its own particular use, you see. But a lot of it depended on what time of year it was. Some fish, of course, were simply too fat to be pickled, so they would be smoked, often as a bloater. The cure at their level of fish just went rancid.'

'Do you realize that you are probably one of the last people in England still using these words?'

'Well, I don't, to be honest. I should write a book about it all one day. That would be a good idea.'

Yes, Colin. An excellent idea.

We reached the smokehouse, and Colin had arranged for a

magnificent pyrotechnic display. The room looked fairly anodyne from the outside, but open the door and there is an ancient smell, a deep tang of tar and smoke. Its walls were positively congealed with layer upon layer of thick, bituminous, jet-black tar. It made me worry about my lungs. Looking upwards from the inside I could see lines of herring impaled on wooden speets, all placed with military correct-ness, row upon row, tail downwards, waiting to be blasted by the smoke. On the floor of the smokehouse lay six or so little mounds of wood dust, and as we spoke Colin stooped down and gently lit them, disappearing into the smoke himself.

'We don't use oak here,' he explained. 'I don't think it's the best wood to be honest. It's too old and full of pollutants. I'd rather use this.' And he handed me a pile of sawdust — whitewood, he called it.

After being locked in for however many hours tradition dic-tates, the kippers or bloaters or whatever they have become are sold on to feed the diminishing number of people who like these things.

If the herring are now gone, so is the market in Kinshasa. So are the Scots lasses who worked the shore, the fishing fleet, the drifters, the smacks, and the local knowledge. Gone too are the merchants, the skippers, the coopers and the sail menders. But rejoice, for Lowestoft does have a spanking new Birdseye factory. And you can still buy a mean bloater or two among the tap wholesalers.

20

BRECKLANDS

Anglo-Saxon Feasting

THE NEXT DAY I ATE THE FATTEST, FRESHEST MUSSELS I HAVE EVER eaten in a pub in the Norfolk village of Stiffkey (pronounced Stu-key), languishing in front of a blazing wood fire. The village is actually more famous for its cockles, Stiffkey blues, but there weren't any for sale in Stiffkey that day.

'You'll have to go up the coast to buy some,' they told me in the pub.

But north Norfolk exudes such a mellow air that I just shrugged my shoulders and ordered the mussels. If you go there, just be careful that nobody tries to show you their stewie.

So relaxed was the barman that he forgot to tell the kitchen that somebody actually wanted to eat, and after waiting an hour or so I thought it was about time I mentioned the fact. Despite this, and despite the rain and the sodden atmosphere, I felt calm enough not to blaze myself. No doubt the kitchen staff were all lying prone on the floor, whimpering, and dreaming of relaxing things to do.

On I drove, to the weird Christian village of Walsingham, where Our Lady was once known to hang out, and where everyone smiles at you so fervently. The abbey stands stark, and still, a mere remnant of what it once was before Henry VIII decided to destroy so much of our heritage in order to marry the next lucky woman on his list. Oddly, very oddly, the post office in Walsingham was selling a magnificent selection of Russian dolls, icons and enamelled pots – this apparently because the owner's old line in second-hand Soviet cameras wasn't doing too well. Cley next the Sea, Wells next the Sea – it's all exquisitely nice and English up here.

The coast is desolate, with curious ancient harbours, and enormous churches that speak of wealth and days long past. There are vast expanses of reeds, rich with birds, and marshes flush with samphire. Long pebble beaches lie along the coast from Cromer northwards. It is a truly blissful sight. Inland, windmills dot the horizon, but few of them work in any meaningful way any more. Those that do function are curiosities that live off tourism, and mill only half-heartedly. The summers can be long and dry. East Anglia is dogged by an unnaturally desiccating and frost-bearing east wind. A good drying wind, though. Norfolk was once famous for its biffins, apples that were dried in the breeze and snacked upon through the year. Long gone? Why, of course!

I set off on an unplanned wander and ended up in a curious part of Norfolk called Brecklands. A brown sign had appeared out of the blue. I swerved, and followed it, with little idea as to either what or where it was.

Brecklands didn't turn out to be a mock Tudor suburban residence, but a tract of sandy wasteland that straddles the two counties of Norfolk and Suffolk. Among the stunted trees and flowering gorse I came across the ruins of an Anglo-Saxon village at West Stow, which allows you an excellent oppor-tunity to see if they really were the wayward lot of popular legend, warriors who liked nothing more than slaughtering one another, singing around a fire, and telling Danegeld jokes. My misconceptions surfaced quickly. I discovered, for example, that the people who originally built the village were more likely to have been Angles than Anglo-Saxons, and were thought to have come from the area around Anglen in Denmark. It seemed feasible.

The only problem is that it isn't too clear what you should actually call them. Anglians sounds too automotive, so Angles it has to be. Anglo-Saxon is fine too, but it avoids the reality that they weren't actually one and the same. They have been jumbled together historically and have been jointly blamed for the woes of the world by the Normans in particular, but they were never a homogeneous mass. It seems that Angles preferred to settle around the East Anglian coast, while the Saxons, Essex boys at heart, settled slightly further to the south. But together they are known as Anglo-Saxons.

The story goes that the Angles were rowed across the North Sea. They don't appear to have had too many sailing boats in those days, so they paid the pre-bovine Frisians, a tough, sea-faring people, to take them across to the east coast of England. It is said that the Angles and Saxons were originally invited by Vortigern, king of the native Britons, to come and help protect the borders from marauders, for in 410 the Roman emperor Honorius had effectively left the remote British outpost to its own devices in the face of the combined onslaught on continental Gaul by the Goths, the Suevii, and a fearsome lot called the Alans. The Angles and the Saxons graciously accepted the invitation to help, and took the opportunity to invade and occupy much of the eastern part of England. They, together with the Jutes, became brothers in arms, lumped together in the contemporary psyche as part of the barbarian horde from northern Europe, where there was beginning to be a shortage of good agricultural land for their growing population. The collapse of the Roman Empire was therefore hugely significant. Central control disappeared. Coins were no longer issued, so the money economy disintegrated. Britain reverted to an essentially agrarian economy, and became divided into a series of kingdoms. Wars and alliances caused a confusing period about which frankly we seem to know very little. Hence the Dark Ages.

The Anglo-Saxons settled in the east of England during those enigmatic, enticing years. The problem we have is that they weren't too keen on writing, recording or describing their life. They were essentially a culture where the spoken word ruled. Nevertheless, there is one outstanding work that is still much studied and readily available that gives us an idea of who these Anglo-Saxons were. It's ironic that while Europeans will merrily, and often disparagingly, call the British Anglo-Saxons, we, their descendants, seem to have little idea who they really were.

But we can turn to *Beowulf*, the *magnum opus* of Old English. The Irish poet Seamus Heaney has conveniently translated this mighty elegiac creation into modern English. Read it, I was told by an Anglo-Saxon expert, and read it I did. But it seemed to be a spoken tale. I, uncluttered perhaps, or just plain ignorant, could hear the ale-breath, the dark evening wind, and see the huddle of bodies listening rapt over goblets of mead and ale to this classic battle between good and evil.

The Anglo-Saxon village at West Stow was discovered in 1847 when a Suffolk farmer was ploughing the field and saw some relics poking out of the ground. The authorities were called in, and 150 years later they approved the construction of an Anglo-Saxon complex. I walked into its welcoming lobby, took a coffee in the café that was inevitably called Angles, and read a little about the Brecks. The good woman who was at the desk seemed completely unaware of the significance of anything save the cash till, and strongly suggested that I should be a good boy and settle down in front of the video. That would tell me all I needed to know. So I gawped at the screen that told us the crushingly obvious things we all knew about them. That the Anglo-Saxons liked hessian clothes and axes, looked like Billy Connolly, and although thoroughly warlike were also quite domesticated, quite possibly even caring and sharing.

They are understandably keen on reconstruction here. A band of dedicated archaeologists have managed to extract a few crucifixes, jewels and skulls, which are all safely under glass in the museum. Also hidden in the sandy soil — an excellent medium for preserving ancient objects by the way — were the remains of over sixty houses, and a particularly interesting large rectangular hall. Luckily, the land was never ploughed over during the centuries following the Anglo-Saxons and the village has remained buried under piles of wind-blown sand. The soil was simply too poor to warrant anything more than sheep grazing. The founding Anglo-Saxon fathers did not choose their ground wisely.

Now, this hall was not a place to hang your Anglo-Saxon umbrella. Nor to arrange your Anglo-Saxon vegetable show, but was, in a sense, the heart and soul of this enigmatic bunch of northern Europeans. It was about thirty-five feet long, substantially bigger than some of the earlier halls that have been unearthed and whoever built it was a man of some status, possibly linked to the one sword that has been found on the site. Swords were for nobles and lords, not for the everyday lumpenproles of Anglo-Saxon society. It had a central hearth. Everyone sat around the edge, and was warmed, fed and illuminated by the fire. The lord would have sat raised on a dais, for all to be seen, and to be seen to be lordly. Hierarchy was immensely important, and was reinforced by the ceremonial activity in the hall. Steeped in a culture that had its roots in Norse gods and goddesses, epic tales and a fierce warrior spirit, Anglo-Saxons loved to tell tales and myths around the fire, to come together, to drink ale, to feast and to fight. And this all tended to happen in the village hall.

British English speakers are in immediate trouble here, for

the term 'village hall' is ineluctably associated with chrysanthe-mums and amateur dramatics. But, in a way, that's an entirely logical progression, for in both cases the hall emphasizes the villagers' sense of community. And the village or church hall, even the church itself, can be seen as a direct descendant of the Anglo-Saxon hall. People would have constantly milled around outside. It was where warriors met and where many slept, especially those who had yet to set up a family house of their own. And there were times when the hall was used for some-thing more controlled and structured. The feast.

There were two types of feasting: the more formal, structured *symbole* and a looser, more drunken, ale-swilling session called the *gebeorscipe*, held for the *gebeoras*, literally the people who drink together. The etymology of the word *symbole* may also have connections with drink, being a possible mix of the word *som* ('together') and *alu* ('ale').

'*Wisam weila!*' Let us be well. With this, the lord would summon the guests to the *symbole*, first seating the most esteemed opposite him and then inviting everyone to their seats. After this the lady would enter, greet the lord in fulsome tribute and offer him a blessing. Then the feast could begin. A high-status lord would be offered drink from a vessel made of finely carved horn, beautifully elaborate, with richly engraved silver at its lip, or rarer still made from glass with carefully blown edges made to look like a hawk's claw. This drinking horn would be passed around the entire hall for the whole of the feast; indeed it was considered extraordinarily bad form to lay it down and not to pass it on. We perhaps see reflections of this in the tradition of passing the port around the dinner table. And the drinking-vessel greeting '*Was hail*' lives on in the wassail cup. To help the evening trip along, even to give proceedings a bit of an edge, there often appeared the enig-matic figure of the *scop*, half minstrel half poet, the 'laughter smith' as he was known, a man who could flatter and mock his lord but was obliged to stay on his good side if he was to remain alive and working. A delicate balancing act had to be perfected. Many found life as an itinerant traveller rather less stressful, and simply lived off their wits. Since a *symbole* could last for three days, you can maybe see why the British seem to have a deeply held attraction to bantering and binge-drinking. The *symbole* emphasized the strength of the Anglo-Saxon village, of the lord and his guests, and was a time for drinking, endless stories and music, for listening and learning of the world in which they had settled. And if that still doesn't ring any bells for you, you have never been inside a British pub.

The newcomers adopted neither British nor Roman ways, with emperors and lackeys, but had their own distinct hierarchy, with the lord and lady at its head, and the subjects with differing status set beneath them. The lord had to be fed, and part of the lot of the villagers was to produce enough surplus to allow him to live in style. A lord was thus the emblem of a well-run village. But he too had duties to perform, acting as arbitrator, lawmaker and leader, whose survival depended on the success of the whole community.

No Anglo-Saxon meal would have been complete without bread or ale. Indeed, the old English word for lord, *hlaford*, was derived from the Anglo-Saxon *hlaf-weard*, or bread guardian. Servants were often paid in bread; people even ate off trenchers made from bread. To this day a good trencher-man is someone who eats all his food.

For that truly special Anglo-Saxon evening, there may have been roast meat, but it was more likely to have been salted. And we come back to the old cauldron, for in order to become edible, salted meat had to be boiled. The Anglo-Saxons also ate broth, and dumplings, and would have used the guts of animals to make sausages and puddings – all very familiar to us these days. Our culinary roots, it seems, despite the best efforts of the Normans, are deeply entrenched in this Anglo-Saxon world.

Just as each family had to provide a specific amount of food and ale for their lord, so the king, at the very top of the hierarchy, was in turn supported by what were called food renders. This made survival for the community during hard times even more difficult. He might have been paid in cheese, or salted meat, but the most prestigious of all foods was honey, the one source of sweetness then available and the valuable fundamental component of mead. And Anglo-Saxons simply loved their mead. It was the status drink of the times. By the time of Edward the Confessor, the last Anglo-Saxon ruler (1042–66) in Britain, villages were permitted to pay a monetary equivalent of the going rate for entertaining kings, which was the sum of £80 – no mean amount. Money also allowed the king's rights to food rent to be bought by the more successful lords. This food rent, or *feorm*, was an inescapable obligation, and kings travelled widely around their realm to benefit from it. In return, the king, like the overlord that he was, settled disputes, supported his nobles and generally ruled, but he was doomed to perpetual travel if he was to eat. A reever in each village was specifically appointed to collect the food render, which wasn't necessarily a slice of cake or a bunch of dahlias but could range from salted meat to grain, cheese and butter, and would often include high-quality mead. He might have received his rent in other liquid form, as ale which might have been mixed with rosemary, bog myrtle or yarrow to give it a particular flavour. The lords and the kings were involved in constant socializing, which also took place in the long halls that characterize Anglo-Saxon settlements, and whose function profoundly affected the way our ancestors lived.

It was believed that the very act of giving actually increased the fertility of the soil, and was the mark, it seems, of a well-run community. So, feasting was an absolutely fundamental part of Anglo-Saxon life. Each feast became a way of expressing success and superiority over others. If roast curlew or bittern was offered, it indicated that the lord was doing so well that he could afford a hawk. Likewise, venison suggested wealth, for it implied that it had been hunted with hounds. These are the origins of the long-term link between hunting and eating game and the food of the ruling elite.

When I was taught history, there was this assumption that basically it all started in 1066. Yes, we were told that Alfred burned his cakes. That Ethelred was unready. That the Vikings were an unruly, violent, all-conquering people who raped and pillaged. But as far as the Anglo-Saxons were concerned I was told very little. But elements of this immigrant culture remain. The place-names of East Anglia are peppered with their influence, and our days of the week are named after Anglo-Saxon gods – Woden for Wednesday, Thor for Thursday and Freya for Friday. It may also be that the sense of hospitality that derived from hall culture was subsumed into Christianity. Monasteries and churches began to become the centre of a new version of Anglo-Saxon culture, one with a Christian model, with one God, one martyr, rather than a panoply of gods. Hall culture lived on to some extent in the way that the kings and queens of England continued as monarchs in perpetual motion, living off the rents and renders collected by their representatives, which over time became taxes and tithes, money instead of food and ale, as the country began to get urbanized.

But there's more to it than that. There is something deeper about the English that reflects their Anglo-Saxon heritage. Their conscientious love of getting drunk, for example. Of fighting. The qualities of sturdy self-resolve, of the stiff upper lip, the spirit of the Battle of Britain. And there are the more specific details too. We still celebrate Easter, after the Anglo-Saxon spring festival of Oestre, and eat hot cross buns. We still eat crumpets too – quintessential hearth food – and griddle scones, and we still beat the crap out of anyone who dares to cross our paths. Perhaps we are all a little bit Anglo-Saxon to this day, in terms not only of some of the food we

eat but of our restrained, almost uninterested attitude to it —
food as a functional commodity, a *sine qua non* of survival, not
something in whose preparation or consumption one should
invest too much emotion.

21

HEMEL HEMPSTEAD
Caffs and Cookshops

SOMETHING TERRIBLE HAPPENED TO HEMEL HEMPSTEAD: THEY BUILT it. Marooned en route to the airport, I had just enough time for a quick cuppa and to marvel at the sights while a pair of nature-loving swans picked at a pile of nocturnal spew opposite the bus stop. They were snacking when I arrived, and still snacking when I left. It was raining, the sky was an exotic leaden grey, and there was not an awful lot to do but to seek shelter and wait for the bus to Luton.

Hemel Hempstead. It sounds almost rural. Horses might once have happily clip-clopped through the high street and fields of hemp fluttered in the blow, but this town seemed to me to be a profoundly dismal place. Now I'm sure, before I get bombarded with hate mail, that Hemel Hempstead is really a lovely, caring town, full of wonderful people, but with bitter regret I never had time to grapple with its other persona. It is what used to be called a new town, created by 1950s man to cope with the continual desire for urban improvement. And they came up with this.

On the other side of the bus station I saw twinkling lights, and merry faces. It was a good old British caff. At least it was warm. I pushed open the door and stepped in, and quickly ordered tea and a sausage sandwich. This was a voyage of national gastronomy after all.

'Do you want a cup or a mug, luv? Like it strong, do you?' I was asked. The sort of crucial decision that can easily befuddle the early-morning brain.

'A cup, please, and as weak as you can make it,' I replied, committing a dangerous social faux pas. Tea drunk in a caff should be good and solid, throbbing with tannin and laced with sugar. No fine bone china, certainly no lapsang souchong, and keep that little finger well tucked in. And, anyway, real men are supposed to drink tea in mugs.

The woman behind the counter smiled and gave me an old-fashioned look. I moved off to sit down and waited for my cup of tea and sausage sandwich to arrive.

An old man sat listlessly smoking a fag by the no smoking sign, and everywhere, immodestly loud, buzzed an unfettered flow of private conversations.

'Did you see that hospital programme on the telly last night?'

'Eh? The what? No, I done that job.'

'No, the telly! There was this bloke who had his head chopped open, and he was still conscious.'

'Nah! Really? That sounds disgusting.'

I felt free to join in here. I had actually seen the programme and had been utterly transfixed. But not half as transfixed as the poor bloke whose head was being investigated by the neurosurgeons. It was distinctly unsettling. The verbal duet continued.

A heavily made-up woman fresh from the Blitz was looking after a bored kid, and feeding him bits of bacon. His name was Jean Paul. Or possibly John Paul. It all seemed a little far-fetched, but the young JP performed magnificently, scrambling around on the floor and throwing a tantrum. Being the youngest around by several millennia, he was the darling of the caff. Miss Sixty was very tolerant. The head-opening conversation took off again once he had calmed down.

'It's amazing what they can do these days.'

The woman behind the counter had seen it; the bloke next to me had seen it.

'Do you know what, it's amazing what they can do these days,' he repeated, to me this time, and bit into his toast.

I had to agree. It really is amazing what they can do. I told him my own it's-amazing-what-they-can-do yarn. I had seen a programme years ago about someone in Maoist China who had a lung taken out while anaesthetized by nothing more than a series of carefully placed needles. Pneumonectomy by acupuncture. The patient was sipping tea on one side of a screen while indescribable scenes of carnage were taking place on the other. I sipped my PG Tips uneasily.

'Nah! Really? Amazing!'

Everyone chipped in, with different parts of the body taking the lead. I felt absolutely at home here. But time was ticking on. I knew that soon I would have to bite the bullet and move on, to the far and distant town called Luton.

My sausage sandwich arrived, with absolutely no pretence at all. On one level it was a completely charmless thing. A thoroughly unexceptional sausage made from rusk and minced bits of a pig stuffed into a machine, wrapped in plastic, cooked, and then reheated, served with a hint of margarine between two slices of white bread baked in an industrial bakery God knows where. It was lovely.

Now, you may just be wondering why this particular intrepid gastronome is even mentioning this. But, I'm taking the warts-and-all approach here. If we are considering what the British eat and their relationship with food, we mustn't get lost in the rose-tinted elitist stuff. A book about food must include the good, the bad and even the ugly, especially if we are trying to tease out hidden meanings and eternal truths. And here in beautiful Hemel H we had chanced upon what gastronomically speaking was definitely the bad. The British simply love their sausages. They have leapt across the stifling class boundaries of British society. They make us all go weak at the knees, and poetic. They are the *raison d'être* for the millions of bottles of ketchup we consume, and for me they are the only edible thing I always, without exception, crave when I am away from the country for any length of time.

And here I was eating my sausage in a very typical British caff. Formica tables. A smell of grease wafting in the air, mingled with the faintest tinge of carcinogenic cigarette smoke. It is one of what must be several tens of thousands in the land, and they are in a way central to the story. Apart from all those nasty multinational corporate places with yellow arches to their name, the caff is the one culinary constant you will find from Land's End to Lerwick. And I am using the word 'caff' deliberately here. It is a term often used instead of the more complex linguistic sound 'ca-fé', just in case you are actually not at all sure what I am talking about. We don't want to get any false notions of real coffee and croissants, now do we?

And so we come to another universal truth about the British: they love bottled sauces deeply and passionately. Be it ketchup, brown sauce, HP sauce (author's favourite, particularly good with smoked salmon by the way) or Worcester sauce. It would be quite unthinkable to eat a sausage sandwich without a squirt of ketchup, however pharmacological it is to the eye. So the caff is an ideal way to become acquainted with one of our quaintest paradoxes: we are the acknowledged masters and mistresses of the bland, but we also love to thrill our taste buds with something fiercely piquant (hence our adoration of Indian and Chinese takeaways). Which of course allows us to be fed on mushed-up bits of mechanically rendered meat without the slightest murmur, for most of these sauces successfully conceal rather than compliment the taste.

The word 'ketchup' is long established and has appeared in various forms, catsup and catchup among them. It was derived from the Malay for soy sauce, *kecap*, which was used by the Dutch originally for the imported soy sauce, though it came to refer to a whole range of bottled liquids almost all of which, apart from tomato, and mushroom, have disappeared from culinary use.

Tomato catsup

Place two dozen fine, large, sound and fully ripe tomatoes in a jar and bake until tender. Strain off the water and pass the pulp through a sieve. Then add to every pound of pulp:

1oz shredded shallots
½oz shredded garlic
¼oz bay salt
¼oz powdered white pepper
1 pint of chilli vinegar

Boil the mixture until quite soft, then pass it again through the sieve. Now, to every pound of pulp add the juice of 2 lemons and 1 large Seville orange. Boil it again until it has attained the consistency of thick cream, and when cold, bottle, cork and seal well.

from *The Art and Mystery of Curing, Preserving and Potting* by 'RJ' (1864)

As I was nibbling on my sausage, with blood-red ketchup dribbling from its nobby greasy end, I couldn't help but wonder quite why it was that the British seem to hold the concept of taste so far from their hearts. We seem to be increasingly concerned about how food is produced, that our pigs have enough room to lie down and read books before we slaughter them, and that cows are no longer brought up on a diet of minced offal, but it doesn't always seem to link naturally with improving the taste of the food. Can it be that we are actually quite unmoved by taste, happy, indeed, in our preference for the dull and insipid? There seem to be two possibilities here: either it is rooted in our culture, or we have simply had our taste buds gradually anaesthetized by years of eating industrially produced food. Current thinking seems to go along the following lines.

Sadly, most Brits seem to assume that food comes from supermarkets and has little connection with the natural world. It is a product formed and refined in long, hyper-clean factories for our convenience. Who among us really thinks pig when eating a sausage? What fool ever dreams of a tomato as he squeezes the ketchup bottle? The quality of taste, sadly, is simply not high on the list of everyday priorities. We tend to eat when hungry, and as cheaply and conveniently as possible. Not for us the long two-hour lunch break of the French and the Spaniards. Not for us the pointless discussions on the merits of line-caught bass. Although when it comes to drink, that is a different matter entirely.

So let's look at the sausage, and see if it proves the point at all. The eighteenth century saw an enormous increase in productivity from the land. These were the years when Jethro Tull invented the turnip drill, and when cattle cake was first used to increase both beef and milk production exponentially. Yet, despite all the radical changes in farming, the agricultural population was not the beneficiary at all. Land enclosure – when contemporary logic stipulated that farms should be enclosed and worked more rigorously, and that common land should become private property – resulted in a real decline in the quality of agricultural labourers' diet, and of course that of their families. They were actually eating less meat and more bread by the end of the century than they had done at the beginning. The monarch we know as the Farmer King, George III, presided over a distinct deterioration in the lot of country people. Many left the land and moved to the cities, fuelling the industrial revolution. The result of all this was that a huge mass of the working population were fed on off-cuts and carnal waste matter, which never really seemed to be particularly troubling.

And some two centuries later, the fact that the particular everyday sausage I was given in Hemel Hempstead was absolute crap still didn't raise a flicker of disapproval from anyone, myself included. And what an ill-mannered arse I would have been to say, 'Now listen here, my good woman, this sausage is quite possibly toxic. It is swimming in fat, and tastes of absolutely nothing at all!' Of course, if I was paying more money for my sausage, and if it were covered in gravy and mash and served in a fine country gastro pub, it would have been scandalous to have served said sausage, and yes, I would have bellyached to the ends of the earth. But, here, in a caff, one just doesn't do this sort of thing.

The British sausage is curiously homogeneous, and is seldom, if ever, cured, smoked or fussed over. Probably its most distinguishing feature is that the British have for some time added cereal in the form of breadcrumbs, or worse, to bulk it out and keep it cheap. It is in fact the classic way a poor family can play the cultural game of meat and two veg without breaking the bank on a joint of fresh meat. Yet, strangely, we have virtually no regional charcuterie at all. (It should not surprise you that, as with 'cuisine', we use the French word here.) Why is this? Climate plays a part. Damp, warm winters are not ideal curing weather.

But sausages are fighting back in the regions. Cumberland sausages appeal to the revivalists among us, but shockingly are seldom sold as they should be, in long, curled spiral links. In my own backyard, the Oxford sausage, a mix of veal and pork plus a herb or two, has been given the kiss of life by one butcher in the covered market. In fact, I suspect they employ butchers solely for the purpose of making sausages all day long, so popular are they with the city's diverse population. The archetypal British sausage was invariably made from off-cuts, fresh, to be cooked rather than stored for consumption during the lean season. Much of this art has of course been taken over by processors using industrially reared pork, but butchers around the country are now vying for sausage status, and entering prestigious sausage competitions.

While curing sausages might never have been in the housewives' domain, bacon was a different matter, for it was the best way to preserve the family pig, by packing it in salt and letting it spend the winter being gently smoked over the fire. Bacon was also a key component of cauldron cooking, imparting saltiness and providing protein long after the pig had been killed. It also remains a firm British food favourite, equally at home sandwiched between two slices of industrially produced bread, with a squeeze of tomato ketchup.

An eighteenth-century recipe for choice breakfast bacon

Take a side of pork and rub both sides of the meat well for a week with the following mixture:

1½lb pounded bay salt
1lb coarse sugar
1lb minced shallots
1oz saltpetre
1oz sal prunelle
2oz bay leaves

Turn every other day, and after a week add 1lb common salt and 1lb treacle. Rub again daily for another week, then take it up, dry with a coarse cloth and rub it all over well with peas meal and bran mixed in equal quantities. Hang it, to be smoked with:

2 parts oak lops
2 parts dried fern
2 parts peat

After three weeks of smoking, commit the side to your ham and bacon chest, where it can be kept for three months and longer, well embedded in malt coom or charcoal. It will never be rancid.

The sausage (not to mention a slice of bacon or two) is now an absolutely essential gastronomic linchpin in our famous Full English Breakfast, beloved of B&B landladies the length and breadth of the country. Apple and leek, sage and onion, venison and cranberry varieties – all can be found spilling from the supermarket shelves.

We are, it seems to me, an accepting lot at times. The British enjoy the distinct good fortune that one of their mother tongues, English, is fast emerging as the global lingua franca. But, not entirely immune to the normal ebb and flow of language, we still have a few very mundane everyday words that are very much franca in origin. There is, for example, *cul de sac* which quite clearly translates from the French as 'arse of bag', and although we have adapted it to describe a road without issue, to some it suggests a place often with tightly designed, rather anal suburban houses of dodgy architectural worth. We eat beef, derived from the French word *boeuf*, not cow. And pork not pig. We are aware of, though not too fond of demonstrating, our *joie de vivre*, and we just love to eat out in *restaurants*, and sip our overbrewed tea in *cafés*.

Let's look at this word 'restaurant', one we have accepted almost without question, and one that seems to recognize that the French most nobly came to our rescue (thanks to Monsieur Boulanger, whom we have met before) and showed us how to eat out, and how to spend our money on crappy food. But is it really true that this notion of eating out came joyously to our unsophisticated shores from across the water?

The story is well known, a little hackneyed even, and briefly goes like this (forgive me if you know it). In 1765, M. Boulanger decided to offer his clients the opportunity to eat as well as drink in his establishment on the corner of the Rue du Louvre in Paris. He was well aware of the power and influence of the city's *traiteurs*, who had grown rich on supplying the French aristocracy and the growing bourgeoisie with cooked dishes of what was at times immensely complex food. (We have a word for them in English. It is marginally less evocative. We call them caterers.) One thing *traiteurs* did not do was to offer their clients the opportunity to sit down and eat. They had, however, formed a powerful guild that protected their trade with scrupulous thoroughness, and fought off any rivals to their domain.

Until, that is, M. Boulanger came along. He had the brilliant notion that if he offered but one dish – his boiled sheep's feet and marketed it as a food that was good for the health, he wouldn't necessarily be treading on their toes. The *traiteurs'* wrath was such that they entered into a long and pro tracted legal dispute which they eventually, on the ruling of Louis XVI, lost. The results were predictable: restaurants appeared in cities throughout France, and it wasn't long before they appeared in London.

The story could just rest there, while we give eternal thanks to French beneficence, but it doesn't actually stand up to analysis at all. We possess a remarkable collection of ancient documents that describe British life in town and country in great detail, particularly from the early Middle Ages onwards. One of these was written in the late twelfth century by William Fitz Stephen, who describes London as a city of bucolic happiness, full of learned students playing football, skating on animal bones, and carousing as they still tend to do; a city full of wells with water 'sweet salubrious and clear'; a city where strangers – the word 'stranger' and the French *étranger*, or 'foreigner', are close in meaning – arrived, river-borne and often hungry. And so, we are told, by the bank of the River Thames, not far from the ancient fish market at Billingsgate, there was to be found a public eating house. This is how it is described in an eighteenth-century translation:

> Here according to the season you may find victuals of all kinds, roasted, baked, fried or boiled. Fish large and small, with coarse viands for the poorer sort, and more delicate ones for the rich, such as venison, fowls, and small birds. In case a friend should arrive at a citizen's house, much wearied with his journey and chooses not to wait, as hungered as he is for the buying and cooking of meat, the water's served, the breads in baskets brought.
>
> No number so great, of knights, of strangers, can either enter the city, at any hour of day or night, or leave it, but all may be supplied with provisions.
>
> Those who have a mind to indulge need not hanker after sturgeon, or a guinea fowl, or a *gelinote de bois* [godwit]; for there are delicacies enough to gratify their palates. It is a public eating house, and is useful to the city.

I found this extract quite revealing. We had our own public eating places long before restaurants came along and saved our culinary souls, but what on earth happened to them? They were called cookshops, and in London alone could be found in their hundreds. It was somewhere where all could go and eat, and was often just about the only place the poor and the travelling public could afford. Most Londoners lived in houses crammed into small spaces, where kitchens simply didn't exist; fuel was hard to come by, and families often shared this limited living space with others. If they were to eat at all they were often obliged to eat out. Cookshops served this market perfectly, and they began to be avoided by the more affluent members of urban society who would in all likelihood have been rich enough to cook in their very own kitchen, or to employ cooks and other domestic staff.

Cookshops flourished. Every city had its fair share of them. Families could even bring food to be cooked, just as in the Blackpool B&Bs in their heyday, and were charged a set price for doing so; when funds allowed, punters would choose choice pieces of meat. In London many were located in Eastcheap. The Great Fire of London in 1666 started in Pudding Lane, in a cookshop. One of its great specialities was the pie, portable and cheap, made from the off-cuts of the carcass.

Have these cookshops simply disappeared? I don't think so. For me, they endure in spirit in the caffs and greasy spoons of Britain, where people go to eat and to live, though they definitely don't live to eat.

22

COTSWOLDS

Double Gloucester and the Food Platter

OH YEA, OH YEA, AND IT SHALL COME TO PASS THAT THE TIME they call half term filleth multitudes with deep dread. And the roads shall be full of MPVs, and ye ancient sites will be visited, with mewling children who showeth no respect and knoweth not how to be grateful for their parents' elaborate planning. Oh yea, oh yea.

Yes, it was yet another Bank Holiday Monday, and I felt an urgent need to see something suicidal. The easiest option was to jump into the car. This is the traditional thing to do. The idea of a bank holiday is quite simple really: you join everyone else and go on a journey — not too far, mind — until you come across a traffic jam, at which point you assess its length and join the queue. It's what the British like to do.

The summer bank holiday is when traffic jams really come out to play. Everyone leaves the city to seek the calm of the countryside, which they do in such numbers that it neatly defeats the whole point of the exercise. Calm is the very last thing you will find. Every rural nook and cranny will be full of ogling folk, oohing and aahing and dreaming that life surely must be sweeter here. And they are happy, of course, because the banks aren't open. What an odd lot we are. While Italians drag religious effigies from the sea and swoon and the Portuguese sing *fado*, dance demurely and cook huge feasts in the name of Saint John, the Brits prefer to celebrate the fact that the banks aren't open. None of this saint's day non-sense that they have on the Continent! Bah! We're British! We're different!

Holidaymakers in caravans trundle south to see the sweet little ponies of the New Forest before they get sent off to be eaten as horsemeat in (boo, hiss) Europe. Brits don't eat horse-meat. That's the sort of thing they do over *there*, on the Continent. Some travel to savour the purple flowering heather moors of Scotland, maybe even to meet a purple-nosed Scot who is just a little too fond of the whisky. Bikers amass, ramblers ramble, ancient cars rally and teashops and seaside piers begin to fill up, sighing a collective sigh that they have managed to survive one more miserable British winter.

The chances of a fine bank holiday are pretty slim. But come rain, hail or even sunshine, on every bank holiday you can catch a glimpse of Britain at its most British: smug, mildly chaotic, but with a streak of defiant anarchism in the air. It has become one of our quaintest traditions. Not long ago budding journalists took themselves down to the sea to witness another curious ritual, the tribal combat between mods and rockers. Mods rode scooters and looked like Liam Gallagher. Anoraked and fur-hooded, they were pitched against the muscular grease-balls known as rockers, leather-jacketed, tattooed, hair heavily gelled, visibly more threatening. Each had their own band of babes. Beaches all over the country turned into battlefields and the press trumpeted and bleated, as it only knows best, and decried the sickness of society while merrily and hypocritically poisoning what was in reality a fairly light-hearted bout of aggression. The rest of us veer between apoplexy and courtesy for the whole weekend, until Monday evening comes along and aggression rules once more as we cross back into the urban world that is home. For most of us at least.

For one particular car, author at the wheel, three kids in the back, it was off to the Cotswolds, the driver still determined to visit the country's furthest corners to witness the oddest things, and the finest things. The Cotswolds are a happy mix of blue rinse and green welly with some staggeringly beautiful and much-visited villages where people like to see how rural Brits hang out. Petunias thrive in their well-watered baskets. Antique shops have set forth and multiplied. All is well and serene in these ever-popular little settlements. The towns and villages have peaceful, easy names: Bibury, Burford and Broadway, all hardcore Cotswoldian settlements that once prospered on the wealth of wool. They do not have many dark secrets. But travel further out, to the western edge of the Cotswolds where the Severn drives its aquatic wedge between Wales and England, and things change.

Gloucester, despite being the shire town, is a surprisingly dismal place that most people now associate with mass murder. Some with cheese. Not usually close bedfellows, I admit. The house of the slaughter-happy West family is now destroyed, but the cheese lives on. There is a Single Gloucester and a Double Gloucester. One is thinner than the other (guess which), and the other is often coloured to resemble carrot lite by adding a little annatto dye to the form.

In one particular village, Cooper's Hill, not far from Gloucester, Bank Holiday Monday means but one thing. Tough and happy people gather on a small and precipitous slope to witness the bizarre spectacle of cheese rolling – a local cheese, that is. The idea is quite simple really: a seven-pound Double Gloucester cheese is rolled down the hill, followed by a screaming sweaty horde, and the first to the bottom gets the cheese. To say this hill is precipitous is an understatement.

From afar you can see a swathe cut through the woods, a scar down the side of Cooper's Hill. On cheese-rolling day, crowds of people line both sides of the track, waiting and watching for the run to begin.

As I was stuck in my own private traffic jam, a young Nepalese man called Padan Shreer was limbering up for his first attempt at the run. This Gurkha soldier was lithe, super fit, and knew a thing or two about mountains. At twelve o'clock, the runners were called to the line by the master of ceremonies. The Cooper's Hill Cheese Rolling and Wake 2004 was about to begin. With a one to be ready, a two to be steady, and a three to prepare, the cheese was sent on its way.

'Four to be off!'

The mass of human muscle plunged down the hill to the belting roar of the crowd, theoretically trying to catch the cheese. It bumped, tumbled and climbed into the air, falling with ferocious speed, bouncing wildly far away from the grasp of anyone at all. The sight up the hill was truly medieval: limbs flailing, wide-eyed, crazed men slid and rolled and tumbled down and down towards the bottom, but all was made even more harebrained by the added fun of there being not a simple space on which to end, but a fence, so no gentle landing could be made at all. It all seemed very fitting for a Gurkha soldier used to the vicious steepness of the Himalayas to win the honour of being the first to cross the line, and to win the cheese of 2004.

A rescue team from Search and Rescue in Disaster stood by, hardened professionals more used to dragging bodies out from rubble left by earthquakes than off the slopes of an English hill. But they took the cheese pursuit in their stride. The busiest stall of all was the St John Ambulance Corps, who are usually required to stand by and do nothing at these quaint rural happenings. Here, however, there were queues of wincing people waiting to have their bodies and limbs checked over.

Heat two, the women's race, was won by a Kiwi. Then the kids had their turn, junior champions of the future. At last this mad scurrying was won by a local lad. This was originally supposed to be a bit of local fun, a tradition for the workers of Brockworth, but the secret is out now and people come from far and wide every year to test their ability to break their limbs. At the end of the day, the announcer told us over the loudspeaker that no limbs had been broken this year, and it was all over. But not quite, for almost as soon as he had signed off the crowd roared once more as an entirely naked man, scrotum flapping, entertained us with a final leap for fame. We all admired his balls.

In a word, it was a strange event. I saw no police. No signs saying cheese rolling this way. Nothing, but we did the bank holiday thing, joined the jam and used our noses. And I thought, how very British it all was. Amateurish. Wacky. Challenging in an entirely meaningless way, and vaguely medieval. Irreverent. Irrelevant.

We sat down on the grass, marvelled at the world and the scudding, cloud-filled sky, had a drink and chilled. After so much time spent trekking around the country, I had come to expect that at such a happy moment, while cheeses were being thrown down steep English slopes, we would be hard put to find anything to eat, even so much as a chunk of Double Gloucester. And sure enough, there was nowt but an ice-cream van. But life was sweet, and we climbed back down again to eat in the local pub. Again, nothing that smacked of place and location. Just corporation. To make the day go with a memorable swing, the pub had arranged for a giant bear – a human-in-costume type of bear, that is – to wander around while everyone was eating, giving out balloons and sweets. My kids thought this so funny that they had real difficulty eating their bowls of ice cream with multicoloured edible things liberally sprinkled on top. And that was quite an achievement.

We then took to the car and drove on. It is strange

sometimes how you find yourself doing the same thing you did when you were young, and used to think was so unutterably boring. We visited a village fête, as sedate as the cheese rolling was wild. South Cerney is a very typical Cotswolds village, its fête a very typical fête. There was a tea stall run by men in straw hats who panicked at the sight of a ten-pound note. Piles of lovely soggy flapjacks, and slices of sponge cake, with jam oozing from the middle. Just as it should be. Scones and cream. And vile jugs of orange squash to keep the children alert. Stalls outside ran along the side streets, plate-smashing, strength testing. It was all delightfully amateurish. The church was filled with flowers, and the vicar looked beatific. He was a little uneasy though, for one of his congregation was busy unburdening herself, telling him how she had become used to the fact that her fifteen-year-old granddaughter was pregnant. He shifted on his wobbly posterior and preached forgiveness.

I hadn't actually meant to get involved with either the village fête or a woman's confidential confession, but having been born with an acute sense of nosiness, both had rendered me rapt. I had in fact been vaguely looking for an old friend of mine who ran a nearby farm, which to our great joy was called Butts Farm. 'They're up at the village fête!' I'd been told when we dropped in, entirely unannounced. Butts Farm has successfully morphed into a place where you can go to see animals cavorting, lambs in the spring and piglets when they appear, and happy chickens. It is run by Judy Hancox and Gary Wallace, whom I had met long ago during my British food festival at Sir Terence Conran's Chop House. We spent a very pleasant afternoon there *en famille*.

In the morning, in the true spirit of democratic endeavour that grips families on holiday, I decided it was time for a henge, so we made our way to Avebury, following a very deliberately sentimental path. I had been dragged along exactly the same roads in my early days, when motorways hardly existed and we drove a VW Beetle with a split rear window. I was determined to make my kids suffer too. I remembered that somewhere nearby there was a thwacking great pork factory where pigs were mushed and mashed in the name of the sausage, and a fetid, greasy smell hung in the air. I think it was the Harris pork factory at Calne. They've gone all farmers' market down there since those raw, uncouth days in the sixties.

Now, a henge is, as you probably all know, a collection of huge stones whose significance no-one can really explain, and we have a fabulous one at Avebury, with junior relations at nearby Stonehenge and Woodhenge. Avebury had for no particular reason completely escaped from my must-visit list until that day, when I joined the ranks of the semi-stressed and took to the roads to entertain the children.

First stop Marlborough, a fine market town (though sadly without a market that day) that once straddled the main road from London to Bristol, an ideal location for one of the country's better private schools, or as we should say with the true logical force of the English language, public schools. Marlborough high street shows a delightful disdain for architectural conformity, with splashes of Jacobean and Georgian vying for the eye's attention, which in my case was scouring the vista for traffic wardens, for I had committed the everyday social blunder of leaving home with absolutely no change at all and had to slip off to buy a bunch of locally grown parsnips. This is a sort of food book after all.

A need for coffee attacked me when buying my one-quid vegetable deal, so off we trekked looking for some caffeine, deciding against Polly and her tea room as being far too twee for a modern family. We settled for a little caff in the back streets being manfully manned by a skateboarding champion with dreadlocks, and a terribly polite way with the customer. And, it has to be said, particularly fine cranberry and white chocolate cookies. They actually resembled what I used to know as rock cakes, and as the kids entered into the let's-criticize-absolutely-everything spirit of the day with glee, we tore into the use of the word 'cookie', took a bite and hastily shut up, since it hit the spot with force. The coffee was good too, and there were even jugs of fresh water to hand. Feeling less nervy by now, we set ourselves this challenge: could we find anything to eat in the town that suggested local food – Marlborough Pies or something like that?

So off we went, to a brilliantly well-lit shop with brown paper bags that sold a wonderful selection of fresh breads and cheese. An excellent start you may think. But the thing was that everything in it was Italian. Exquisite rounded loaves with springy crusts, and a fine yeasty smell, but with strange, remarkably strange, names.

'Excuse me,' said I, 'but can you tell me where you get your bread from? It looks gorgeous.'

The good lady behind the counter showed me her Neapolitan sourdough, her *pignaccio* and her rye mixed loaf, and replied, 'Oh yes, it's all baked locally you know, in Devizes. There's an Italian baker down there who supplies us every day.' She even let me smell her loaves.

The shop was brimming with weird and wonderful things from Italy – *salsiccie*, sun-dried tomatoes (of course) and piles of pasta. All typical everyday British food. Plus the usual range of dried mushrooms from the excellent Antonio Ubiquito, well known to us over here for being the rotund godfather of mushroom picking, the restaurateur Antonio Carluccio.

Down past an inn, a magnificent building where I told my kids about stable blocks and the difference between inns and taverns, only to see them looking at me with distinct disdain, that 'yes, Dad' look that comes over them when I get going, as they probably wished I would. We found cajun chicken, lasagne, chilli, curry and pizza, but still absolutely nothing at all that suggested anything local, apart from a row of raspberry jam in good old Polly's Tea Room. It would have been far easier to cook a scintillating Tuscan *ribollita* that day in Marlborough than anything even vaguely English, let alone British. It all became intensely annoying, particularly when we came across another delicatessen, once again an all-Italian shop, full of the local bread of Devizes and run by somebody who looked as if they had done bird in Tuscany. Mission most definitely not accomplished.

Marginally disgruntled, we set off towards Silbury Hill. The sight of this extraordinary, man-made neolithic pustule on the local landscape is deeply etched into my memory. We always used to stop there when I was wee, especially when we needed one. We would jump out of the car – it was a tight fit, and bottom-numbingly uncomfortable – and climb skywards. That's how I remember it anyway. My kids looked seriously aggrieved when I suggested doing the same.

When we got there, I pulled into the lay-by, looked over and began fondly to eulogize. My daughter tapped me fiercely on the arm. 'Move, Dad, move. Drive on, *please*. That's disgusting.' She pointed out that I had pulled up right beside the bruised corpse of a young deer wearing a benevolent, mildly shocked expression, with bloody spume oozing from its gaping jaw. Roadkill, I assumed. Florrie is a vegetarian for the reason, I once believed, that she found chewing meat far too demanding, but it has become a fiercely reasoned belief and she refuses to rise to the temptation of bacon sandwiches despite my and her brother's constant suggestions. She is made of sterner stuff.

We screeched away from the carnage, only to discover that Silbury Hill is now closed to the public and the lay-by was about as unattractive a place as a lay-by can be. So we nibbled on another excellent local delicacy, an Italian *cornetto*, breathed in the air, only lightly tinged with dead deer, read the notice explaining just how old the hill was and thought how crazy, forlorn and neglected this magnificent sight seemed now. Older than the pyramids perhaps, mysterious, but entirely unloved it seemed, judging from the scuzzy lay-by that welcomed visitors. Silbury is as enigmatic a sight as you will see in England, massive, green and ancient, and we mused about how useful it would be if somebody could hurry up and invent a time machine so we might be able to answer the unanswerable question: what on earth is it? Silbury lies on the edge of a veritable complex of profoundly ancient, unfathomed man-made creations that have given us the chance to elaborate on, even create mysteries where perhaps there are none.

A mere minute or two away, you can park in greater comfort at the entrance to the mighty Avebury henge, and will immediately notice that you are not only positively cosseted but not alone. Indeed there were hundreds of others doing the same half-term thing, and some of them actually appeared to be enjoying themselves. Creepy. Avebury henge is a collection of massive rocks set in a circle on top of a man-made ditch, so ancient it almost defies imagination. Most experts reckon it is between four and five thousand years old. We thought we had discovered something deeply significant by pacing out the distance between the massive, rather wild and disreputable-looking standing stones and realizing that with spooky regularity they were nine paces apart. Until, that was, we found one that was seven, then one that was eleven, etc., so our theory went to pot. But theorizing has often brought out the best in us. The kids were also revelling in the idea that they were placing their fingers in Neanderthal finger holes, until a small thought occurred that we were severely misrepresenting the skills of the inhabitants, forgetting that the Neanderthals actually were supposed to have died off, and we are really talking descendants of Cro-Magnon man and woman here. We actually meant neolithic. Sorry, Neanderthals. You really are history. These henges were built way past their sell-by date.

My kids have perhaps a stronger interest in eating than most, and both began to bombard me with the dreaded what-are-we-having-for-lunch? mantra, then demonstrating a remarkable aptitude for being able to read the word 'restaurant' from distances of up to two hundred metres.

'Is that restaurant open, Dad?' they asked, assuming me to be omniscient, as I was always telling them I was.

I had no idea, but I gave a suitably anodyne answer, followed the signs and noticed that no light shone from the windows at all. Bad news. Crisps again? But I couldn't help but check out the menu, to see what we were missing. And here at last was local food at its finest. On the children's menu, the option was either 'small main meal' or 'small soup and bread', while we grown-ups would have been spoiled with Big Soup and big bread, plus 'a selection of vegetables, Vegan, and gluten-free'. Shame it was closed, we thought.

Off we went once more, searching again for the Holy Gastronomic Grail, up the village high street and past a shop that offered henge tours, significant Celtic crosses, incense and books on King Arthur, for Avebury has, rather speciously, become attached to the Arthurian heartland, a story that gives it Avalonian credibility in some people's eyes. There seemed to be little option since the kids had been so viciously denied their small main meal but to try the local pub, so in we walked. Never have I been so forcibly struck by an atmosphere of wild panic. The bar was piled high with filthy glasses. The food counter had a notice warning that food would take at least forty minutes. The place was nearly empty.

'It's the same even if you asked for a basket of bread,' said the waitress, gently caressing her nose ring. 'Sorry, but we're a bit busy today!' She was unaware, apparently, of the legion of empty tables close by.

Well, surprise, surprise, I thought. Forward planning would be absolutely out of the question. Half term is such a newfangled thing, only hundreds of years old.

We looked at their menu, pondered its glories, and ordered.

'One vegetable tiddlies, one fish bites, both with chips, and I'll have the Food Platter, please.'

We wandered off onto a blustery terrace looking out on to the stones to wait out our forty-minute sentence. On the way we stopped at the bar to see if we could at least slake our thirst.

The barman was sweating profusely, jaw clenched as he saw yet another customer coming his way, and knew that there was no place to run. The washing-machine engineer had called in to try to mend his glass washer. The barman had told him to just get on with it, don't bother him, he was far too busy. And then he began talking to a morose bar-propper: 'You've got the best place in 'ere, Malcolm. It hasn't stopped all day. Do you know, I poured myself a coffee at eleven and I've 'ad two bloomin' sips all mornin'. I ask yer.' That made Malcolm take a walk through the door. Maybe the barman had been trained to talk like this to create an atmosphere of British bonhomie, but it failed dismally. Perhaps the customer wasn't called Malcolm after all. I commiserated as much as I could with his plight, ordered the drinks, paid and went outside.

Within fifteen minutes or so, our dishes appeared. I assumed they had got it all wrong and were merely intent on tantalizing us, giving us a touch of gastronomic foreplay, but no, this was indeed our very own selection of tiddlies, fish bites and chips, and my very own Food Platter. Wow. Nearly half an hour ahead of schedule.

Now, I don't want this chapter to turn into a mad rant, but this food really was one of the most awful things I have ever pushed into my long-suffering mouth. Grease sprayed from every particle of my Food Platter. Sausages cut up and lying in greasy onions, filo pastry grease, meatballs, two dips – emulsions, really – and something that presumably once had shape but was now simply sitting formlessly on my plate. I never did manage to work out what it was supposed to be.

'What's that, Dad?' Sid asked.

'I've got absolutely no idea. It's horrible anyway. It's got cheese in it, that's just about all I can tell you. Swap it for a fish bite?'

Bursting with the pure energy of grease, we set off to take another look at the ring. And this was a ring that had suffered. It seems that our immediate ancestors behaved as if these huge stones hardly existed at all, as if they were somehow offensive rather than amazing. Which they were to them, for there really does seem to be something in the air down here, and it has absolutely nothing to do with Christianity at all. The Church knew this and encouraged the village to pay the stones no attention – unless it was to use the raw material in the building of the village houses, and even the inn. It just wanted to carry on regardless and create a jolly Christian agricultural community with a handsome church, and continue to usurp the location of what were probably the country's most important pagan sites. The village developed with a deliberate lack of tact. A fact that has not been forgotten by the nation's growing band of pagans, who flock down here on solstices and especially pagan days to worship at the temple of something.

So much has been surmised over the years that there are some wonderfully bizarre explanations about what the Avebury stones actually signify. The reality seems quite simple, and can be summarized as follows: the stones are obviously significant, but nobody knows what they signify.

Archaeologists have found both Roman and Saxon remains on the site and suggest that while the Romans might have visited out of curiosity, the Saxons seem to have used the henge as a defensive site (they called it *weala dic*, meaning 'moat of the British'). But as soon as the Dark Ages became illuminated by medieval tolerance and wisdom, the Christian world fought constantly against the idea that there was any other form of religion permissible, and encouraged the neglect and gradual destruction of the site. Despite all this, pagan names still abound: the Devil's Stone, the Devil's Chair and the Devil's Brandirons can be found in the Avebury complex. It seems that much of the destruction was carried out during the Middle Ages since all the pottery found under the stones dates from that period, as does the unfortunate man called the barber-surgeon who was found buried under one of the stones, crushed to death.

So, as magnificence became embarrassment, we committed an act of crass stupidity in the name of religion – which reminds one of the theocratic nonsense that inspired the Taliban to destroy equally significant ancient sculptures in one of their final moments of power. One brisk sunny December morning in 1649 the antiquary John Aubrey came across the forgotten henge while riding to hounds with friends. He was immediately struck by what he saw: 'The chase led us (at length) through the village of Avebury into the closes there: where I was wonderfully surprised at the sight of those vast stones: of which I had never heard before: as also at the mighty bank and graff [ditch] about it. I observed in the enclosures some segments of rude circles, made with these stones, whence I concluded they in the old time had been complete. I left my company a while, entertaining my self with a more delightful indignation.'

John Aubrey, who is best known for his *Brief Lives*, was an early member of the Royal Society and mixed in enlightened circles, so when he wrote about the stones, the word spread. King Charles II summoned him when on a visit to Bath and asked to be shown around, which he duly and with due reverence did. But like his *Brief Lives*, Aubrey's major work on the British landscape, *Monumenta Britannica*, remained unpublished in his lifetime, though it still exists in gloriously scribbled manuscript form. In it he wrote at length about Avebury, and was quite awestruck by the extraordinary mass of stones. Like many since, he began to try to put meaning to it all and formulated the idea that was to hold sway for generations – indeed it still does – that these buildings were druid temples, and thus represented but little threat to

Christianity as they were believers in the same God. Unfortunately, we now know that's impossible for the very simple reason that the stones precede the druidic religion by a matter of millennia. It is quite likely that druids did, and still do, feel that both Avebury and Stonehenge are part of their heritage, but the truth lies elsewhere, in those mysterious days two millennia before Christ walked the earth. And the sea, come to that.

When we were walking around expending our massive calorie intake, we looked at the stones and pondered, and saw quite clearly, as thousands have done before, that some of them have faces. Now the thing that is supposed to distinguish this particular set of stones from Stonehenge is that they haven't been worked at all, neither sculpted nor altered, and if this is true they might well have been chosen for the very reason that they had in their natural form a distinctly human appearance. I like this idea. And so do others. Of all the theories I have come across it is the one that suggests the stones have character, and represented – conjecture, of course – the good old universals of sex, and copulation, of male and female energy. As recently as the early eighteenth century there stood, for instance, in the middle of the Avebury circle a giant stone known as the obelisk that would have been a suitably proud and phallic centrepiece. Some of the outer stones have slits and holes that have an obviously female association, so there's balance there of sorts. Apparently, the position of the stones is such that the shadow of the male touched the female during the summer solstice, and that some of the others, the Goddess stone in particular, faced the midsummer rising sun with uncanny accuracy. The sun was then quite possibly thought of as male rather than female, so you can begin to see that therein lies an answer to what it all signified for our neolithic ancestors, untroubled by Church and Bible, and science.

It has been estimated that it would have taken five hundred men ten years to build Silbury Hill, which suggests a level of commitment to something. It seems to my innocent brain that there also has to be some connection with the location. And there are few more intriguing ideas than that of the system of ley lines that exists in this part of the world. Again, no-one is quite sure what ley lines are – prehistoric tracks linking meeting-places, or markers for the Earth's imperceptible energy currents? – and you might not like the idea of them and think it all just too pagan, but take a look at the evidence. There is a line that runs all the way from St Michael's Mount on the Cornish coast up to Glastonbury and on to Avebury – a coincidence, perhaps, but is there just a little truth to it that has simply disappeared from our collective consciousness? A consequence of our visceral inability to accept that our ancestors might have had knowledge that is beyond us, skills we simply cannot easily accept?

Which has a distinct echo in our food culture. Britain – so proud of our history and traditions, yet so neglectful of them. We certainly seem to have almost completely jettisoned a culinary tradition that was once rich in local variety, and permitted, nay encouraged, to take its place one that is nationally, and monotonously, almost entirely homogeneous. It's a pasta and pizza, burger and curry culture that has triumphed. But it is, I think, a shifting dialectic. Regionalism is lurking in the shadows, feeding itself for the big fight. The problem is that the shadows are so monumentally dark it may be but a pathetic elitist revival that has little relevance. It had certainly proved a struggle to find a sizeable groundswell, in the Cotswolds and in the country at large.

When we left Avebury, having had our fill of neolithic rambling, I was still flummoxed by my Food Platter.

'What did you think of that meal then?' I asked Sid.

'Neanderthal,' said Sid.

Neolithic, thought I.

23

CORNWALL

Pilchards and Oysters

'RUN HER UP TOWARDS THE GRIBBIN, ME BOY!'

Even though the 'boy' was ninety-one years old, he tweaked the wheel expertly.

I was out fishing for pilchards, on a beautiful, calm, pristine summer's day with the little Cornish port of Mevagissey in the background. While hundreds of tourists munched on their ice-cream cones, a crew of three had walked purposefully past them, down to the *Lyoness*, to do a spot of gentle fishing.

Meet the crew. There was the skipper, Andrew Lakeman, Mevagissey born and bred, a passionate entrepreneur whose family has been working these waters for thirteen generations. He had proudly shown me the family tree that stretched all the way back to 1705. Then there was Cyril Hunkin, an ancient man, full of vim and sparkle, the oldest working skipper I had ever come across. Also one of the smartest, dressed in a suit, tie and trilby – not always typical Cornish fishing gear, but I guess we were just being sociable. And then there was me.

I just watched, soaking in the fishy tales of derring-do. An odd team, perhaps, but this light-hearted fishing gave us the time to talk about the old days, when Mevagissey's thick harbour walls were stuffed full of fishing boats that worked the huge shoals of pilchards offshore.

The old pilchard fishery started in the summer. Lookouts were posted along the coast up purpose-built towers on top of the cliffs. These were the huers, and they would spend hours searching for signs that the pilchards were arriving on their annual visit, watching for the sea to turn what they called a 'royal purple', the colour it took on as the vast shoals swam up eastwards from the Lizard. Gulls circled overhead. The sea seethed as the fish were bombarded by birds from above and by tuna and dolphin closer to the shore. As soon as the shoal was sighted, the huer would begin the hue and cry of 'Hevva! Hevva!' down a tin megaphone towards the fishermen. He would have two gorse bushes covered in white canvas to hand that could be used to give the precise location of the fish, using a complicated set of semaphore signals. The huer, along with the skipper of the fishing boat, was paid in part by wages and in part by a share of the money from the fish, so he had a real interest in getting to the pilchards as soon as possible.

The fishery was worked by rowing boats, carrying a seine net. Sails were not needed, since the fish swam so close to shore, and it would often take only minutes to get out to them. A net was cast around the shoal, the keep net, made of a fine cotton filament, and the skipper would then take a look at the fish. Too lean and they would be useless for salting; too fat and they would turn rancid in no time at all, so his judgement was important. No-one would buy them unless they could be used to make that great local speciality, the Cornish salted pilchard.

If the catch looked good, the boats would cast a second inner net, to dip into the boiling mass of fish, and pile them high into the boats to be rowed back to shore and taken up to be salted. It was an uncomplicated business. The pilchards were cast into huge pits and containers, covered with great mounds of French bay salt, and left to suppurate for eight weeks. The next stage called for little more expertise: the pilchards were taken out and pressed to squeeze out the oil and moisture, leaving a salted, desiccated fish that was admirably long-lasting. The oil — train oil it was called — was burned in lamps, and used to waterproof canvas.

Although salted pilchards were considered by some to be a delicacy, they were not one the British ever really fell for; they preferred their pilchards out of a tin. Yes, they were renowned, but mainly in Italy. There was a local Cornish market of sorts. Jousters would tramp the countryside laden with anything up to twenty kilos of salted or sometimes fresh fish to sell to the remoter outposts of the county. But the bulk was shipped across the sea to Italy. Salted pilchards, *salacche inglesi*, have been boxed and distributed all over the country for hundreds of years, to be eaten with polenta and pasta, and were admirably suited to satisfy the demand for fish far inland, away from the sea. They were always cheap, and became a particular favourite during the meatless fast of Lent. But in Britain they were and still are virtually unknown. Their decline has so concerned the Italians that the Slow Food movement is coming to their aid. It has created a presidium in their honour.

The idea of a presidium is to put all the producers of a particular endangered food in touch with one another, and to inject some capital that would aid its economic survival. Every two years in Turin, Slow Food arranges a spectacular event, the Salone del Gusto, where producers from all around the world — it is hard to keep pace with the speed at which Slow Food is expanding — congregate. It is quite the most invigorating food event of all. Yes, the majority of producers are Italian, and there is a marked predominance of pungent and deeply obscure Italian cheeses, but in the International section you will find the salted pilchards in all their glory, being nibbled and commented upon with true Italian gusto.

But is Britain as fertile a ground for the Slow Food movement as Italy? I'm not too sure about that. Regional food culture in Italy is alive, not entirely untouched by fast food culture but far more vibrant than the equivalent in Britain. In fact, to be absolutely frank, there is no true equivalent in Britain. Many of the most enthusiastic regional food producers are refugees from cities with careers that are entirely unrelated to food, passionate and often highly effective people who learn on their feet. Amateurs again, inspired, and individualistic. Some of the finest foods we produce actually have a very recent past. Britain's cheese culture was so nearly annihilated by years of centralization and government control (remember the Milk Marketing Board?) that we almost lost the art of making farmhouse cheeses altogether. So the salted pilchard really is a particularly unusual case, helped by the fact that its market was never a domestic one. Needless to say, it would really thrill me to see a similar mass movement in the UK that would help revive the brilliant ancient culinary heritage that exists now almost solely in the written word. To make those singing hinnies sing once more . . .

But, back to the fish. In Mevagissey the fishing has declined markedly over the years.

'The harbour used to be thick with luggers,' Cyril recalled. 'You could walk from one side to the other along 'em, moored up. But the fish started to disappear in the 1950s. No-one really knew why.' He then told me how he'd spent a few years cruising around Europe on the plush wooden yacht of a local lady. 'It was a gentleman's yacht. If you see what I mean.'

How things had changed. A few years back you would have found it hard to find anyone fishing sardines down here at all. They were mostly caught in Portugal, and Brittany, but the Lakemans and their company Ocean Fish decided to encourage some of the local boats to give it a go, and back they came with their holds positively brimming over with sardines and pilchards. By the way, you all know this I'm sure, but a pilchard is nothing more than a slightly older and possibly slightly wiser sardine. They are both of the species *Sardinus pilchardus*.

And how bizarre it is that not long ago I was busily shipping fresh sardines from France into Britain when we had our own fishery all along. But it became confused by nomenclature. If the fish were caught down in Cornwall they tended to be called pilchards, which had the distinct psychological disadvantage of their association with canned fish, poverty and smelly dustbins. But if they came from France, well, that was different. Thoughts of striped sweaters, crusty baguettes and fabulous food. The difference lay in one or two centimetres, only this time it was the shorter the better. But wisdom has for once prevailed. What once would have been called pilchards are now being sold as Cornish sardines, and sales are booming. In 1997, only eight tons were landed. By 2004, this had rocketed to 540.

Sometimes it amazes me just how easily we forget that, simply put, Cornish fish is among the finest in the world. And, just to remind me of how glorious it can be, I spent the morning with Steve Griffiths, Ocean's buyer at Looe Market, a little way to the east of Mevagissey. I knew the port well. Last time I was there I met its oddest merchant, a one-eyed seal called Sammy, who liked hand-lined mackerel so much that he would arrive in the autumn with the shoals that swam offshore. Looe is a very special port, and has a fine reputation to uphold, but the key to it is the blindingly obvious fact that its harbour dries out and there is simply no way big fishing boats can use it without getting stuck. Which means that the fishing fleet is made up of small day boats that fish overnight and come back with the following tide. The result is that their fish is quite gloriously fresh.

All the stars of the fishy firmament were there at the

market. Tropically bright red mullets, turbot, brill, and monk tails as firm and mysterious as ever. The story goes that the whole fish is so ugly that its head is chopped off to avoid upsetting the customers. In fact, far from sending people into fainting fits, monkfish generally cause gaggles of excited people to gather in wonderment. They are a fantastic sight, and a fantastic fish to eat. Then there are the lugubrious John Dorys with their nasty spikes and weird telescopic mouths, but here they lay before me, still with that gorgeous golden glow to their skin – which is, by the way, why the French call them *jaune doré* ('golden yellow'), from which we get the anglicized John Dory.

Before we all go fish crazy, we need to reflect a little on the complicated business of looking after the world's fisheries. Down here, as everywhere else in the world, some of the fish stocks have been declining. But, happily for us all, the sardines appear to be in blooming health, and the word is that this fishery is being worked at sustainable levels. And fish that are landed by day boats are in most experts' opinion being caught by a thoroughly sustainable fishing method, so that's good news both for our stomachs and our consciences.

It wasn't tales of the enigmatic pixie folk I spied at Gnome World nor the serene calm of Screech Owl World that drew me to nearby Falmouth, but the tale of the finest bivalve in the land, *Ostrea edulis*, the native oyster. This elegant mollusc had me donning my wellies and stepping out into the autumn tides, to wade among the wafting wands of seaweed, and to check out just how the oyster beds of the Fal estuary had survived the summer.

The beds belonged to a local oysterman called Les Angel, Cornish through and through, who with a summer tan only lightly faded was one of the few licensed fishermen still allowed to work the oyster beds. The real joy of this fishery is that it was decided way back in the nineteenth century that no motorized boats were to be allowed to work it at all. It has proved to be a wise decision, for that is how things still stand. And they still have their oyster beds.

Les came to oyster dredging late in life.

'I heard that the owner of one of the boats was giving up, so I thought I'd give it a go,' he told me. 'The oil business wasn't doing too well and my great-great-grandfather used to work the beds, so I knew how it was done. I bought my boat, the *Three Sisters*, and started fishing.'

There are now seventeen licensed sailboats and seven punts working the beds, and they all know precisely who works what bank by using little more than peer pressure and tradition. The writ is totally informal but completely respected. They don't really like the idea of anarchy down there. Upstream you will see a few sticks that act as markers, and that is all that's needed. No-one dares cross the bounds and usurp other people's oyster beds. It's just not done. Quite impressive really.

'It works,' Les confirmed. 'There are still oysters out there and everyone agrees that it's the best way to run the fishery. All you do is lay the line and pull in the dredge. It's that simple really. When I was young I used to work one of the punts – winkboats we used to call them. That's how I first got to know the beds.'

Winkboats have a rudimentary winch on the back that can pull in the dredge, but they are nothing like as attractive as the Falmouth work boats. With bowsprits, gaff rigs and good solid hulls, they are the essence of the oyster fishery, superb chunky sailboats that work the river. But they are not, as I thought at first, all built to the same design. Some of them have come from other Cornish rivers and estuaries, and there's still a boat builder at Mylor who makes the modern glass-fibre version, not quite as ravishing but a beautiful boat nevertheless.

Everyone knows that the oyster boats are incredibly in-efficient and only work about 15 per cent of the oyster beds.

But isn't that just fab? To worship at the altar of inefficiency for once! Perhaps this might seem very quaint until you reflect on what's going on here. Everyone knows that motorboats could hoover up the oysters in no time at all, but with characteristic Cornish stubbornness they have doggedly stuck to the dictum that this must never be allowed. Ever. Technically, any sailboat could work the river, but the Falmouth oyster boats suit the water. They are shallow-draught, and can easily ply the creeks and estuaries that stretch way up to Truro to the north. So long as there is wind, that is.

Les told me somewhat disparagingly, 'They don't all work the beds any more. Some of them have been bought by solicitors and doctors and the like. They just use them to race. On weekends mostly, except for the festival week.' Which is held between 16 and 19 October and is timed to coincide with the start of the oyster-harvesting season. Oyster tasting, cookery demonstrations, live music, an oyster ball, local produce and craft fairs are accompanied by the Working Boat Race. Strange one, this. I had witnessed cheese rolling without tasting a cheese, and spent hours watching people weighing giant gooseberries without eating a single one; here, at last, was a festival, three days long no less, where the culinary star, the immaculate Falmouth oyster, can actually be eaten.

Oyster loaves

Make a round hole in the tops of some little round loaves, and scrape out all the crumbs. Put some oysters into a tossing pan, with the oyster liquor, and the crumbs that were taken out of the loaves, and a large piece of butter. Stew them together for 5 to 6 minutes, then put in a spoonful of good cream, and fill your loaves. Then lay the bit of crust carefully on top again, and put them into the oven to crisp.

from *The London Art of Cookery* by John Farley (1796)

It is said that Britain has the finest native oysters of all. Said, that is, by the British, who rarely taste a Belon, or a wild Tralee oyster. The Romans liked them too. There are records of oysters being packed off in wicker baskets, covered with ice, to be eaten by the gourmets of Imperial Rome — an early example of what we do best with our best: send it all abroad. They were said at the time to be from Rutupiae, the Claudian bridgehead that was built by imperial troops in AD 43 and which gave its name to the oyster which any dedicated Roman gourmet sought out. Rutupiae evolved, and became the Saxon port of Richborough, whose ruins can still be seen near Sandwich, in Kent. Sadly, its glory days didn't last too long, but it must have been a pretty awesome sight. Claudius ordered the construction of a vast triumphal arch to greet the arriving imperial warriors. Embellished with bronze on marble, it recorded the apparent submission of the eleven kings of Britain, a disparate bunch who nevertheless gave the Romans an excuse for this early triumphalism. It seems likely, however, that the oysters sent from the port were actually harvested from the rich oyster beds at nearby Whitstable.

Talking oysters does make one a little hungry. After a day's wading in the river Fal, I needed mollusc, and I needed them bad, so it was with no real difficulty that I ordered a plate of natives and one of rock oysters on the banks of the river. To compare and contrast. Served perfectly, on a bed of crushed ice, in a deep tin dish so you weren't drenched in crustacean melt water. Pulsating still, the fat bivalves slipped down my throat, followed by that strong mineral rush that is pure sea, and iodine, with just a tiny touch of sperm. Just the thing for a healthy Sunday lunch. To appreciate an oyster at its very best it should be eaten freshly shucked, and will indeed be alive or at the very least reactive to a squeeze of vinegar or a sharp drop of fresh lemon. But a live oyster hardly dances and prances like a scallop. They are entirely passive when they grow, just endlessly filtering edible matter through their apparently rather uniform flesh.

But hidden among this amorphous glob is an animal of startling complexity. Did you know, for example, that the oyster is one of the few members of the animal kingdom to have a rotating organ? First you must open your oyster, by prising open the shell; one of its weak spots is the hinge that joins the two shells. For this you will quite probably need a stout oyster knife, which may well cost you more than the oysters (never mind, they have a hundred other uses). Then slice through the strong muscle that connects the two halves of the shell – which is why they are called bivalves – cutting it as close to the upper shell as possible. This is true for both rocks and natives.

A word on this distinction. Yes, it's true that oysters and poverty were once soul mates, way back in the nineteenth century when London's urban poor could afford little else, but pollution and overfishing soon began to push the prized mollusc beyond the pockets of the poor and it became an exclusively luxury item. It is hard to imagine that oysters, like salmon, were ever food for both the rich and the poor, without becoming stigmatized as poor food, but such were the quantities of oysters caught that it led to a flourishing pickling trade that enabled them to be sold all year long.

In France, the techniques of oyster cultivation were far advanced, but the French had for obvious economic reasons decided to concentrate on the faster-growing but non-indigenous species *Crassostrea gigas*, the Pacific or rock oyster. This oyster more closely resembles the popular but by then disease-prone long-shelled Portuguese oyster, but since it doesn't reproduce naturally in British waters – they are too cold – the seed has to be produced en masse artificially in a hatchery.

And now back to oyster biology. I became utterly absorbed by the details of it all, a tale of sex change and enormous strength, of the animal kingdom's most enigmatic and rarest rotating organ, for the oyster may be a glob but it's nonethe-less a complex glob, one that manages the unthinkable in human terms: it changes from female to male, and continues to do so on an annual basis for the whole of its life. If you think about it, the mere feat of creating layers of tough shell, the mollusc's exoskeleton, is startling enough given that its diet is but an endless procession of microparticles. Then again, if a whale can thrive on krill . . . We must remind ourselves every now and then just how awesome nature can be. So, glance down at your oyster and take a close look. Become a biologist before you devour your molluscs.

Oysters filter water through a set of fine lamellae, or gills, that are covered in a protective layer of mucus to protect them from the damaging effects of any larger and rougher particles that may come their way. These cilia simply exist to waft both oxygen for the circulation system, and particles into the gut system to be digested. When the particles are too big for the oyster they are wrapped up cosily in mucus and ejected, as pseudofaeces. What is deemed good to eat by the oyster is then passed into the stomach (more wafting here), a curious organ if ever there was one, with a weird rotating stile and an ever-changing proboscis that helps pull particles into the stomach, ensuring that they come into contact with the stomach wall. Then, with an almost Christian sense of biological nobility, the stomach proceeds to liquefy its own end in response to the reduced level of acidity that food particles bring, thus releasing a series of digestive enzymes that enable the oyster to convert any starches found in, for example, plankton – a primary food source – into the sugar glucose.

Another biological curiosity is to be found in the behaviour of the oyster's blood cells. They don't just circulate in the oyster's system but can enter the stomach as a phagocyte, and surround and consume any edible particle – much like an amoeba – before returning to the blood system, passing once again through the stomach wall.

And then there is the amazing story of oyster reproduction. In fact, the ability to change sex is really down to the extreme simplicity of the reproductive system, for all that really changes is that the reproductive follicles produce immobile sperm, or eggs, which are simply ejected into the water when a critical temperature has been reached. This is rather higher in the case of the rock oyster than for the indigenous native oyster, which is why we need to breed rock oysters artificially and bring them on to a few centimetres in width before they will survive our relatively cool seas and estuaries. At first the oyster is male, then it becomes female, hence the popular confusion over their sexuality. Technically speaking, an oyster is a protandric hermaphrodite – which will conjure up an image of wild tantric mollusc sex parties with Sting for the more vividly imaginative among you. Perhaps.

When the time and temperature is right, the process begins with a mighty mass ejaculation of oyster sperm, which is then filtered in by the female oysters. As the eggs are fertilized they simply drop to the sea floor and slowly develop. The Pacific oyster, and others of the genus *Crassostrea*, expel their eggs straight away (naughty eggs). Relatively few manage to develop, which is a good thing, for millions upon millions of eggs and sperm are released and the world would have been overrun by oysters.

I know all this by experience, for some of my formative years were spent working for an Irish oyster company, and I was given the sole responsibility of looking after the storage plant that was built in a down-at-heel part of west London. Come the warm summer months, our little oysters became sorely tired of being confined to their tank and did indeed ejaculate en masse, mostly over the weekend when I was similarly occupied. Come Monday morning, I would open the shed and be greeted by waves of oyster froth, a Delphic mix of oxygenated water and sperm whose scent will live with me always.

There are times of the year when eating oysters is deemed wrong, i.e. when (in English) there isn't an R in the month, and I'm sure it won't surprise you that the reason why is closely linked to this mucky old business of reproduction. This isn't because the oysters become toxic; it is because they become spermy. Milky, some call it. Others – fishermen, I am told – call it white sick. And when the oyster has fertilized eggs inside, it darkens to become what is called, equally romantically, black sick.

Happily, all this gastronomic squeamishness has had the serious ecological advantage of preserving our oyster beds from complete destruction. When fertilized mini oysters – technically called spat fall – are sent on their way into the brutal marine biosphere, they naturally settle on any hard substrate, a hard oyster shell being ideal, which if allowed will cause oysters to grow on top of one another in a rather confused orgiastic mess. So the business of oyster cultivation actually involves rather more than sitting back and watching your oysters slowly grow.

The dedication of the Falmouth oystermen to preserving the old ways has been helped by the arrival on the scene of a new company that has helped them market their molluscs, for that, they say, has been the trickiest part of all. The Falmouth Oyster Company works from the edge of the docks, and is keen to tell us all about this quirky fishery on the river Fal. They pack, deliver and pump away at the local markets, and have even sent their oysters to France. Despite all this, Falmouth oysters are rarely seen. But the story still warms the environmental, and the gastronomic cockles of my heart.

DORSET

Bread

WHAT HAS HAPPENED TO OUR MASLIN, DEMESNE AND WASTEL loaves? I wondered one bright morning as I stepped into Greggs the bakers and surveyed the monotonous selection before me. There can be a real sense of excitement when you step into a baker's as you take in the sensual bling – the freshly made loaves, the shapes, the odd names. But something seemed to be missing here. What characterizes Greggs is a studied uniformity. Each loaf is like the next. Identical weights. Standard shapes. Each shop is the same. Greggs seeks a corporate identity, and they have got it in spadefuls. From their early days in the north-east they have evolved to become a fairly typical modern British bakery, probably selling more meat pies now than bread. Their commercial acumen is notorious. Not long ago they offered their lucky customers a special deal: four cream buns for a pound. And the normal cost of one? Twenty-five pence.

They epitomize the industrial approach to baking. A

centralized plant serves satellite bakeries. The pattern is repeated all over the country, and the aim is simple: it is to get bread as cheaply and as quickly as possible to the shop, and this they do by using the notorious Chorleywood Process, a mechanical mashing so rapid that the dough is ready in minutes. Long, slow, malingering fermentations are out. And that is how most of the bread we eat is made. Even though the flour used may be low in protein, it doesn't matter at all, because modern science can deal with it. There are a whole range of additives and enhancers to get that loaf rising in no time.

It is a shame that we have become so distant from the art of making bread. Once, the bakers of Britain worked in towns and villages to ancient rhythms, and bread was tipped and tapped from their ovens from the early hours, which might even have been used to roast the villagers' Sunday joints. The baker was a quintessential part of everyday life, part of the community. The idea is pretty laughable now.

Since the days of the Plantagenet kings, bakers were closely surveyed to keep them from the wayward art of villainy, from fiddling the weights that is. And also, to keep the population fed and not starving, it was essential to control the price of both wheat and bread. Not that all bread was made from wheat. A maslin loaf was half wheat half rye, while a wastel was all wheat. Even then there was status among loaves. The rich ate white bread if possible. The poor would have, but had to make do with a rougher and, ironically, more nutritious unrefined loaf. The *Liber Albus of London*, written in 1419, clearly states that all bakers should make bread with the stamp of their seal on it, and that absolutely no-one should light their ovens with fern or stubble. On no account were they to bid for corn before the prime was sounded. Rules and regulations, however, have their own meaning. And it was quite simply the case that the reigning monarch found controlling the population that much easier if they were off that dreaded bread line. Loaves were to be sold at either two or four to the penny, which when you consider that a penny could also buy you four larks, a dozen finches or a snipe may seem even from this remote perspective rather expensive. So the temptations of the baker were many.

But even now there is among us a band of dedicated people who take their bread very seriously, who want us to appreciate the loaf and use the time-honoured methods to create something that really, and triumphantly, tastes. Slow-rising dough and carefully bought flours are the hallmarks of the growing band of artisan bakers who have emerged all over the country. And then there are the homebakers. Some of us downsizers have time to bake bread at home, and actually enjoy it. Come the weekend, I for one want to don my baker's apron, plunge my hands into a bowl of sticky dough and sprinkle the house with flour. Friday is flour day.

But, hey, Doc, I've got a problem! I have been trying to perfect one of the most challenging of all loaves, a thick, crusty sourdough that uses high-gluten flour and natural yeasts to make the dough rise. But my sourdough is invariably too sour, my crusts are too thick, and they don't stay hard. My loaf is not bubbly enough, and my oven is unpredictable. How can I face the world? Let's face it. There is nothing more inviting than a kitchen suffused by the warm, gentle, yeasty smell of freshly baked bread, and over the years I have heaped piles of dough, kneaded hundreds of kilos of flour, added this and that, but have singularly failed to make what I consider to be the *ne plus ultra* of the baking world, the sourdough loaf.

It was time to consult one of the country's leading artisan bakers. I had heard somewhere on the culinary grapevine that there was this dedicated baker who had created magic from the simplest of ingredients, and who was happy to help us amateurs get to grips with the tricky business of bread making. He had worked with dough for years but was no longer an active baker; he had become a teacher, and had opened his very own bread-making school in Dorset. All you have to do is contact him and all your bread-making problems could be solved. That was the idea anyway.

So, welcome to the farinaceous world of Mr Paul Merry, an Australian by birth, and although the years in Britain have taken their toll, he no longer walks around in shorts. The gentle burr is still there, but softened now, and with his stretch Steve Martin looks and long, sinuous hands, he seemed to have just enough gravitas as far as I was concerned. Paul's small baking school is called Panary, and it has risen from a converted barn set in the lush green fields of mid-Dorset, just to the south of Shaftesbury.

Dorset has given me the very fondest of memories. I did the harvest there once, at a chaotic, ramshackle farm on a dung-caked road that swooped down to the sea at Kimmeridge, just past the little Purbeck metropolis of Worth Matravers. It was a blisteringly hot summer at a time when my muscles worked with the energy of youth. Well before the days of giant straw Swiss rolls, we leapt about in Dutch barns and stacked the prickly bales, a curious mix of Londoners, students and locals who became crippled by days of endless riotous laughter that so annoyed the unfortunate farmer who had taken us on that he seemed to be on the verge of suicide by the end of the harvest and couldn't even bring himself to bid us Godspeed.

The one thing I will never erase from my brain was having a cream tea in this staggeringly beautiful part of the county, where Dorset meets the sea. Neither an isle nor an island, Purbeck rises from a chalky escarpment that you can see from afar, especially around the heaths and sandy moors to the north of Poole and Bournemouth. The soil is poor, sheep are happy, and the sea is home to crabs and lobsters that can be eaten sweet and freshly boiled if you're lucky. And once there was a farmer who actually made his own clotted cream. It's all gone now. White-hatted farmers now need to finance a multi-million-pound investment enclosed in plastic walls to avoid the incredible dangers clotted cream could pose.

Over time, they began to bake the lightest and freshest of scones as well, serving them moist and still warm with home-made strawberry jam, and tea in those clumsy angular green cups that were far too small for a decent cuppa. I can feel the heat from the sun, hear the larks sing, and see the distant blue sea fanning out in Kimmeridge Bay below as I write. I can feel the thistles, and sense the dried cow dung and those enormous suede-coloured flies that seemed to be at their happiest when lapping from the well of a freshly produced liquid cowpat. The stunted, wind-sculpted thorn trees blossomed in the spring, and we picked vinous purple berries and sloes in the autumn. In the summer there were the tourists, hundreds of them, but despite it all Purbeck remains a ravishingly beautiful part of England that part of me still loves after all these years.

But this was a trip that had no time for romantic memories of scones or cream. It was meant to hone my baking skills. Paul Merry's bread-making school is set next to an old water-mill that still grinds and sighs on demand, and offers courses making the basics along with some traditional British breads such as the cottage loaf, the London bloomer, cobs, as well as milk cakes, saffron dough cakes and the gloriously gooey Chelsea bun; he will even teach you to make pastry, to bake your own baguette, or to fine-tune your *panettone* during the occasional French and Italian bread two-day special. It is all very informal, and relaxed. Some excellent flour pours from the dusty heights of the mill opposite, convenient for one and all. I arrived just in time for the final day of an Italian baking course, and was quickly enrolled in making *panettone*.

It soon became obvious that one of my big mistakes when it came to baking was a tendency to be imprecise. I am terrible at following recipes and like to believe that you can feel and improvise your way out of most problems in cooking, but I admit that at times this is complete and utter tosh. Especially when it comes to bread and pastry making. So I began to get slightly panicky when Paul started asking me seriously searching questions such as, 'Now, William, how many grams of yeast and salt will we need?' I was the late arrival and had picked up that the required amount was 2 per cent, but was getting a distinct feeling that I was being class dunce here.

'So you have to add all the dry mass weights together? OK. Right . . . erm . . . six grams?'

'No, sixty. You're a nought out!'

I could have been sent into the corner, but was allowed a bit of time to pull myself together.

With the *panettone* stuffed into tall pots, and a southern Italian loaf called *pane altamura* on its way, I began to come over all profound, and to wonder about what we were all doing here.

'Paul,' I said, 'since we are making a bread from Puglia, how do we really know whether we are succeeding? I mean, surely it's very difficult to create a bread that's so specific to a particular place?'

'Well, you're right and you're wrong, really. Yes, it's true that the flour, the water and the yeasts all vary from place to place, but then there are still quite a lot of things you can do to create a bit of variety. By combining different flours, for example. By moulding the dough into different shapes. Yesterday we made some *pan bigio* using a *biga*, or a sponge as you would call it in England. That creates a bread that really is quite Italian.'

And as we started thinking about this, he pulled out a *pan bigio* and let me nibble a little. It was true. This bread did indeed have a special flavour about it. The devoted students had created a loaf not only with startlingly large bubbly holes in it, but also with a fantastic taste. And they went on to achieve a rare state of *panettone* bliss. We talked about this north Italian delicacy, half cake half loaf, studded with dried fruit and fennel seeds, and its complex flavours, how it is so often tinted and tainted with additives, and has this ability to be kept for centuries with no apparent ill effect, which always makes me a little suspicious of what it contains. So it all felt perfectly legitimate, this exercise in Italian baking, here in deepest Dorzit.

As the session drew to a close, everyone began to pack up and stuff their cars and stomachs with bread, baking stones, dough cutters and all the accoutrements of baking. I couldn't help but wonder who would actually be true to the cause and carry on with baking in the years ahead. In fact, it probably is fair to say that baking bread actually stopped being a domestic activity long ago. Fuel was often too expensive to waste on maintaining the high temperatures needed, and life was hard enough without having to get up and bake bread in the middle of the night. Leaving it to the experts was an expedient thing to do.

Since Paul had generously promised me a one-on-one session the next day to get to grips with my sourdough, I wandered off to try and find a B&B nearby to rest my weary fingers.

The road down to Blandford Forum was in the old sense of the word lush. I drove on into the evening sun with the rape glowing in the distance, and looked at the fields on either side of the valley of the river Stukely. It was cow bingo time. Every single one of them had its eyes down, head firmly stuck to the grass, and what a deep and very appetizing green it seemed to be. They really seemed to love that grass, licking it and nibbling it with a sensuous fervour. Lovely. This was England at its most beautiful. Woodpeckers dipped from the woods – well, OK, one woodpecker. Diseased rabbits looked up from the roadside. And there was the endless rural hum of tractors speeding along the highways, dropping piles of manure to fertilize the asphalt. I could have taken a Ph.D. in yokelry and rural studies quite happily that evening, but there was still the small matter of getting somewhere to sleep for the night.

Blandford Forum has an unusual architectural purity about it. Burned to a cinder in the eighteenth century, it has a Georgian sturdiness as well as one of those particularly evocative names that are just, like, so Dorset. Where else would you find a village called Binghams Melcombe only a few miles away from Melcombe Bingham? I liked the idea of sleeping in this quiet market town and seeing if Blandford had succumbed to the *cappuccino*, but shock horror, for some utterly inexplicable reason Blandford seemed to be full of young men in shorts all looking for a bed. I think there was either a curious epidemic of fashionitis that completely passed me by, or a conference of footballers, but whatever the truth – and I did try to find out – all beds were full, to me at least. Maybe I should also have been in shorts. I had to escape to the next town, Sturminster Newton.

You might have realized by now that I was developing a profound passion for that mighty British institution the bed and breakfast. And as luck would have it, I was to find a real cracker in Sturminster. It was a little on the pricey side, I admit, so I haggled. But there was something about the place that drew me in. I beat down the asking price to what seemed a decent sum and went to rescue my laptop and toothbrush from the car – all I thought I would need for the night.

The lady who ran the B&B spoke in a voice with just the faintest hint of long-term tobacco abuse, and a distinctly urban accent. Somewhere in s'arf London I would place it. Her house was clean, and carpeted. The beds even had duvets. And she was the most attentive of hostesses.

'Can I get you a cup of tea?' she asked.

'Oh, thanks. That would be lovely!' For there are times when tea really hits the spot. This was one of them.

Off she went to brew, returning with a little tray of biscuits. Classy stuff.

'If you need anything, do ask,' she kindly told me,

rounding her vowels, adding a growing layer of posh over the south London.

Now attentiveness is all very well, but it can get a little disturbing. Every time I opened the door the landlady appeared like a smiling, silent phantom.

'Off to the car, then?' she asked on my first foray.

'Yes, just getting my wash bag, thanks!'

Half an hour later, hunger beckoned me to try out the no doubt highly developed local eating scene.

'Out for something to eat, then? There's a very good Indian up the road if you like that. There isn't a Chinese though. Oh no, we don't have a Chinese here at all. Anyway, you're welcome to come back and eat it here if you want, you know.'

Another Dorset composite, with its own dinky market square and a town hall with a thatched roof, Sturminster Newton's golden days are well and truly over. Sadly, the Artificial Insemination Centre has closed, as has the country's largest calf market. As a result, there is little to do other than race around the town in raucous cars. I really think the Prince of Wales should stand on the street corner and shout, 'It's appalling!'

But as I walked through the town's busy streets, I grew to love the quintessential dichotomous nature of Sturminsterness. A committee of local worthies sat on one side of the town hall, bristling in blazers and sensible shoes, probably trying to solve the problem of the market cross and the spiritual feebleness of the town's youth. On the other, the cars spun by and everyone joined the queue for the kebab house. As did I, before you accuse me of non-participation. My conversation went along these lines:

'I'll have a doner, please.'

Something shouted in Turkish.

Then I added, 'And have you got any mineral water?'

'Sorry?'

'A mineral water.'

A look of mild panic came over the kebabmeister, who had obviously never heard of this effete luxury drink, and his English wasn't quite up to asking me more about it. The guvnor chipped in and said sorry, no, we don't do water. We've got Coke or Fanta.

'Thanks,' I said, and sadly turned down these almost exact equivalents.

Meanwhile, someone else had come in. A regular, for the guy behind the counter, the selfsame chap who had struggled with the expression 'mineral water', then began speaking fluent glottal stop: ''Allo, mate. Or right? 'Ow are you? The usual?'

I wandered through the town, and sat in the pub, slowly asphyxiating in the smoke, then decided to wend my way back to my B&B. It seemed a more attractive proposition.

Perhaps I had an overactive thyroid or something, or I had been reading too much Stephen King, but since the bedroom door had no lock on it I decided for the first time in my life to jam a chair underneath the handle. Just under the note that said 'I live on the top floor. If you need anything in the night, please don't hesitate to ask.'

The following morning at eight o'clock sharp I arrived for breakfast as promised. As soon as I stepped out of the door, there she was ready and waiting, husky and smiling. She silently padded after me. I went into the dining room, with its solitary place set – she had brought out her best china, and the linen napkins (or were they serviettes?), neatly ironed and pressed on the side plate – and off she went into the kitchen. The TV was blasting out gory pictures from Iraq. Beheadings, bombings and blood weren't my ideal breakfast companions, so I reached for the remote and turned the effing thing off. I have yet to stay in a B&B that doesn't assume you are simply gagging to watch telly in the morning.

Within seconds the good lady was in. She took a long, hard look at me and said, almost conspiratorially, 'Would you like to listen to Radio Four?'

'Is it that obvious?' I said. 'Oh dear.'

'Well, I thought you looked as if you might!' She smiled as she delivered this hammer blow, then fiddled with the zapper and went back to her sizzling bacon.

And a fine breakfast it was. She had sculpted a melon with geometric precision, and brought the ritual Full English in, with the baked beans tastefully set aside in a warmed pot, cherry tomatoes (get you!) and an egg with a decent yellow to its yolk. The toast was thick, and although not quite home-made sourdough it was at least a step away from the industrial pap you usually get in a B&B. No sliced white loaf – wow! Pretentious or what? A first in my B&B experience.

I took her lovely antique bone-handled knife to the butter and lovingly spread a little on the bread. Ping! It snapped in two; the brittle blade had had enough. Time for some quick thinking. Should I pocket the whole thing, and leave post haste? Or should I come clean? As if by magic, in she came.

'I am really, really sorry,' I gushed, 'but your lovely butter knife broke.'

'Oh, no, no! *I'm* so sorry. That's awful. Are you all right? You're not hurt, are you?'

Marvellous.

This dance of manners continued into the realm of the surreal, both of us blaming ourselves, practically flailing our bodies with remorse. I hurried through the meal, packed and left. I was about to start the car when someone rapped on my window, frightening the life out of me.

'You forgot this!'

And she handed me the receipt.

I began to wonder about the B&B. Who are all these gallant amateurs who decide one day to up sticks and open a B&B by the sea, or in the depths of the country? And why do I love them so? I think the answer is that they are so quintessentially British. Amateurish, and governed by ludicrous rules, they seem to be a woman's domain, an extension of domesticity, often run by an incomer full of enthusiasm and just good old-fashioned nosiness. We British still seem to have this marvellous laissez-faire attitude to life. We can set up a business overnight, practise as an organic witch doctor with impunity. After all, we do have this expression 'jack-of-all-trades, master of none', and while I know the restrictions on running, say, a B&B exist, they aren't half as overwhelming as they could be – dare I say it? – over 'there', on the Continent. After all, we don't do things like that, do we now?

But, almost without exception, they get it just ever so slightly wrong. I remembered the B&B in Great Yarmouth where the first thing you saw was the husband watching the telly in a vest with a huge pile of cigarette butts by his side. I recalled too a Scottish lady and cupboards that fell apart, a bed with bedsprings popping out of the mattress. All human life was there.

And they are not all sweetness and light. The B&B can be full of hidden meaning. For example, if you live in a B&B full time – on benefit, that is – it is interpreted as the modern equivalent of being in the workhouse, to be down and almost out, supported by the state and filling the pockets of an often absentee landlord. It is a pretty rough life. Seaside resorts are full of B&Bs like this, stuffed with people whose lives teeter on the edge.

But there are the B&Bs that live off people passing by who like their cheapness and hospitality. However much some land-ladies might be just a little over the top, a smile and a real human being is a marvellously welcoming way to begin the night. Far better than a dowdy receptionist in a hotel chain whose heart is seldom so deeply involved in your one-night stay. What really needs to be celebrated is our absolutely dogged love of being the amateur, the free spirit who tries his or her hand at anything, for this is a freedom we hold dear. The bed and breakfast landlady belongs to the same world. Some are monstrous failures, others misguided, but many have got it all just perfectly right. So, to any of you who worship at the temple of the anodyne, cheapo hotel, I urge you – no, I beseech you – to take the plunge and enter the wacky world of the British B&B.

This spirit of amateurism is infectious. Enthusiasts easily convince themselves that they can run restaurants, raise pigs or make cheese, and amazingly it often works. It's just that once in a while – well, maybe more often than that, come to think of it – you will meet abject failure, crass, misguided, mistaken enterprises. My journey had introduced me to one or two of them. And lo and behold, we are now shipping this talent abroad. So grossly inflated have property prices become in the UK that thousands upon thousands of intrepid home-owning Brits are selling up and living the dream, opening *gîtes* and B&Bs all over the sunnier parts and quite probably the less sunny parts of the continent of Europe.

This congenital lack of respect for professionalism is quite possibly why we seem to find cooking so challenging. We devour cookbooks with almost unseemly greed; Jamie Oliver tomes tumble off the shelves by the thousand. But if we all love the idea of buzzing about metropolitan London with our tongues hanging out, publishers will tell you that any recipe must be detailed down to the very last nanogram. Gram by gram, litre by litre, everything must be clearly laid out, for we have so little culinary memory at our disposal. Hence, perhaps, the demise of my beloved dishes. Take a look at an Italian cookbook one day and you may notice that two letters, *qb*, appear rather often. *Quanta basta*, or as much as you need, which is entirely meaningless in a culture that has lost its culinary roots.

Back at the mill, my sourdough day was due to begin. I marvelled at the glorious morning light and the depths of the colour green, to whose beauty we can all become quite immune – until, that is, we step off that plane back from the annual holiday in Tenerife and marvel at the comforting fertility. Imagine England glorifying its brown and pleasant land. No worries here that the prickly pear may replace the blackberry. I can handle that. But it would be a sorry day indeed if our grass was to change colour. And what would we do with all our lawn mowers?

I should try to explain why I have this thing about sourdough. Firstly, what is it? Sourdough bread is made by a technique widely practised all over the world, especially in those poor, deprived areas that haven't yet discovered the bread machine, and quick yeast. It is slightly — well, massively — laborious, a complete contrast to the busy person's way with bread, to pour everything into a bowl and mix and wait. It requires time, patience and experience to get it right. Paul, justifiably, thought it unwise to hand out a recipe: 'You cannot deal with it properly without all the background about how the leaven is raised and nurtured, ratios of food, etc. It's just too big and complicated a topic to arrive out of nowhere in a so-called recipe. Frankly, I'm against such simplification.' But with perseverance, and by mastering your brief, the rewards are a loaf of awesome beauty, with an alluring, mildly sour taste and a firm, leather-brown crust. It keeps for days rather than seconds, makes the best toast in the world, and children don't like it so, adults, you can eat it all yourselves. By using natural yeast, you create a starter, which is then used as the source of leaven for baking the loaf. This will become your constant companion, a household pet that needs to be fed every now and again or it gets too sour. It needs to be kept alive, and to be used; it can easily become the sole source of your weekly bake. So chuck away the easy yeast. Cancel all social engagements and join the quest for the perfect loaf.

But before we get down to the sticky business of sourdough, we should, I think, add this. It is by no means a British invention, and has in fact infiltrated from the United States and France, a blessed bipolar attack from which we can all profit.

Although the San Francisco sourdough loaf is now offered in bakeries around the world, it is in a sense a complete con. It is said, and I for one see absolutely no reason to disbelieve it, that the bacteria that are particular to the damp Bay Area in San Francisco give the bread a unique flavour, so that it's really quite impossible accurately to reproduce the San Francisco sourdough. Bread will vary according to where you live, but you can still follow the techniques used in San Francisco. Anyway, it sounds such an attractive idea.

When European immigrés first settled in the area they brought with them the tried and tested techniques of making bread from a starter, using natural yeasts, and might even have brought chunks of live dough or buckets of yeasty brew with them back in the early settler days. It was mainly the Germans and the French who used this method of bread making. And if you do find one of the diminishing band of artisan bakers in France, look out for the bread made *au levain* – that is, with leaven rather than with *levure*, or added brewer's yeast.

The notable exception are the Italians, who have never really developed a taste for sourdough bread but who are more familiar with the halfway house the French call *à la poolish*. This is when you make a little dough the day before baking using added yeast, then let it rise overnight. The next day you add all this to some more flour to make a new batch of dough, and knead and shape as usual. The point behind all this is the taste of the bread – greatly improved, subtle and less pervasively yeasty. As is the structure and elasticity of the loaf. Big bubbles may seem to some to be a damned nuisance, a mere butter drain, but they are proof of a well-made, slowly maturing loaf where the elasticity of the dough is just strong enough to capture the gas produced by the fermentation of the yeast. This was why the *pan bigio* from the day before proved to be such a rip-roaring success. It was elastic, well crusted and superb.

The mere fact that many of us are struggling with the idea

of creating our own sourdough tastes is in itself invigorating, and tells a heartening story of globalization for once, that a loaf brought by immigrés to America can return to Europe and cross over to Britain, a country that has begun to appreciate the fact that not all bread comes in plastic bags and keeps for weeks. Some is made with care, and attention, slowly worked to perfection by the growing band of artisans who have chosen one of the most exacting professions of all.

If you watch and listen to a dedicated baker you will quickly become enthused by the sense of passion, and the skill. It is a process so full of variables and pitfalls that you can in a way understand why the industrial bakery was created, with its improvers and additives to bake a loaf that is invariably the same – equal weight, equal slices, a product devoid of that human touch. Bakers can be bombarded with challenges. On my sourdough day, Paul decided to test some of his ciabatta flour, which had been used the day before and had made a series of particularly anaemic-looking loaves. They tasted fine, but looked pretty insipid. It was almost comforting to see Paul start it all again, checking the flour, moulding and manipulating the dough, feeling it, pinching it, and then, in the final process before he placed it in a banetton to bake – we had deviated from the true ciabatta slipper form here – taking it in his hands for a final session of baker's love.

'Keep the manky bits to the right,' Paul told me, 'and push it up the table. Tuck your fingers on the edge of the ball and you'll get a perfect round shape, then place it in the basket. No, keep your elbows in. You should be able to do two at a time.'

You could begin to sense the rhythm of the baker as he worked in his dark and dusty basement, warmed through by sweaty kneading, exhausted by the exacting heat of the oven – as Paul put it, chasing the perfect loaf.

The mass of slightly sour dough had been left to rise overnight, slowly, as befits such a noble loaf, and was ready in the morning to be cut and shaped, then baked. A gentle yeasty whiff emanated from the mass as we sliced through the knocked-back dough, placing a precise 500g in each basket, covering it in the softest linen and leaving it to rise while we attended to the troublesome ciabatta. This was a great go-and-have-a-fag sort of rhythm to be working at, and it left us not only solving all the world's problems but talking a little about Australia's great gastronomic revival. Paul, you may remember, is an Australian by birth.

Here is a country that was once almost automatically associated with the British way of cooking. Dull, in other words, with an over-reliance on canned meat. And then, in the 1970s, something extraordinary began to happen. Greeks, Vietnamese, Thais, Chinese, Italians and Croatians, among others, arrived in their thousands and created a terrifically vibrant culinary culture, in a country that is blessed with space, beauty and an incredible range of natural resources. As well as a scant disregard for their own indigenous food culture. It provides a startling contrast to the UK. While Australia is creating a real beaut of a fusion down under, Britain fiddles and fuses while its culinary heritage burns.

Our loaves, however, were a startling success. Absolutely impeccable thick crusts, lovely springy interior. The only problem is that I still can't do it at home. Maybe it really is my oven. Or maybe I'm just too much of an amateur.

25

WEST WALES

Sewin and Welsh Cakes

MRS POWELL MADE A MEAN SEWIN SANDWICH. NOW YOU MAY not know what a sewin is, which is quite understandable. Hopefully a sandwich will be more familiar. But don't fret, a sewin isn't a rare velvet water vole, or a solitary, semi-extinct amphibian; to the Welsh, it is an iconic, glorious, migratory fish that the English call the sea or salmon trout. And it is about as fine a fish as you will find in Britain.

When the opportunity to go fishing for sewin was dangled in front of my inquisitive nose, I leapt at it, and looked forward to a relaxing day in the depths of the wild west Wales coast, on the river Tywi, just below Carmarthen. Relaxing it proved to be. But the endgame was more than I'd ever hoped for.

Every year, as the sewin started to run up the Tywi, the redoubtable Mrs Powell would welcome the local seine netters into her pub at Ferryside with a round of crusty, freshly made sandwiches. They were so delicious that people talk about them still. Especially when marooned on a sandbank waiting for a fish to entangle itself in the net, starving hungry, and in full view of the pub where all this took place. I was out casting a net across the river with one of the nine remaining boats licensed to fish sewin, with father Ozzie and his son Dan. We had been on the sandbank for a couple of hours already when hunger began to bite. The fish, however, resolutely refused to do so.

Bearded and as tanned as a pirate, Ozzie's soft Welsh voice was telling tales of days long gone when the river was full of fat, fabulously beautiful sea trout. He turned to his son, who was pulling in the net from the river. 'Do you remember Mrs Powell's sandwiches, Dan?'

Dan was the brawn of the two-man team, his dad the brains. As his dad talked, Dan continued to pull in his net, while we all watched hoping for a sign, that special splash a sea trout brings.

'I don't know what she did with them, mind. They were so moist. Kind of uncooked, like. Delicious they were. You see that building over there? That's the pub, the White Hart. Nice pub it was once, you know. I could just do with one of Mrs Powell's sandwiches!'

We were not alone. Only metres away a lazy seal snuffled and writhed in the water, waiting too, to snatch a fish from the net. These Welsh seals seemed strangely respectful of the law. This part of the Tywi was in a strictly controlled sea bass preservation area, and it was expressly forbidden for us humans actually to take anything but a sea trout. The only problem was that we had not yet caught a single one. But there were bass aplenty, fiercely entangled in the nets, along with a dopey grey mullet or two. It seemed so tantalizing. I had spent years of my life searching for fish of such supreme freshness, and now I couldn't touch a single one of them, let alone cook them. I watched, mightily respectful, as Ozzie and Dan struggled to free each and every fish caught in the net, spiking their hands bloodily in the process. Bass and grey mullet there were, but not a sewin in sight.

So we all dreamed of platefuls of Mrs Powell's sandwiches and draughts of cooling beer, delivered by magic, conjured up from nowhere in the still afternoon on this wide-open sand-bank, with crabs scuttling around our feet, razor shells gaping in the sand, and the tide gently flowing upstream.

In the distance lay Pendine Sands and the land of Dylan Thomas. Beauteous it was, quite beauteous, with scudding clouds, gentle waves and a huge stretch of gently rippling sand underfoot.

A seagull squawked. A stomach rumbled. No-one had spoken for a while.

'I wouldn't mind a plate of cooked sewin either, mind, and some fresh-dug Pembroke potatoes,' Ozzie added after a moment's silence, and off we all started again on this infectious fantasy.

'Or some cockles, bacon and laver bread. Now that's lovely!'

A rollercoaster of snacks and desires flowed. Yup, we were definitely in hungryland. So was the seal that was eyeing us up, snorting into the coffee-coloured water of the Tywi.

I had been driven down to deepest west Wales through the strange Forest of Dean, past the abbey at Tenby and down to Ferryside on the motorway – the 'slab', they called it.

'I'll take you down the slab, I think. We're a bit pushed for time.'

Horace Cook, founding father of the Severn and Wye smokery, was whirling through the lush green forests to buy the fish that had been caught on the Tywi the night before. The fishermen liked to be paid promptly, and it was in his interest to keep them all happy and flush with cash. Loyalty is a fickle thing with fishermen. As we started off that morning Horace's son Richard, energetic, entrepreneurial fellow that he is, had shown me a box full of shimmering, fat sewin that were to be sent off to London that night. Less than a day before they had been drawn by unseen forces back up the Tywi and had landed slap bang into a net. Tragic really. But what a wild and adventurous life they must have led. I felt infinitely sorrier for their flabby cousins, salmon, cooped up in fish farms, fed on grim little pellets, swimming round the eternally tedious pen where they are fattened for the table.

There is something more than a little intriguing about the sewin. Biologically they are nothing more than a brown trout, but one that has added an entirely new dimension to its life by migrating to the sea for a few years, feasting off the local shrimps and prawns, and fattening itself to a luxurious silver sheen. And then, back they come to the river to spawn. Almost indistinguishable from a wild salmon, these sleek, powerful fish are, despite their rareness, always sold for less than salmon, but are just as good to eat. The easiest way to tell them apart is to look at their mouths. The sea trout's runs well behind the eye; the salmon's doesn't. Other than that it's tricky, but a salmon tends to be sleeker and will grow much larger – if allowed to, that is, by the life-challenging obstacles in its way.

The unfathomable precision with which these migratory fish swim back to their own home river will always amaze me. And here I was in their very own aquatic backyard, hoping that just one of them would swim into the nets and give my fish-capturing soul a real buzz of satisfaction. The mystery of fish migration has volumes of wise words written about it, explaining it all in terms of molecules and magnetic poles, but I will simply doff my hat respectfully and continue to marvel at the way nature has evolved, at how with such unerring and unnerving accuracy sewin and salmon return to the rivers of their birth when their time comes, leaping over falls and battling against man and all his evil ways.

The sun was beginning to set, and we had a choice: one

more shot of the net, or back to have something to eat? The seal joined in the discussion and implored us to stay. We pondered, and decided to shoot the net just one more time. Dan rowed out into the river, and we all stood, watched and waited. The tide was flooding gently now, and over on the next bank another boat had struck lucky. This spurred us on. Although netting requires little skill, it does call for a lot of patience.

You can probably guess what happened next. A sewin did the decent thing and swam into the net. There was a gentle tug on the floats midstream, and Dan sprang into action. For this was to be a fierce battle between man and seal, and when a seal senses fish it has the unbearable advantages of speed and sight, as well as an awesome set of teeth. But this particular seal had been distracted by the other netters upstream, having given us up as a useless bunch of sandwich-obsessed amateurs. Dan quickly glanced over his shoulder, saw that the seal was away with the ferries, and began to pull in the net, brow sweating, muscles rippling.

Then the seal began to sense that something was amiss. Bitter and angry now that he had been outwitted, he sped over. The race was on – Dan and seal. We prayed to Neptune for some munificence. The seal closed in.

Mrs Powell would have been proud of Dan that day. After three hours of setting the nets, pondering, chattering and seal cursing, our reward finally came in the form of one gallant sewin, netted on the way back to its ancestral river. Sorry, fish. But at least you weren't mauled to death and half eaten by a seal. You were simply caught in the fishing net of destiny, and you live on in the spiritual oneness of the printed word.

That was most definitely to be it. We piled into the dinghy, and Ozzie pulled at the Seagull. For the non-nautical, that is an outboard engine, the marine equivalent of a Morris Minor, reliable, simple and almost sexy. It took me back to days of pottering about in Chichester harbour, of sailing-club teas and sunburn. And the sweet fatigue of the sea.

Horace, who had been snoozing and networking by the looks of things, said, 'Get any fish did you now?'

We showed him what must hardly have been an encouraging sight if your business is selling fish. One paltry sewin, approximate weight four pounds.

Then we set off, to get a bite to eat.

How to cook sewin

The best and easiest way is to bake the fish whole in the oven. Scale and gut the fish, and clean the gut cavity well with water and kitchen paper. Sprinkle outside and in with sea salt, add a splash of white wine and dot the cavity with butter. Wrap tightly in silver foil, and bake until the fish is just cooked down to the bone. Serve with new potatoes, and a wedge of lemon. That really is the finest way, and the simplest too, to enjoy a sewin.

The netting was supposed to be only the half of it, for Horace had also arranged that we should go upstream to see the weirdest fishing of all that night, and I was in boyish mode at the prospect. The Tywi has some of the last remaining commercial coracle fishermen in Wales, and they were set to fish the tide at two in the morning. The night was to be long and tense. And so it proved to be, but in the end it had nothing to do with coracles at all.

Just as we were setting back I received a text message from home: 'You'd better come back. My waters have broken!' Ever blasé, I had been saying, 'Oh no, the baby isn't due until the weekend. All the others have been on time.' But in the back of my mind, aware of the good old law of the sod, I suspected it was a risky approach. And usually my risk-taking fails.

This time it was Horace who did the decent thing. Without hesitation, he said, 'Come on, we've got to get you back.'

So we got ourselves together. They passed me a little symbolic bundle. It was the sewin. And noble old Horace drove me all the way back again down the slab, with impeccable generosity, for which I will be forever grateful. And how nice everyone was. I'll drive him; no, I'll do it.

This was, in a way, a piscatorius interruptus. Instead of the coracle fishermen, I met my youngest daughter, Lola, who will, I fear, always be told about how her irresponsible father went off fishing just as she was being born. In fact she waited just long enough. The waters had broken, but labour didn't start for another day. We had time for a quick Pimms by the Thames, then a curry, and almost as soon as the bill was paid labour started in earnest and a new life was on its way.

The coracle story was, however, simply too good to let slip. It rankled. A few months later, on a whim, I set off once again. The baby had arrived safely and was off in France, agooing bilingually with her *nany et papy*. So it was time to finish the story, and to round off my gastronomic travels. I had heard that there was to be a coracle regatta on the river Teifi, further west than the Tywi in the county of Ceredigion (we used to call it Cardigan, but this is Wales, and we play by Welsh rules). I thought this could be my best chance to see a coracle.

A week before I left, a friend had been to Wales and returned, so that was encouraging too. She had brought with her a pack of Welsh cakes, a more affordable gastronomic icon than a whole Welsh lamb.

'Here, I thought you'd give these a good home.'

Kind thought. I took a bite. They were disgusting, really and truly horrible. This is what happens when a cake falls into the wrong hands. Is that really what a Welsh cake should taste like? With the density of a cream cracker, studded with the odd currant, it was all just too jaw-stoppingly unpalatable.

Welsh cakes

The Welsh cake was something to be cooked and eaten quickly. They simply do not keep. So, back at home, I dug out an old recipe to see if they were any better if freshly made. The results were beyond denial. They were defiantly edible.

1lb white flour
6oz lard
½ tsp salt
1 cup sugar
1 cup currants
½ tsp bicarbonate of soda
½ pt buttermilk

Rub the lard into the flour and add all the other dry ingredients. Dissolve the bicarbonate of soda in the sour buttermilk and work into the dry ingredients to make a soft dough. Turn out onto a floured board, roll out until it is about a quarter of an inch thick, and cut into small rounds. Bake both sides on a lightly greased bakestone over a moderate heat.

from *Welsh Fare* by S. Minwel Tibbot (1976)

I piled into the car determined to get the truth, and even more determined to get to see a coracle, if not actually in the process of fishing then at least doing something. My computer had seized up again, so I was celebrating a false freedom for a couple of days.

Off I travelled down the very roads I had taken in the opposite direction to catch a glimpse of Lola being born. I thought about how nearly I had missed the birth, but luck had been on my side. One hour and forty minutes after the Indian she was alive and kicking, and almost immediately fell asleep. Her little face and wisest of looks will always be with me.

I got stuck in Cheltenham again and thought of the mad vision of the cheese rolling down Cooper's Hill. Then, hours later, I passed Carmarthen, and nodded towards the sea and the sewin. New ground at last. I took to the hills and the road along the Teifi Valley. I began to feel out of place in a car. The roads were buzzing with tatty old 4×4s, working, muddy even, almost all of them towing a squat little sheep trailer called Ifor Williams.

It rained. In fact, it more than rained. It deluged. Not far away, on the other side of the Bristol Channel, the little village of Boscastle hit the headlines when it was nearly washed into the sea by a flood of biblical proportions. Global warming, we are now told, will bring us more extreme weather. A blessing for doom merchants and satellite television.

The Teifi was on the verge of ill humour. It swelled and fidgeted, licking at the riverbanks and pushing away the lazy twigs and branches that had sought eternal peace. The Teifi was once one of the finest salmon rivers in the land, good too for the great sewin, but the days of plenty are over. While farmed salmon have been pushed into ubiquity by corporate profiteers, the drama of the sewin's life cycle has become almost forgotten. And its taste too. We eat a Ford Prefect, and have forgotten the Aston Martin.

Most of the salmon we eat is cheap, and horrifically fatty. I will not eat it, and will not let my children eat it either. It's not just that the colouring agents may be dubious. Nor that the chemicals used to control sea lice are highly toxic, and become embedded in the food chain. Nor is it simply a matter of taste. It's this that really bothers me: salmon have to eat. They are not a marine cow, and cannot exist on a diet of seaweed. They need protein. In the wild they eat prawns and crabs, and their flesh turns a delicious red from the keratin in their shells. We now have to colour the flesh of a farmed fish to make it red. Grey-fleshed salmon does not sell well. Farmed salmon are fed on fishmeal, a marine gallimaufry, a mix of fish trawled from the deep oceans, fish such as the sand eel upon which much of our sea bird population thrives. This unfortunate species has been so grossly overfished that the Danes, industrial fishers par excellence, cannot even fulfil their EU quota. That tells you two things: EU quotas are unrealistic, often hewn from political compromise; and the sand eel is in trouble. But that's not all. A salmon takes more protein out of the food chain than it can ever render, so a three-kilo fish will need more than that in wild fish for it to be brought Billy Bunter-like to the table. It is therefore simply unsustainable, particularly when the catching of the fish that make the fish-meal is so poorly controlled. Enough said.

Well, not quite. Let's also add that here in Wales the sewin population has plummeted even more than the salmon. And why? Us again. An axis of evil exists in the sea too. Drift netters, fish farmers, polluters – isn't that enough for a fish to battle against? The deep-sea netters take too many fish. Salmon farming has allowed the sea louse population to explode, and they have proved to be particularly fond of Welsh sewin. Even the Teifi has been affected by nitrogens running off into the water, and the dyes once used in the woollen mills upstream. Cheap food isn't always as cheap as it seems.

The rain moved into a thumping cyclonic rhythm, and I began to wonder about the wisdom of this coracle regatta. Then I had a moment of heritage happenstance. The Coracle Centre was close by. My heart leapt like a sewin on speed. Squeezed into a seventeenth-century mill on the Carmarthen side of the river, it looks down on the Teifi at Cenarth Falls, one of the few places in the country where you can actually watch salmon leap from a car park. It has to be said it is a particularly lovely car park, built on crumbled slate. To get to it you have to cross the bridge, and the border into Ceredigion. The bridge is wacky, and sublimely beautiful. Built in the eighteenth century with local stone, it glows and hums in the wet, as the river cascades over the falls. There are two cylindrical holes built into the bridge that give it its peculiarity, but they serve a particular purpose: to relieve the pressure from the floodwater when things get too overwhelming. It seems to have worked. The bridge still stands.

I got out, stretched, and soaked it all in. By the time I had done this I was also soaked, but the coracles beckoned. I stopped and asked the man who was overseeing things, 'Any fish running today?'

It was an easy chance to check out his accent. Softer, mellifluous Welsh – *musicaaal* one might say. He was eating an ice cream. I was to see him quite a lot over the next couple of days, and every time he was eating an ice cream. I suppose it didn't help that his kiosk was just by the ice-cream shop.

'Yes, there's been some this morning actually,' he replied.

So I hurried on over to the falls and looked and waited. Nothing. A few anglers stood on the riverbank downstream, cogitating. None had any fish.

'Any fish running today?' I asked them.

The Teifi boomed over the falls in the distance. The air had that mild freshwater pungency, half pond half newt. There was a seamless world of water from the river to the sky.

'No, nothing at all. There's just no fish about.'

I walked over the bridge and took refuge in the Coracle Centre, knowing that we could always take to the water if it all became too much.

Although the days of fishing for salmon are now over at Cenarth, coracle building is not quite a moribund art. In a land of wandering shepherds and valleys the coracle kept man mobile by using materials that were ready to hand. The inner shell is built from willow and hazel branches, and the outer waterproof cover on the wooden frame was once made from hide, covered in tallow, but those coracles were heavy. These days calico cotton is used; boiled in a cauldron of pitch, it's far lighter.

A coracle is a strangely paradoxical creation. It may seem to belong to the neolithic age, but it is practical, and there are many variations on the theme, from the Spey curragh to the Iraqi *guffa*. They are all strictly functional. The coracle can be carried on the back – that's rare for a boat – and they have myriad uses. They can be used for fishing, working in pairs at night, setting a net to catch any fish swimming upstream. They can even help guide sheep across the river. These days the law restricts the number of boats allowed to work the river – twelve pair licences are permitted on the Teifi – and any fishing must be carried out on tidal waters, which means that Cenarth is too far upstream. So coracles now work from Cilgeran and Llechryd downriver.

As you would expect, the Coracle Centre will tell you just about all you need to know about coracles. All the information is stuffed into one room, and when I walked in a family was just leaving. The kids had been kept amused by Rosie and Jim doing something natural in a coracle. A relevant video nasty.

Martin Fowler, the owner, came in and told me, 'You get a little bored with that after twelve years!'

I asked him the old any-fish-running question, and got a more global outlook.

'Well, there's no point asking any of the anglers. They never give you a straight answer. But there have been a few fish about. Whenever I go fishing I always try to go with him. You always get more fish that way.' He pointed out an article that had been pinned on the wall: LOCAL MAN CROSSES CHANNEL ON CORACLE. 'You should talk to Bernard. He lives at

Llechryd, a few miles down the road. You can't miss his house. There are always a few coracles outside.'

Tough, wily Bernard Thomas put the coracle to possibly its toughest test by crossing the English Channel in an astonishing feat of perseverance. It took him thirteen hours, and to record the fact he planted a Welsh flag in the sands at Cap Gris Nez. He is sadly one of the last of the old school of coracle makers. Even more sadly, he was taken to hospital on the day I called. My coracle trip was floundering a little.

The sun was setting somewhere behind all the gloaming, so I drove on to Aberteifi, a.k.a. Cardigan, and walked into the tourist office with practised ease. They quickly sorted out a bed for the night and I marvelled at the sound of a whole family speaking Welsh. It shattered the illusion that Welsh was a dying language. Ceredigion is apparently one of the bastions of Welsh. But what do we outsiders know of it? A profound and absolute nothing, I suspect. We have more idea what the Greek for yes and no is than the Welsh. Even the greeting *croeso* was pathetically as unknown to me as the Kikuyu for dog.

I had left on this journey with many assumptions. One was that urban mores rule, and that it is the south-east of England that predominates culturally and linguistically. True in one part of England only, I think – the south-east. This much-derided, self-perpetuating myth now seems a little dated. I can even begin to see the logic of peculiar ideas such as regional assemblies. Wales and Scotland seem well on the way to independence by stealth.

Somehow, Aberteifi seemed smaller than it should be. I was expecting a bit more pride about its one contribution to world fashion, wool, but no-one made any mention of the cardigan. The iconic happy grandfather's favourite, that dull old piece of wool, to be worn while waiting for the grandchildren and skipping through the weekend *Telegraph* obituary column. Is it too shameful a thing to be proud of? Can anyone ever put the cardigan on the fashionistas' map? Of course they will, one day. You wait.

Aberteifi was once a county town, and apparently a port. Now that is hard to believe, to be honest. The river has silted up, and there is little to remind you of the fact. It's a town that is on the sea, but not of the sea. The castle is crumbling, pinned up by a vast metal truss. It was entered into the For God's Sake Help Me section for the BBC's *Restoration*, a terrifically enthusiastic revelation of extraordinary buildings that share one thing, the fact that they are all decrepit and will soon be but rubble and dust. The castle didn't make it through.

But let's talk location and food. The sea, Cardigan Bay and the setting sun should have meant but one thing – fish. Cardigan Bay, after all, has some exceptionally fine bass and sea bream swimming out there, as well as all that sewin. Would I, could I, find some on a plate among the winding roads and the blustery clifftops? It was the last trip of the trip. It had to be a special, beribboned finale.

I asked at the tourist office for their recommendations. The two women looked at each other, seeking inspiration.

'Fish . . . Well, I think the Cliff Hotel at Gwnmar serves local fish, doesn't it? I'm ever so sorry, but I don't eat fish. Anyway, it's very beautiful down there.'

Her colleague came gallantly to the rescue.

'Yes, that's the best bet, the Cliff. Or you could try the Teifi Blu here in town. It's in an old boat just down on the water by Somerfield's. They do fish, I'm sure.'

Silly, I know, but I had vowed to keep my foot off the accelerator pedal for a while. I am addicted to odd corners on the map, particularly wild, remote beaches and blustery cliffs, to seeing the sun set and hearing sea birds squawking uncommon cries. And here there was more. A substantial chunk of Cardigan Bay is a protected area. Dolphins can splash about unmolested by fishing nets. Seals too, the fisherman's least favourite animal, can cavort without fear of being shot. And intrepid walkers can tramp all along the coast. Miles of windswept wandering can be all yours.

So, pulling on my walking boots, I set off to tackle the ups and downs and the glorious beaches as the sun began its leisurely descent, triumphantly visible now, sloughing off its grey, cloudy animus. I took the coastal path to Mwnr, and just hoped I didn't have to ask whether this was the right way. I wasn't too sure whether it was anything more than a cluster of houses. But it is. Mwnr sits atop the sea, with a crowning headland and a church of brilliant white, an ancient building, low slung, protected from the sea by a slate-grey wall, and full of tombstones, each one inscribed in Welsh. What a grand place to be buried. But laid to rest? I doubt it. The winter storms must be as fierce as hell. You can dip and dive into some perfect little sandy bays, wander for miles along the coast, and lap it all in.

Inspiring? Indeed. The wind forces itself into your every pore, your inner soul. It makes you want to dream and ramble, to cover yourself in seaweed. You too can have your Dylan Thomas moment up here. But try to be sober. I had, after all, already been struck by the passion of Burns, though less so by Wordsworth. All this nature was getting to my soul. And my appetite was beginning to stir in the vortex of my gut.

What better way to finish off a day than with a brisk blast along the clifftops and a plate of gloriously fresh fish, sitting on or even by a pub table with a fabulous view? Further along the coast, a band of neoprened surfer warriors craned their necks, checking for that mythical wave. I tramped on towards a pub in Aberport and glanced at the menu. There was a goodly fug inside, beer and smoke, and a thrum of clinking. I was sorely tempted.

I could have chosen a pizza from Hawaii, lasagne, or chicken and chips, but with true grit I thought I should stick to my brief. Hawaii didn't quite fit the desire of the moment, the need for that glorious something, a surprise, a plate of exquisite freshness. I should have known by now, but I have a unique capacity for fantasy. There was, as so often, simply nowt on offer.

Trekking back seemed the best option, to the Cliff Hotel. I really had been told 'It's lovely!', but to my eye the hotel was a gruesome, sloppy building with no form – just a simple statement of economics. More bedrooms here. Annexes there. And lording it over such a glorious view! Inside at the reception desk was the usual girl dressed in black with a wavering, semi-welcoming smile.

'I was wondering whether you serve local fish in the restaurant?' I even added a contemporary touch by raising my voice at the end of the sentence. She was young. I wanted her to understand me. I hoped she'd answer, 'No, sir, fish never book!'

Instead she hesitated, then said, 'Yes, we have some snapper on the menu tonight. I'll show you the menu if you like.'

What can I say? How can you offer a fish that has been caught thousands of miles away, off the coast of Africa, when you are perched right on top of one of the most beautiful stretches of sea in the world? And how can you offer fish caught by a boat that has been licensed to gulp up diminishing shoals that were once the very lifeblood of little fishing communities along that African coast? I couldn't really justify morphing into a Meldrewish 'I don't believe it!' or a McEnrovian 'You cannot be serious!' Nor could I bristle, ask to see the manager, and beat him over the head with a newspaper. I suppose I could have fallen to the floor and torn out my hair, but what with receding hairlines and all that . . . So I did the British thing and excused myself, thanking her profusely.

But, snapper? Pathetic.

As a facetious parting shot, I did ask her, 'Is it caught

locally?', half expecting her to reply, 'Yes, we have our own fleet of trawlers working the coast of west Africa.'

She disappointed me once more: 'I'm sorry, I haven't got a clue. I'll ask if you like.'

So, I set off back to Aberteifi feeling that my ribs were poking through my chest once more. Don't worry, it was an illusion.

But the Teifi Blu brought me a measure of gastronomic closure. Stuffed into an airy converted old fishing boat, it sits on the river and looks seaward, a distant prospect over the muddy estuary, but they do at least defiantly admit to using local produce, even if they are a little too keen on studding everything with slices of orange. I ummed and aahed between a slice of locally caught swordfish – slightly sceptical about that one, but giving them the benefit of the doubt – and the black bream, a fish that can be depressingly insipid. The grilled swordfish won it. It was served with a bowl brimming with fresh vegetables. You could tell they were fresh because the runner beans actually tasted of something. So, it took some effort, and yes, I could have stayed in town all along, but in the end all was well.

The next day started with another 'Full Breakfast', as tradition has it, for I did wonder just what they called it. It's easy just to say 'Yes, I'll have the Full English, please!' and forget that you are in Cymru. Full Welsh Breakfast should be the thing to say, I guessed. The lady assured me that it was all made from the finest Welsh produce and was therefore definitely a Welsh Breakfast. I flipped on the radio and caught the end of somebody enthusing about coracles, and the regatta day at Cilgerran.

After breakfast I wandered up the high street and bought some of the sweetest-looking mountain lamb I could find. You could almost pick it up, with its bright red, fresh, pure, inviting flesh, and gnaw those little bones.

A brief digression on the theme of Welsh lamb, if I may.

A few days later, back in Oxford, we sat down to eat the diminutive roast carcass, the air filled with the sizzling smells of the lamb, crispy roast potatoes from the allotment, rosemary and garlic. It was blissful. The meat was tender and succulent, but my thoughts turned to the travails of the hill farmer. Hill farming is, and always has been, a highly marginal business. We have become so used to our chops and roasts being a certain size that Welsh mountain lamb is struggling to maintain its market. A mountain lamb may well have as many as twenty chops on it, while a lowland sheep is more likely to have ten. Now this could easily traumatize an unwitting consumer. Just as sheep will bleat, so does a supermarket buyer when confronted with something that simply does not conform in any way to what he or she expects a consumer will expect. It can be a very tautological world out there. This is Britain, and there is said to be but a minuscule market for Welsh mountain lamb, and little chance that one will fall happily into the lap of the gastronome. It is far more likely that they will be sold, as they have for long been sold, to the markets of Greece and Spain where these dinky but infinitely tasty little lambs are spit-roasted and devoured with pleasure. And so long as disease doesn't ruin even that market, there may just be a few Welsh mountain sheep around at the end of the next decade. Otherwise the future looks pretty bleak.

When I finally arrived in Cilgerran it was bedecked in flags, as you would expect of a village that was celebrating its annual coracle regatta. A gaggle of people gathered around the front of a pub. The rain had stopped. It all looked promising. The Teifi cuts through a steep escarpment here, which is why a medieval warlord decided to build a castle that still stands, perched above the river on what was once the upper tidal limit. The castle will immediately make you think of armour, and pouring barrels of boiling pitch over a recalcitrant enemy. However, it was quite likely that the enemy was none other than the rightful locals, the Welsh, and it is said that this castle was attacked and partly destroyed by Wales's most enigmatic hero – not Bryn Terfel, but Owain Glyndwr. Born into relative wealth and privilege, Glyndwr waged a spectacularly successful guerrilla war against the English Crown in the first decade of the fifteenth century, and in the midst of this campaign, in 1404, he was crowned the King of Wales. The war continued for thirteen gruelling years, and it wasn't until the fall of Harlech castle and the capture of Glyndwr's family that his will seemed to desert him. He was neither killed nor captured, but faded back into the countryside.

Owain Glyndwr has become the classic Welsh hero, brave, highly educated and with a fiercely loyal following. It is said that when word of the uprising became known, Welsh scholars studying in Oxford sold their books so that they could return to join the fray. Welsh workers from all over the land returned home to fight the eternal enemy, the English. Hence, of course, the reason why a group of Welsh radicals who took to burning second homes in the 1980s called themselves Meibian Glyndwr, the sons of Glendower.

From high up on the castle, the river looked turgid. A thick, completely silent, cold cocoa stream of Teifi water flowed with Amazonian stealth. In fact I have never seen a river anywhere that looked so Amazonian save the Amazon itself. Trees flopped into the water, and bubbles tanned with spume sat on the surface and floated by. But such silence! Not a gurgle. Not a whisper.

Walking down through the village, I stopped by a stall selling my own very special culinary friend, the Welsh cake. Thinking that I could at last solve the riddle of these deceptive treaty things, I asked the ladies on the stall how they made them.

'Well, we don't actually. We get them all in from a lady in Aberdore.' And all this in a rich American accent. 'Are you here on holiday?'

'No, I've come to see the coracle regatta. It's down by the river, isn't it?'

'No, it's been cancelled. The river's too high. Shame, isn't it?'

A shame. Yes, a shame. What was it about coracles and me? Fate.

I grabbed my Welsh cakes, pulled them close to my chest, walked down the road to the river, sat down and thought about what might have been, and bit into my Welsh cake. It still tasted remarkably like a blend of chalk and currants to me. Still, I could almost sense the farmhouse ovens, the bakestones, the ancient ladies warming themselves under woollen shawls, the bleating sheep. I wondered what they would have thought of life in twenty-first-century west Wales, where their tiny lambs are frozen and their beloved Welsh cakes are mass produced.

AFTERWORD

BOOKS ARE A LITTLE LIKE BABIES. A PAINFUL BIRTH, A HURRIED delivery, and then they are out there, living, breathing things over which you gradually lose control. You criticize and regret, but for all that you love them passionately.

While I was fiddling about with the final draft of this book, we took our human baby Lola off for a few days, profiting once more from the crazy world of cheap flights. Even crazier in this case, since an infant cost twice as much as an adult. And where did we go? Why, Italy, of course. I needed to breathe the air, to drink a real *macchiato* and cogitate. So off we flew to Verona in the north-eastern province of Veneto, the city of Romeo and Juliet, with its glorious Roman arena, bizarre sky-high tombs of the medieval rulers the Scaligeri family, and a phenomenal number of clothes shops which, this being Italy, were buzzing. I noticed once again that even dustbin men had a certain elegance about them.

I was, needless to say, more drawn to the food of Verona, to its intricacies and odd little quirks, so I set off to the local bookshop and riffled through the shelves. There was not one but three well-written, comprehensive tomes to choose from. *La cucina Veronese*, it seems, has its roots in the extreme poverty of the Veneto, which was a little hard to imagine in Verona of all places. It is also marked by a distinct fondness for the horse. Eating them, that is, not riding them.

The story goes that there was an ancient battle of such barbarity that the rulers decreed that all the broken, blood-soaked horse flesh left in the field should not be allowed to go to waste, and should be cooked, stewed in fact, long and slow. This is the origin of the great local dish *pastissàda de caval*, a magnificent, unctuous stew spiced with cloves and nutmeg and eaten with a slab of polenta, a distinction that can be explained by Verona's proximity to Venice, for long the centre of the eastern spice trade in Italy. Twice we ate in a restaurant where the menu was studded with bits of horsemeat. Even Lola had her first mouthful. Which set me thinking. If I had arrived in, say, Chichester, a beautiful city in the south of England, as rich in history as Verona even if with fewer balconies, would I have encountered any regional culinary identity at all, let alone any books describing it? You know the answer to that one by now. A resounding no.

And what of this business of eating horse? To most northern Europeans it is a disgusting and, yes, an immoral idea. Horses are our friends, and we don't eat friends. We are happy to let them steeplechase their way to their doom, but we should never eat them. Just send them off to the knacker's yard to be eaten by dogs. It's much easier on the conscience. The British are, if nothing else, a hypocritical lot when it comes to food. So why do the good citizens of Verona, immaculately dressed and coiffed as they are, happily tuck into a plate of horse without, apparently, the slightest qualm? It is evidence, I think, of something that has sadly singularly failed to occur back home. What you could call everyday proletarian cooking has triumphantly survived almost entirely intact, and is nurtured and indulged by all Veronese. It has become mainstream, and helps give the Veronese a unique identity and a stronger sense of self than their British counterparts, if indeed such things exist in this country at all.

What happened to the gastronomic counterpart in Britain? As I travelled around the country I did get a sense of a revival in regional food but it seemed a very one-sided, haphazard affair indeed. Yes, farmers' markets are springing up all over the place, and these arenas at least allow us to talk to producers and begin to amass a degree of awareness about food, nutrition and seasonality, but at a price. Much of the produce seems so insanely expensive to most of us when compared to the mass-produced pap we are accustomed to buying in the local supermarket that we often find it hard to get it into perspective. In other words, any good food movement is perceived to be elitist.

The real equivalent to Verona's horse stews is to be found in the tripe and onion culture of the industrial north, the sooan sids of Orkney, the Hindle Wakes, the parkins and fat rascals of a Yorkshire tea – all part of an almost lost but evocative past. It isn't really the wild boar prosciutto from Cumbria, however fine a product it is. Is it just too late for us ever to revive this disappearing gastronomy? Quite possibly. We have all become too geographically mobile, and too inured to the evils of M2VS, to be able to recreate what once was. But we can nag. And rootle around and search for this golden grail, a renascent British food culture that has to be more than just the ability to buy carrots with mud on them, and the odd farmhouse cheese.

After all my travels and travails, I only really felt a true sense of place north of Manchester, and that is where the heart and soul of British cooking will live or die. Sometimes I think I have become a gastronomic fascist, seeking purity where none ever existed, seeking that authoritative dish but finding none. That is not for me to judge. But what I can say is that now we have some decent raw materials around again, why can't we learn to use them, to cook those fantastic dishes with such wonderful names that obsess me so painfully? For God's sake, can someone, somewhere out there, at least put Hindle Wakes back on the culinary map?

A GLOSSARY
of British GODs (Great and
Obscure Dishes)

SO WHERE DID THEY ALL GO? WHY ARE ALL THESE DISHES WITH
such fabulous names so hard to find? I thought it would be
worthwhile to set it out in stone, and provide albeit a far from
exhaustive list that is merely meant to whet the appetite; one
day someone out there will bite the bullet and start cooking
these great and almost totally forgotten dishes. Like all great
GOD movements this one needs an evangelical soul prepared
to suffer huge indignities and frustration. But, I'm busy, sorry.
And I've just written this book.

   Some of these dishes are in particular danger of extinction,
which is often down to the obscurity of their principal
ingredients. Muggety pie, for instance, simply doesn't work
without umbilical cord. Some of them may seem a little perplexing: 'boiled baby' doesn't sound too enticing a dish.
Others live on, but need wider recognition. And don't forget
all the clearly named dishes – tripe and onions, for example –

that fail to qualify as GODs due to the lack of mystery in their meaning. They too need help if they are not to disappear for ever.

Our culinary heritage needs mollycoddling. I would encourage you to join an informal adopt-a-dish programme and nurse your very own British GOD back to full cultural health. Create a fuss.

Eat wisely, eat well, eat a GOD!

Bawd bree Scottish hare soup.

Bere bannocks Orcadian rolls made from bere barley meal, and sometimes buttermilk. See page 122.

Biffins Norfolk biffins are slices of apple wind dried, then slowly baked and pressed, and coated with sugar. See page 253.

Blaand A Shetland drink of lightly fermented buttermilk whey that is slightly sparkling, and said to be refreshing.

Boiled baby A boiled suet pudding with nutmeg, raisins and cinnamon.

Boxty Irish; a mix of raw and mashed potato fried in bacon fat. There is a rhyme that goes, 'Boxty on the griddle, boxty in the pan / If you can't make boxty, you'll never get your man'.

Brown Betty Layered baked apples, spiced breadcrumbs and Demerara sugar.

Cabbieclaw A Scottish dish of cod with egg sauce and horseradish.

Ceuthes Orcadian word for young coley, sometimes eaten blawn, or lightly off. See page 117.

Clanger A suet crust pasty from the beautiful county of Bedfordshire, with meat at one end and jam at the other, made for the hardworking menfolk by their ever-loving wives to keep them fuelled up for a hard day's work on the farm.

Clapshot Orcadian mashed potato and neeps. See page 120.

Cockaleekie A soup originally made with an old cock stuffed tight into a pot, surrounded by leeks, potatoes, barley and water, and cooked until it all disintegrates, bird included.

Colliers foot(s) Transportable pasties eaten for lunch in Lancashire mines. Often called Lancashire foots. Made with meat, potatoes, onions, bacon fat and beer. See page 24.

Condimacke Quince paste, a.k.a. quince cheese, a.k.a. *membrillo*. See page 238.

Crappit heids Stuffed haddock heads (Scottish origin).

Crubeens Slowly cooked pig's trotters, once eaten in Irish pubs with Irish fingers.

Cullen skink A GOD that has quite a high public profile. It's a thick smoked haddock and potato soup that comes from the Morayshire village of Cullen.

Dormers A fried mixture of cooked beef, suet, boiled rice, egg and breadcrumbs (Lancashire origin).

Elder Sold in the offal stalls of northern England until recently. Not the floriferous and useful indigenous fruiting tree, but pressed udder.

Fat rascals A Yorkshire cake, half scone half rock cake, studded with raisins. See page 98.

Figgy dowdy A Cornish plum pudding with a nautical connection.

Flummery An ancient thickened pudding originally made from boiled oatmeal, and tarted up with the addition of cream and sugar, as well as – occasionally – orange flower water. It became a classier dish in the seventeenth century when it was often set in elaborate moulds and served to much applause.

Frumenty A thick, sweetened, porridgey goo made from cracked wheat, almonds, cream, currants, sugar, rum and saffron, of great antiquity. Was once served as an accompaniment to meat, and even roast porpoise. Sometimes called furmenty, or furmity.

Gallimaufry One of several terms ('hodgepodge', qv, is

another) used in pre-twentieth-century cookbooks to mean a mixture of cooked or hashed meats. In Kettner's *Book of the Table* (1877) there is an elaborate and not entirely convincing explanation of the origin of this word and its connection with an ancient pre-Sanskrit language that suggests it has something to do with small birds. Confused? Try reading his fourteen-page exegesis.

Hasty pudding A pudding that could literally be made hastily before packets of Instant Whip were invented. It was made with flour and milk, then sweetened, or spiced, and often had an egg added. It was such a fine creation that it travelled across to the New World. It can still be found in America, where it is often called mush.

Hindle Wakes A deeply evocative, totally unfindable dish of boiled fowl, with a spectacular combination of black, yellow and green. The fowl was once stuffed with pig's blood (black) but later prunes, and after a protracted boiling was taken out, covered with a rich lemony butter sauce (yellow), garnished with greenery and served on Wakes Night. Said to originate in the Bolton area. See page 25.

Hodgepodge, or hotchpotch Yet another term for an indeterminate mixture that is stewed. Mrs Beeton brings some precision to the term and describes it as a dish of mutton, peas and onions. In northern France a similar term is *hochepot*.

Katt pie A traditional pie made on Templeton fair day in Pembrokeshire, Wales, from mutton, sugar and currants. No feline connection at all.

Kickshaws An anglicization of the French word *quelquechose*, for a little something served with a banquet when that meant a meal often taken outside in studiedly beautiful surroundings when all that was eaten were little bits of this and that, generally sweet. One type of kickshaw was a small piece of quince cheese fried in puff pastry.

Kitchels Small cakes made in East Anglia to hand out to

children during the Twelve Days of Christmas. Puff pastry, currants, chopped peel, ground almonds, cinnamon and nutmeg.

Krappin Nothing scatological about this Scottish dish, which is a sort of marine haggis, made of fish liver, oatmeal, salt and pepper stuffed into the 'muggie' or fish stomach and then relentlessly boiled.

Lobscouse, lobby or scouse, Inextricably associated with the great British seaport of Liverpool whose inhabitants are still to this day known as scousers. It is a maritime dish said to have come across with German sailors, being known in north Germany as *labskaus*. A one-pot stew, though its exact constitution is varied. Sometimes made with mutton, or beef, and thickened by the addition of cowheel or pig's trotter; it is also said that crumbled ship's biscuits were used. Potatoes, onions and other root vegetables would have been added as well. See page 23.

Muggety pie A truly extinct GOD this, made with the umbilical cord of a calf.

Mulligatawny A mildly spiced Anglo-Indian soup made from chicken stock, lentils, tomatoes, garlic, cumin and ghee.

Olio podrida I became mildly obsessed by references to this dish in a number of cookbooks from the sixteenth to the eighteenth centuries, and seriously planned to revive the olio by cooking it and inviting the whole of Oxford for lunch. It is obviously Spanish in origin, derived from *olla podrida*, which if literally translated means 'rotten pot'. It is a classic example of a dish adopted then anglicized, and is essentially yet another mixture of this and that. Often immensely laborious, and these days costly. Early references include those by Robert May in his *Accomplished Cook* (1660), where it consisted of an astonishing variety of meat, slowly stewed and spiced. It would have fed a good number of guests, but recipes were often more complicated than necessary, for chefs liked to portray themselves as having skills ordinary mortals could not acquire. These days the exact opposite is true: recipe books must not seem too daunting. The olio was a dish for entertaining, not one for private consumption. So widely used did the term become that it was also used in much the same way as hodgepodge (qv).

Pan haggerty A fried mix of potatoes, onions and Lancashire cheese, from the north-east of England. Findable and delicious. See page 23.

Panakelty A Northumbrian corned beef hash, according to some, or a variation on pan haggerty (qv). It calls for spuds and onions, plus either bacon or corned beef, and was a supper dish.

Parched peas Great street food from Lancashire, made from black, pigeon or Carling peas, also known as gutter slush. See page 16.

Parkin A Yorkshire teabread. See page 83.

Rum nicky Cumbrian pie. Sweet pastry, dates, butter, crystallized ginger and rum.

Sad cakes A Lancashire speciality, Sad cakes were often taken on Wakes Weeks holidays (see page 27) and were a particular favourite of Rossendale. The basic recipe is flour, suet, sugar and currants, baked until golden.

Salamagundie An inexact, improvised salad of inexact, improvised spelling, traditionally eaten during Lent. It has been called anything from sallid magundi to Solomon Gundy, but refers to a cold dish made from eggs, anchovies, onions, chicken, grapes, almonds and raisins. Like a salad niçoise really – except that the French dish can be found on menus all over Britain whereas the English version can't. A Lancashire recipe I have seen mixes boiled herring with anchovies, capers, chopped onion and chopped mushroom, the grated rind of a lemon and some pickled oysters. It must have been incredibly easy to make but is now rarely found in any form at all. Ready and ripe for a second coming.

Sally Lunns Quite well known as a bap-type teabread that comes from Bath. The origin of the word is interesting. Although some commentators say Sally Lunn was the name of some buxom woman who made a fortune wandering the streets of Bath selling her teabread, other accounts say it is derived from the French *soleil et lune* (sun and moon), after the look of a Sally Lunn, with its golden bottom and flour-dusted top.

Scouse Liverpool's own evocative stew that is a derivation of lobscouse (qv) and is still made at home, but never with ship's biscuits. It is basically a meat and potato stew.

Sea pie An English curiosity in that it was never made with anything from the sea at all, but was eaten on board, by sailors and more particularly by canal boatmen. It was generally a one-pot meat stew of varying constitution sealed with a lid of suet or pastry.

Seftons 'Veal custard' best describes this exquisite-sounding GOD.

Senior Wrangler sauce A Cambridge term for brandy butter. Senior wrangler being, as you will know, the term for the highest achiever in the Maths Tripos.

Shoe horns Eighteenth-century hors d'oeuvres made from anchovies, manchets (bread), bottarga (salted tuna roe), snapdragons and herrings.

Sids Not really a GOD, but important nevertheless. The chaff of black oats. See page 143.

Singing hinnies Griddle cakes made in the north-east of England with flour, bicarbonate of soda, cream of tartar, raisins and milk, and cooked on the griddle with a little mutton fat. They were often given to children with a small coin hidden inside.

Skillygally Oatmeal gruel. Not a very appealing-sounding GOD.

Sooan/sowan Another oatmeal gruel, made from sids, now rarely found but still living on in Orkney. See page 143.

Spotted dog A suet pudding similar to the inimitable

spotted dick, whose spots are nothing more than raisins.

Stap A dish from Shetland, of cooked haddock liver mixed with the meat from boiled haddock head. The livers are generally steamed, or cooked in a jar, to preserve their flavour which would be lost if boiled.

Stotties Not that obscure if you are from Newcastle, these are soft bap-type rolls with a milky dough, made into all sorts of highly nutritious specialities such as bacon and egg stotties.

Syllabub Essentially a sweetened mixture of wine (or sherry) and milk, or cream. They can be made in one of several ways, but recipes often call for the milk to be poured into the wine from on high to allow as quick a curdling as possible. I was particularly struck by an account of Charles II riding through a London park, and stopping by a cow to partake of a freshly made syllabub.

Tatie pot A northern English pie unusual for its combination of different sorts of meat (e.g. mutton and beef) layered with black pudding.

Throdkins A speciality of the Fylde, made of oatmeal and bacon, and served with syrup. Peculiar in my book not only for its combination of sweet and savoury, but for the fact that the mighty world wide web has no reference to throdkins as far as I can see.

Umble pie Umble is an ancient word for offal and has nothing to do with humility at all.

Wet nellies A Liverpudlian version of bread and butter pudding made in honour of Admiral Lord Nelson, still to be found lurking in the streets of Walsall. See page 24.

Whim wham An English pudding made from boudoir biscuits, sweet wine, cream, roast hazelnuts, angelica and sugar.

Wow wow, or Bow Wow sauce Great name, great story. The sauce is made from stock with a dash of vinegar, port, mustard and pickled walnuts, and served with roast meat. It gets its name from the Cotswold village of Painswick and its ancient enmity with nearby Stroud. The Painswickians were said by the Stroudians to have once been in the habit of sacrificing dogs to propitiate the god of shepherds. Fed up with the taunts, they once asked the good villagers of Stroud to a jolly get-together and served them a pie made from real puppies. Yum yum.

Yellowman An Irish toffee made at Lammas Fair. According to the *Rhyming Irish Cookbook* (at www.recipesource.com):

> Yellowman is thick and sweet,
> And much tradition lies behind it;
> For centuries at Lammas Fair
> In Ballycastle, you would find it.
>
> To make this toffee, first you melt
> The butter in a heavy pan;
> Add sugar, syrup, vinegar,
> And start to boil your Yellowman.
>
> To test it, take a spoonful up
> And in cold water let it fall:
> It's ready if the mixture turns
> Into a crisp and brittle ball.
>
> Now put the baking soda in —
> You'll find that it will foam and froth;
> So take a spoon and rapidly
> Keep stirring up the bubbling broth.
>
> Now pour it in a well-greased tin;
> Cool, then break in bits to eat.
> You'll soon know why, at Lammas Fair,
> The Yellowman was such a treat.

RECOMMENDED READING

General works on British food and cooking:

Ayrton, Elizabeth, *The Cookery of England* (Penguin, 1977)

Dallas, E.S., *Kettner's Book of the Table* (London, 1877)

David, Elizabeth, *English Bread and Yeast Cookery* (Penguin, 1996)

———*Spices, Salts and Aromatics in the English Kitchen* (Grub Street, 2000)

Davidson, Alan (ed.), *The Penguin Companion to Food* (Penguin, 2002). Indispensable.

Dunn, T.C., *How to Become Plump* (1878)

Hayward, Abraham, *The Art of Dining* (1852)

Girouard, Mark, *Life in the English Country House* (Yale University Press, 1993)

Grigson, Jane, *English Food* (Penguin, 2004 edition)

Hagen, Ann, *Anglo Saxon Food and Drink* (Anglo Saxon Books, 1995)

Hartley, Dorothy, *Food in England* (Little, Brown and Co., 1999)

Kitchener, Dr William, *A Cook's Oracle* (London, 1821)

Mason, Laura, *Traditional Foods of Britain: an Inventory* (Prospect Books, 2004)

May, Robert, *The Accomplished Cook* (1660)

Mennell, Stephen, *All Manner of Foods* (Illinois University Press, 1995)

Raffald, Elizabeth, *The Experienced English Housekeeper* (1786)

Smith, Michael, *Fine English Cookery* (Serif, 1998)

Tickletooth, Tabitha, *The Dinner Question* (London, 1860)

Women's Institute with Michael Smith, *A Cook's Tour of Britain* (Collins Willow, 1984)

A selection of the best books on regional food and cooking:

Lancashire

Poulson, Joan, *More Old Lancashire Recipes* (Hendon Publishing, 1976). All books by Joan Poulson are useful, and thorough.

Lakeland

Poulson, Joan, *Lakeland Recipes Old and New* (Countryside, 1978)

London

Wheeler, Alwyne, *The Tidal Thames* (RKP, 1979)

Scotland

Bichan, Alan, *An Orkney Feast* (Orcadian, 2000)

McNeill, F. Marian, *Recipes from Scotland* (Albyn Press, 1946)

Yorkshire

Poulson, Joan, *Old Yorkshire Recipes* (Hendon Publishing, 1978)

Wales

Freeman, Bobby, *First Catch Your Peacock* (Lolfa, 1996)

——*Welsh Fish Y Lolfa Cyf* (1988)

INDEX

NOTE: recipe titles are indicated in **bold** typeface. Page numbers followed by italic *g* indicate glossary items.